STATISTICS

OF THE

STATE OF MICHIGAN,

COMPILED FROM THE

CENSUS OF 1860,

TAKEN BY AUTHORITY OF THE UNITED STATES.

Condensed for Publication by the Secretary of State of the State of Michigan, in pursuance of an Act of the Legislature, approved March 16th, 1861.

LANSING:
John A. Kerr & Co., Printers to the State.
1861.

Office of the Secretary of State,
Lansing, October 1st, 1861.

In pursuance of an act of the Legislature of the State of Michigan, entitled "An Act to provide for publishing the Statistics of the State of Michigan, taken by authority of the United States in the year one thousand eight hundred and sixty," approved March 16th, 1861, the following tables have been compiled from the census and statistical returns made to this Department, and are believed to be correct.

JAMES B. PORTER,
Secretary of State.

ALLEGAN COUNTY.

TOWNSHIPS.	Dwelling Houses.		Number of Families.	Number of Inhabitants.				
	Whole number.	Number in Cities.		Whole number.	Colored.	Deaf and Dumb.	Blind.	Insane.
Allegan,	167		165	896	10	1		
Allegan village,	190		171	940	16		1	
Casco,	67		6[illegible]	29[illegible]				
Cheshire,	144		143	670	30			1
Clyde,	18		17	74				
Dorr,	143		139	700				
Fillmore,	136		134	668				
Ganges,	148		147	759				1
Gun Plains,	228		214	1,068				
Heath,	81		77	382				
Hopkins,	126		119	587				
Laketown,	66		5[illegible]	267				
Lee,	9		9	43				
Leighton,	134		129	676			1	
Manlius,	67		65	349				
Martin,	17[illegible]		160	794				1
Monterey,	18[illegible]		18[illegible]	927		1		
Newark,	156		159	8[illegible]6		1		
Otsego,	324		287	1,429		2		
Overisel,	92		89	489				
Pine Plains,	24		20	103				
Salem,	83		82	430				
Trowbridge,	179		167	897		1		
Watson,	176		183	902				
Wayland,	194		185	917			2	1
Total,	3,308	.....	3,163	16,091	56	6	4	4

ALLEGAN COUNTY.—Continued.

TOWNSHIPS.	Value of Real Estate owned.	Occupied Farms.			
		Whole number.	Acres improved.	Acres unimproved.	Cash value of.
Allegan,	$342,900	115	4,053	6,715	$246,790
Allegan village,	425,750		..	.	.. ...
Casco,	64,935	22	698	1,579	40,800
Cheshire,	105,866	84	1,592	5,671	75,010
Clyde,	9,900	8	144	784	6,900
Dorr,	115,460	91	2,251	4,582	87,400
Fillmore,	126,235	72	1,709	3,855	85,080
Ganges,	207,795	49	1,914	3,254	113,175
Gun Plains,	437,200	153	8,371	7,341	426,900
Heath,	74,720	44	1,080	4,819	62,730
Hopkins,	141,210	84	2,353	5,872	116,000
Laketown,	36,070	26	700	1,412	24,500
Lee,	4,350	Not	report'd	..	
Leighton,	139,700	92	3,041	5,825	127,200
Manlius,	120,190	40	1,143	3,395	63,490
Martin,	306,300	117	4,561	6,179	321,500
Monterey,	265,520	117	4,919	5,853	258,440
Newark,	279,800	45	1,209	3,364	65,100
Otsego,	418,760	150	5,777	6,772	291,600
Overisel,	105,025	77	1,517	4,339	82,975
Pine Plains,	28,200	15	485	2,434	23,100
Salem,	58,050	60	1,101	2,432	48,500
Trowbridge,	291,800	139	4,491	9,047	250,750
Watson,	229,600	140	4,659	6,839	248,500
Wayland,	296,920	88	3,036	5,872	134,550
Total,	$4,624,156	1,828	60,804	108,226	$3,200,990

ALLEGAN COUNTY.—Continued.

Value of Farming Implements and Machinery.	Live Stock, June 1st, 1860.							
	Horses.	Asses and Mules.	Milch Cows.	Working Oxen.	Other Cattle.	Sheep.	Swine.	Value of Live Stock.
$11,520	151		278	119	362	406	409	$34,635
997	13		41	26	47	213	72	4,155
2,949	44		127	103	124	87	276	13,750
179	2		9	8	12	2	40	1,280
6,042	38		188	151	163	147	399	18,404
4,474	53		226	92	244	68	253	16,345
4,107	48		112	60	148	303	204	15,174
19,035	305		438	142	577	2,355	993	62,595
2,652	27		72	45	74	38	169	8,380
4,502	48		207	103	256	301	406	18,281
1,697	19		72	26	68	22	74	5,575
5,829	66		194	141	205	394	579	22,410
2,219	37		72	40	69	86	179	9,080
16,659	186		297	166	314	1,900	904	43,545
12,232	145		281	148	331	636	920	39,446
1,833	28	2	71	48	65	30	165	8,687
10,794	210		364	158	469	1,259	885	44,083
4,522	46		230	110	283	73	232	14,554
1,055	14		27	16	15	8	75	3,298
3,109	15		92	115	98	89	346	10,908
8,757	212		316	182	375	612	694	41,239
11,733	138	14	319	194	297	459	816	29,840
6,198	101		209	127	212	401	616	25,270
$143,097	1946	16	4242	2,320	4,809	9,889	9,706	$490,934

ALLEGAN COUNTY.—Continued.

TOWNSHIPS.	Produce, during the Year						
	Wheat, bushels of.	Rye, bushels of.	Indian corn, bushels of.	Oats, bushels of.	Barley, bushels of.	Buckwheat, bushels of.	Potatoes, bushels of.
Allegan,	8,977	1,164	22,523	2,499	188	947	9,937
Allegan vil.,							
Casco,	1,387	371	2,830	255	[illegible]	127	1,692
Cheshire,	1,800	397	8,041	655	[illegible]	194	3,640
Clyde,	553	144	672	46		55	760
Dorr,	4,395	464	11,829	2,066	34	221	3,571
Fillmore,	3 071	725	3,545	1,271	39	303	3,188
Ganges,	3,830	1,586	10,090	995	..	787	5,360
Gun Plains,	26,404	829	34,445	6,640	70	547	10,406
Heath,	884	647	4,815	40	40	269	1,974
Hopkins,	3,796	34	10,213	2,356	68	533	4,052
Laketown,	1,469	565	1,440	273		178	1,298
Lee,				..			-
Leighton,	7,349	287	14,564	2,350	78	508	4 599
Manlius,	[illegible]	372	5 400	1,145	3	303	4,033
Martin,	18 042	93	23,045	6,373	433	312	7,382
Monterey,	15,060	414	28 325	6 400	1,111	[illegible]	6,534
Newark,	1,428	1,397	5,393	214		373	3,887
Otsego,	14,167	249	22 029	2,999	135	265	8,634
Overisel,	4,577	1,099	3,220	2,271	4	801	3,383
Pine Plains,	85	286	640			110	630
Salem,	2,961	57	8,550	1,496	60	72	3,252
Trowbridge,	9,299	889	21,949	2,420	133	497	7,028
Watson,	10,405	386	20 389	5,419	261	776	7,603
Wayland,	6,154	760	10,597	1,430	8	442	4.562
Total,	147684	13154	274532	49,611	2,682	9,704	107405

ALLEGAN COUNTY—Continued.

ENDING JUNE 1ST, 1860.							
Wool, pounds of.	Value of Orchard products.	Butter, pounds of.	Cheese, pounds of.	Hay, tons of.	Clover seed, bushels.	Maple Sugar, pounds.	Value of home made manufactures.
1,235	$1,478	21,350	2,840	97[illegible]	19	19,440	$132
....		...					.
664	183	3,290	230	11[illegible]		2,950	
33[illegible]	131	10,370	650	307	8	[illegible],334	
10	50	930	60	23	..	290	
130	133	13,350	3,180	543		22,84[illegible]	100
168	88	18,095		53	7	1,330	
818	1,338	10,440	30	43		2,750	6
6,657	2,089	32,135	9,914	[illegible]		2,900	640
69	46	7,115	43[illegible]	160	20	1,205	
550	5	16,77[illegible]	1,640	69[illegible]		33,450	300
58	30	6,485		197	.	50	...
.					.		.
57[illegible]	3[illegible]	15,962	1,000	809		23,120	179
237	416	6,91[illegible]	30	342		680	.
5,459	653	23,500	1,830	1,380		34,180	200
1,872	82[illegible]	29,360	857	1,271	16	15,150	150
111	548	6,694		171		1,670	..
3,20[illegible]	835	26,160	2,19[illegible]	1,534		24,190	92
130		17,320	..	677	2	501	..
17	30	1,243		62	.	20	.
30	...	6,970		120		4,782	150
1,800	2,100	25,378	1,885	1,512	.	32,728	1,0[illegible]2
1,218	545	26,660	3,515	244		31,238	204
813	31	15,200	780	811		5,183	106
26,162	12,205	332,731	31,069	15774	72	272065	$3,311

ALLEGAN COUNTY.—Continued.

TOWNSHIPS.	Flouring Mills.							Saw Mills.			
			Power used.			Annual product.			Power used.		
	Number of.	Runs of Stone.	Water.	Steam.	Capital invested in real and personal estate in the business.	Bbls. flour made.	Value of.	Number of.	Water.	Steam.	Capital invested in real and personal estate in the business.
Allegan,											
Allegan vil.,	3	6	3		24,000	4,065	37,375	1	1		20,000
Casco,											
Cheshire,								1	1		3,500
Clyde,											
Dorr,								1		1	10,000
Fillmore,											
Ganges,	1	1	1		3,000	88	16,716	1		1	3,000
Gun Plains,	2	3	2		12,000		26,700	2	2		4,400
Heath,											
Hopkins,								1	1		1,500
Laketown,											
Lee,											
Leighton,								1		1	10,000
Manlius,								2	1	1	9,000
Martin,								2	1	1	2,600
Monterey,								2	2		3,000
Newark,	1	1		1	1,500		5,950	7	1	6	77,000
Otsego,	2	5	2		12,000	*1000	37,660	5	5		13,000
Overisel,											
Pine Plains,								1	1		3,000
Salem,											
Trowbridge,								3	2	1	21,000
Watson,								1		1	3,000
Wayland,								4		4	30,000
Total,	9	16	8	1	52,500	5,153	124401	35	18	17	214000

* By one, the other is a custom mill.

ALLEGAN COUNTY—Continued.

Saw Mills. Annual product. Feet of Lumber Sawed.	Saw Mills. Annual product. Value of.	Aggregate of all kinds of manufactures, Mills included. Capital invested in real and personal estate in the business.	Hands employ'd. Males.	Hands employ'd. Females.	Value of annual products.	Estimated value of Real and Personal Estate. By Assessors.	Estimated value of Real and Personal Estate. By assistant Marshals.
800,000	68,000	$99,950	116	4	182,723		
200,000	2,050	3,500	2		2,050		
1,000,000	4,000	10,000	7		4,000		
400,000	3,250	6,500	11		21,366		
450,000	5,600	21,900	16		39,100		
600,000	2,400	1,500			2,400		
2,000,000	21,000	10,000	20		21,000		
1,320,000	7,900	9,000	14		7,900		
450,000	2,000	3,600	5		5,000		
600,000	3,000	4,000	5		2,800		
12,290,000	88,190	100,300	142		126,191		
1,350,000	7,200	35,500	26		59,660		
500,000	2,800	3,000	4		2,800		
2,100,000	13,000	21,000	17		13,000		
100,000	700	3,500	6		1,900		
3,300,000	18,800	33,000	24		24,300		
27,460,000	249890	366,250	415	4	516,190	*	3,021,847

* Not returned.

ALPENA COUNTY.

TOWNSHIPS.	Dwelling Houses. Whole number.	Dwelling Houses. Number in Cities.	Number of Families.	Number of Inhabitants. Whole number.	Colored.	Deaf and Dumb.	Blind.	Insane.
Fremont,	108	....	49	291				

ALCONA COUNTY.

TOWNSHIPS.	Dwelling Houses. Whole number.	Dwelling Houses. Number in Cities.	Number of Families.	Number of Inhabitants. Whole number.	Colored.	Deaf and Dumb.	Blind.	Insane.
Black River,	24		12	50				
Harrisville,	51		22	131				
Total,	75	....	34	181				

BARRY COUNTY

TOWNSHIPS.	Dwelling Houses. Whole number.	Dwelling Houses. Number in Cities.	Number of Families.	Number of Inhabitants. Whole number.	Colored.	Deaf and Dumb.	Blind.	Insane.
Assyria,	185		179	959		2	1	
Barry,	247		212	1,101	37			
Baltimore,	118		123	61[illegible]				
Carlton,	136		129	678		1		
Castleton,	161		141	781			[illegible]	
Hastings village,	149		142	888				
Hastings,	133		128	663				
Hope,	153		143	689	20	1		
Irving,	165		157	816				1
Johnstown,	197		193	931		3		
Maple Grove,	103		102	621				
Orangeville,	191		181	875		1	1	1
Prairieville,	238		211	1,140		1	3	1
Rutland,	196		147	691		1		
Thornapple,	233		209	1,005				1
Woodland,	189		181	960		1		1
Yankee Springs,	139		129	615	1	1		
Total,	2,933	...	2,707	14,041	58	12	6	5

ALPENA COUNTY.—Continued.

TOWNSHIPS.	Value of Real Estate owned.	Occupied Farms. Whole number.	Acres improved.	Acres unimproved.	Cash value of.
Fremont, ...	$44,600	..	...	.	..

ALCONA COUNTY.—Continued.

TOWNSHIPS.	Value of Real Estate owned.	Occupied Farms. Whole number.	Acres improved.	Acres unimproved.	Cash value of.
Black River,	$10,800			.	.
Harrisville,	44,300		..		.
Total,	$55,100	...	. .	.	

BARRY COUNTY.—Continued.

TOWNSHIPS.	Value of Real Estate owned.	Occupied Farms. Whole number.	Acres improved.	Acres unimproved.	Cash value of.
Assyria, .	$238,600	78	4,833	5,012	$185,980
Barry,	340,980	114	7,152	5,829	261,155
Baltimore, .	123,755	97	3,263	7,138	121,700
Carlton, .	144,730	42	1,976	2,896	86,920
Castleton,	204,095	49	2,209	3,434	110,900
Hastings village,	214,505	.		. . .	..
Hastings, ..	123,745	49	1,867	4 404	83,565
Hope, .	110,475	120	3,151	7,690	109,505
Irving,	208,740	83	4,952	5,698	177,670
Johnstown,	266,455	118	6,500	7,469	271,536
Maple Grove,	125,335	50	2,325	4,857	118,330
Orangeville,	208,845	113	5,346	7,189	194,120
Prairieville,	472,458	123	10,230	5,631	441,418
Rutland,	197,445	118	5,580	6,900	183,860
Thornapple,	315,216	134	5,856	6,109	227,150
Woodland,	228,076	83	3,731	4,567	156,000
Yankee Springs,	167,135	99	5,202	6,589	147,156
Total,	3,690,590	1,470	74,179	91,412	2,876,965

ALPENA COUNTY.—Continued.

Value of Farming Implements and Machinery.	Live Stock, June 1st, 1860.							
	Horses.	Asses and Mules.	Milch Cows.	Working Oxen.	Other Cattle.	Sheep.	Swine.	Value of Live Stock.
... ..							.....	

ALCONA COUNTY.—Continued.

Value of Farming Implements and Machinery.	Horses.	Asses and Mules.	Milch Cows.	Working Oxen.	Other Cattle.	Sheep.	Swine.	Value of Live Stock.
						..		

BARRY COUNTY.—Continued.

Value of Farming Implements and Machinery.	Horses.	Asses and Mules.	Milch Cows.	Working Oxen.	Other Cattle.	Sheep.	Swine.	Value of Live Stock.
$7,092	162		216	136	359	2,656	405	$31,536
9,360	196		261	118	332	2,253	556	38,293
5,825	61		180	180	214	324	494	20,359
2,860	77		143	67	266	1,061	467	17,135
5,274	116		142	44	426	918	635	21,441
4,009	89		134	63	219	542	256	16,232
6,647	43		183	226	127	234	510	19,696
6,602	120		217	165	419	1,972	712	33,966
11,250	187		305	167	423	2,314	638	40,905
4,495	103		161	70	284	457	246	19,435
7,649	135	2	267	210	353	1,775	472	30,812
13,306	310		327	122	424	4,131	584	55,991
6,659	121		235	191	223	462	485	25,959
10,306	172	1	289	194	337	1,210	610	36,166
5,741	169		236	88	464	1,393	712	29,386
6,049	113		206	171	262	883	390	25,936
113,124	2174	3	3502	2,212	5,132	22,585	8,172	463,248

ALPENA COUNTY.—CONTINUED.

TOWNSHIPS.							Produce, during the Year
	Wheat, bushels of.	Rye, bushels of.	Indian corn, bushels of.	Oats, bushels of.	Barley, bushels of.	Buckwheat, bushels of.	Potatoes, bushels of.
Fremont,	.						......

ALCONA COUNTY.—CONTINUED.

TOWNSHIPS.	Wheat, bushels of.	Rye, bushels of.	Indian corn, bushels of.	Oats, bushels of.	Barley, bushels of.	Buckwheat, bushels of.	Potatoes, bushels of.
Black River,							....
Harrisville.			.	.		.	....
Total,	.					.	.

BARRY COUNTY.—CONTINUED.

TOWNSHIPS.	Wheat, bushels of.	Rye, bushels of.	Indian corn, bushels of.	Oats, bushels of.	Barley, bushels of.	Buckwheat, bushels of.	Potatoes, bushels of.
Assyria,	11,959	561	6,745	6,257	231	191	4,235
Barry,	34,746		20,65[illegible]	4,355	1	330	5,348
Baltimore,	7,498	131	12,821	1,896	52	998	6,737
Carlton,	3,349	50	4,650	4,624	637	196	1,497
Castleton,	4,240		7,420	2,174	1,367	176	1,978
Hastings vil.,							..
Hastings,	4,666	688	4,760	2,494	15	306	3,198
Hope,	9,922	448	15,765	1,767	10	1,088	7,260
Irving,	14,561	256	6,045	1,508	94	566	4,657
Johnstown,	23,830	142	14,356	7,101	70	426	7,385
Maple Grove,	3,531	529	5,724	3,217	150	301	1,922
Orangeville,	14,283	1,034	22,142	2,915	103	702	8,462
Prairieville,	40,092	560	31,331	10,009	404	373	7,392
Rutland,	20,554	630	26,597	3,506	118	646	6,769
Thornapple,	17,69[illegible]	2,008	20,188	5,70[illegible]	140	30	7,043
Woodland,	7,395	326	9,755	4,995	459	278	3,066
Yankee Spr.,	11,874	2,508	15,372	85[illegible]		729	8,930
Total,	230200	9,871	224326	63,186	3,959	7,610	85,879

ALPENA COUNTY.—Continued.

ENDING JUNE 1ST, 1860.								
Wool, pounds of.	Value of Orchard products.	Butter, pounds of.	Cheese, pounds of.	Hay, tons of.	Clover seed, bushels.	Maple Sugar, pounds.		Value of home made manufactures.
...	....	... ..	..		.. .	.		..
ALCONA COUNTY.—Continued.								
..	. ..	.	...		.			. .
. .	.		. .					. ...
. .		.	.. ..	.		.... .		.
BARRY COUNTY.—Continued.								
6 708	$ 269	19,696	1,270	1,240	19	5,800		$124
5,863	1,129	21,097	1,940	1,120	14	1,785		239
1,206	247	21,750	400	573	.	15,154		....
2,015	255	11,350	1,015	525	4	24,995		95
1,551	372	13,424	1,210	569		34 220		270
..	. .	.				.		. .
1,274	222	10,540	860	470	8	32,847		113
543	83	18,761	193	1,255		8.235		.
4,854	328	20,077	1 905	1 205	37	9.930		368
5,954	2,881	25,735	2,723	1,364	64	1,884		116
1,252	379	14,375	1,940	501	8	35,065		66
5,203	978	[illegible]	2,287	2,279	2	.		260
11,634	1,321	23,893	2,850	[illegible]	28	100		162
2,222	149	22,708	1,150	1,209	29	4,625		104
3,958	873	20,641	1,465	1,435	11	20 240		195
3,609	692	22,166	2,260	828	38	46,520		410
2,662	437	19.663	1,020	1 371	11	150		88
60,501	10,610	310,138	24,494	17919	273	241550		2,610

ALPENA COUNTY.—Continued.

TOWNSHIPS.	Flouring Mills.							Saw Mills.			
	Number of.	Runs of Stone.	Power used.		Capital invested in real and personal estate in the business.	Annual product.		Number of.	Power used.		Capital invested in real and personal estate in the business.
			Water.	Steam.		Bbls. flour made.	Value of.		Water.	Steam.	
Fremont,								4	3	1	38,000
ALCONA COUNTY.—Continued.											
Black River,							.			.	. . .
Harrisville,					:		. .	1	1		20,000
Total,					. . .	. .		1	1	. . .	20,000
BARRY COUNTY.—Continued.											
Assyria,							. . .	2		2	$3,500
Barry,							.	1	1		2,500
Baltimore,	1	2	1		$1,500	9,000	$900	3	2	1	9,500
Carlton,					. .	.	. .				. .
Castleton,					. . .	. .		1	1		1,000
Hastings v.,	2		2		15,000	8,000	48,000	2	1	1	4,400
Hastings,											. .
Hope,	1	2	1		1,500	*2,000	1,200	4	4		11,500
Irving,	1		1		5,000	1,350	7,038				
Johnstown,						.	.				. .
Maple Gr.,								1		1	4,000
Orangev'le,	1	1	1		2,000	*150000	7,000	2	2		7,000
Prairiev'lle,						. .	. . . . .	1	1		3,000
Rutland,					.	. .	. .			. . .	. . . .
Thornapple,	2	4	2		7,000	*273000	2,500	2	2		4,500
Woodland,					. .	. .		1	1		1,500
Yankee Sp.,						. .	.	2	2		5,000
Total,	8	9	8		32,000	*443350	66,638	22	17	5	57,400

* As returned, evidently a mistake.

ALPENA COUNTY.—Continued.

Saw Mills.		Aggregate of all kinds of Manufactures, Mills included.				Estimated value of Real and Personal Estate.	
Annual product.			Hands employ'd				
Feet of Lumber Sawed.	Value of.	Capital invested in real and personal estate in the business.	Males.	Females.	Value of annual product.	By Assessors.	By assistant Marshals.
2,600,000	23,300	47,500	113		40,437		*
ALCONA COUNTY.—Continued.							
600,000	4,050	23,150	31		14,651		
600,000	4,050	23,150	31		14,651		†219,184
BARRY COUNTY.—Continued.							
1,000,000	$6,600	$3,500	5		$6,600		
300,000	3,000	2,800	4		4,200		
1,330,000	6,550	11,000	9		7,450		
120,000	‡8,400	1,000	1		8,400		
725,000	9,500	35,500	43		93,845		
990,000	5,030	13,000	5		6,230		
		5,000	1		7,038		
		300	3		1,468		
700,000	4,900	4,000	5		4,900		
830,000	4,980	9,000	4		11,980		
400,000	3,000	3,000	3		3,000		
636,000	3,300	11,500	6		5,800		
100,000	800	1,500	1		800		
800,000	5,500	5,000	3		5,500		
7,931,000	61,560	106,100	93		167,211	1724014	2,298,685

*Returned with Alcona County.
†Includes Alpena County.
‡ As returned, evidently a mistake.

BAY COUNTY.

TOWNSHIPS.	Dwelling Houses.		Number of Families.	Number of Inhabitants.				
	Whole number.	Number in Cities.		Whole number.	Colored.	Deaf and Dumb.	Blind.	Insane.
Arenac,	18		18	79	.		1	[illegible]
Bangor, . .	181	.	176	908		2	1	.
Bay City,..	312		318	1,585	6			2
Hampton, ..	73	.	66	316				.
Portsmouth,	35	. ..	33	168				
Williams,	35	.	24	113				.
Total, ...	654	. .	635	3,169	6	2	[illegible]	2

BAY COUNTY.—Continued.

TOWNSHIPS.	Value of Real Estate owned.	Occupied Farms.			
		Whole number.	Acres improved.	Acres unimproved.	Cash value of.
Arenac,	$ 720	6	165	897	$6,400
Bangor,	109,710	36	871	929	25,710
Bay City,	700,600	46	1,054	3,244	78,200
Hampton,	56,100	9	365	597	15,900
Portsmouth,	37,700	5	112	296	7,900
Williams,	16,400				
Total,	$921,230	102	2,567	5,963	$134,110

BAY COUNTY.—Continued.

Value of Farming Implements and Machinery.	Live Stock, June 1st, 1860.							
	Horses.	Asses and Mules.	Milch Cows.	Working Oxen.	Other Cattle.	Sheep.	Swine.	Value of Live Stock.
$ 655	1		9	8	10	8	19	$ 810
2,885	19		74	55	102	37	102	8,350
2,205	56		59	17	51		57	7,423
1,825	15		38	14	63		22	4,150
490	10		24	6	24		7	1,800
$8,060	101		204	100	250	45	207	$22,533

BAY COUNTY.—Continued.

TOWNSHIPS.	Produce, during the Year						
	Wheat, bushels of.	Rye, bushels of.	Indian corn, bushels of.	Oats, bushels of.	Barley, bushels of.	Buckwheat, bushels of.	Potatoes, bushels of.
Arenac, . .	110	34	10	.	.	.	180
Bangor, . .	1,443	1,351	1,935	608	.	5	2,525
Bay City, . .	2,937	55	2,030	3,105	25	248	2,639
Hampton, . .	50	210	525	170		131	720
Portsmouth, .	150	20	155	100		450	340
Williams,	.			.			. . .
Total, .	4,690	1,670	4,655	3,983	25	834	6,404

BAY COUNTY.—CONTINUED.

ENDING JUNE 1ST, 1860.							
Wool, pounds of.	Value of Orchard products.	Butter, pounds of.	Cheese, pounds of.	Hay, tons of.	Clover seed, bushels.	Maple Sugar, pounds.	Value of home made manufactures.
......	....	400	...	36	.	345	....
....	....	3,425	...	213		550	....
......	.....	3 090	...	1,945		..	.....
....	...	1,600	1,640	179		...	...
....	..	1,100	.....	43		...	....
......	..	...	.	....	.	..	.....
......	.	9,615	1,640	2,416	....	895	......

BAY COUNTY.—CONTINUED.

TOWNSHIPS.	Flouring Mills.							Saw Mills.			
	Number of.	Runs of Stone.	Power used.		Capital invested in real and personal estate in the business.	Annual product.		Number of.	Power used.		Capital invested in real and personal estate in the business.
			Water.	Steam.		Bbls. flour made.	Value of.		Water.	Steam.	
Arenac,					..		.				......
Bangor,								4		4	175000
Bay City,	1	2		1	16,000	3,500	25,000	15		15	210200
Hampton,					...		.				
Portsmouth,								1		1	30,000
Williams,					. .						.
Total,	1	2		1	16,000	3,500	25,000	20		20	415200

BAY COUNTY.—Continued.

Saw Mills. Annual product. Feet of Lumber Sawed.	Saw Mills. Annual product. Value of.	Aggregate of all kinds of manufactures, Mills included. Capital invested in real and personal estate in the business.	Hands employ'd. Males.	Hands employ'd. Females.	Value of annual products.	Estimated value of Real and Personal Estate. By Assessors.	Estimated value of Real and Personal Estate. By assistant Marshals.
12,000,000	100500	185,000	120		103,500		
31,350,000	254700	230,600	285		303,865	724,422	800,000
1,500,000	18000	45,000	21		31,750		
44,850,000	373200	460,600	426		439,115	724,422	800,000

BERRIEN COUNTY.

TOWNSHIPS.	Dwelling Houses.		Number of Families.	Number of Inhabitants.				
	Whole number.	Number in Cities.		Whole number.	Colored.	Deaf and Dumb.	Blind.	Insane.
Bainbridge,	168		167	938				
Berrien,	229		223	1 253	27	1	2	6
Benton,	204		200	1,028		1		
Bertrand,	293		277	1,540	6			1
Buchanan,	194		188	818			1	
Buchanan village,	185		190	910				
Chickaming,	70		70	310				
Galien,	142		143	528	3			
Hagar,	89		86	438				
Lake,	151		130	557				
New Buffalo,	196		186	834	13			
Niles,	479		475	2,722	84			1
Niles city, 1st ward	184	184	185	888	75			
" 2d "	120	120	119	660	28			
" 3d "	155	155	153	776	29	1	2	1
" 4th "	85	85	86	465				
Oronoco,	241		240	1,252	4			
Pipestone,	195		19	1,052	50	2		
Royalton,	192		216	964				
Sodus,	127		125	674	49	1		
St. Joseph,	281		279	1,358	17			
Three Oaks,	118		118	539				
Watervliet,	214		200	1,017	13	2	1	
Weesaw	159		153	753				
Total,	4,471	544	4,406	22,274	404	8	6	9

BERRIEN COUNTY.—Continued.

TOWNSHIPS.	Value of Real Estate owned.	Occupied Farms.			
		Whole number.	Acres improved.	Acres unimproved.	Cash value of.
Bainbridge,	$289,790	188	6,698	5,386	$246,550
Berrien,	505,354	135	6,959	8,597	443,155
Benton,	391,700	42	2,200	3,106	162,500
Bertrand,	999,441	140	12,804	5,546	850,380
Buchanan,	319,855	85	3,353	5,078	197,155
Buchanan village	184,665				
Chickaming,	104,130	51	785	6,057	102,438
Galien,	158,550	83	2,494	5,677	154,125
Hagar,	117,990	35	1,184	2,460	65,120
Lake,	121,490	75	1,762	6,027	127,190
New Buffalo,	130,088	74	1,213	5,177	90,810
Niles,	1,107,610	219	11,437	10,431	864,850
Niles city, 1st w.,	321,450				
" 2d w.,	380,730				
" 3d w.,	286,350				
" 4th w.,	200,675				
Oronoco,	431,144	89	5,300	8,298	301,315
Pipestone,	265,330	76	3,850	5,224	191,750
Royalton,	205,130	151	3,460	7,997	212,900
Sodus,	177,950	37	1,965	3,504	114,360
St. Joseph,	477,065	5	224	73	63,500
Three Oaks,	124,108	52	1,433	3,105	92,950
Watervliet,	213,635	80	2,872	3,983	132,150
Weesaw,	158,370	119	3,966	7,169	233,000
Total,	7,672,600	1,656	73,952	102,895	4,646,198

BERRIEN COUNTY.—CONTINUED.

Value of Farming Implements and Machinery.	Live Stock, June 1st, 1860. Horses.	Asses and Mules.	Milch Cows.	Working Oxen.	Other Cattle.	Sheep.	Swine.	Value of Live Stock.
$9,049	193		281	144	278	1,252	778	$36,695
11,782	439		411	83	581	1,154	1,746	61,302
3,560	94		143	62	174	325	373	16,890
25,260	520	5	441	38	588	1,823	1,831	76,108
4,845	210		218	98	347	304	1,075	35,872
1,210	41	2	69	58	82	26	228	8,223
3,862	135		183	104	256	114	569	27,879
2,609	40		84	59	69	105	185	9,277
2,650	120		175	96	292	74	629	18,518
3,575	67		116	74	134	15	315	12,223
23,238	572		690	125	618	1,212	1,795	82,045
8,068	276	2	275	194	477	462	1,159	39,237
5,742	166		253	98	347	521	708	31,819
9,373	195	2	255	141	350	143	859	27,080
2,764	87		122	66	153	407	322	14,848
465	7		12		6	27	21	1,382
3,080	83		133	60	176	114	308	11,962
6,550	107		164	87	214	395	534	19,715
7,775	239	2	303	110	587	229	1,028	36,189
125,457	3591	13	4328	1,697	5,729	8,702	14,473	567,264

BERRIEN COUNTY.—Continued.

TOWNSHIPS.	Produce, during the Year						
	Wheat, bushels of.	Rye, bushels of.	Indian corn, bushels of.	Oats, bushels of.	Barley, bushels of.	Buckwheat, bushels of.	Potatoes, bushels of.
Bainbridge,	17,009	358	23,453	6,370	20	677	16,628
Berrien, .	31,416	20	60,905	10,462	375	250	8,479
Benton, ..	4,828	50	8,000	1,054		104	4,740
Bertrand,	60,024	24460	70,128	15,158	635	184	10,353
Buchanan,	14,624		21,686	3,089	4	189	5,678
Buchanan vil.,	..	.		..			.....
Chickaming	817	8	4,165	230		45	1,775
Galien, ...	8,373		15,215	950		12	2,384
Hagar, . ..	2,631	254	4,558	396		98	2,479
Lake,	3,443	33	12,080	1,451		62	3,813
New Buffalo,	1,293	78	6,052	100		90	3,396
Niles, .	47,221	97	79,805	15,355	490	460	23,261
do city, 1st w..							. .
do city, 2d w	..		.				
do city, 3d w			. .				. .
do city, 4th w.,							. .
Oronoco,	18,067	17	37,698	6,885		61	5,536
Pipestone,.	12,520	96	22,745	3,857		288	3,868
Royalton,	7,858	142	17,258	2,497	50	320	5,907
Sodus, .	5,871	50	9,950	864		91	2,596
St. Joseph,	290	190	480	.		10	343
Three Oaks,	1,812	26	7,002	455	66	21	3,416
Watervliet,	4,424	253	12,315	1,727	40	593	7,341
Weesaw,.	13,574		25,025	1,645		138	6,893
Total, .	255936	26132	438520	72,545	1,680	3,703	118886

BERRIEN COUNTY.—Continued.

...ending June 1st, 1860.							
Wool, pounds of.	Value of Orchard products.	Butter, pounds of.	Cheese, pounds of.	Hay, tons of.	Clover seed, bushels.	Maple Sugar, pounds.	Value of home made manufactures.
4,412	4,438	24,077	3,590	1,259	64½	1,080	$372
3,996	8,111	33,477	780	919	140	5,590	648
1,133	7,590	11,440	640	728		1,870	154
5,928	6,077	41,141	300	1,282	271	2,050	489
....	2,678	18,150	329	690	25	1,978	850
......	.	.	. .		.		
...	550	3,205	....	235		1,830	.
.....	1,139	12,460	1,090	526		6,166	126
384	1,135	8,311	...	256		1,695	114
.....	2,166	8,800	..	543		1,647	.
...	333	7,684	100	421	.	1,475	. .
4,759	8,309	49,760	1,315	1,909	69	9,716	2,737
. .	...	. ..					.. ...
. ..	..	.	.			. .	.
. .	..				.	..	..
......	. . .	. . .	..	.	.		
1,49-	5,835	21,793	1,385	1,480	52½	1,530	158
1,711	1,677	16,070	12,050	524	1	1,755	278
..	4,796	14,690	450	742		3,655	128
1,505	3,958	8,355	1,900	370		2,100	103
58	11,161	856	.	28		...	. ..
.....	1,391	7,975	1,630	389	15	3,187	74
1,305	1,592	15,089	500	542	3	3,470	299
.....	2,329	20,150	4,320	969	9	4,610	....
26,689	75,265	322,483	30,379	13812	648	55,410	$6,530

BERRIEN COUNTY.—Continued.

TOWNSHIPS.	Flouring Mills.							Saw Mills.			
			Power used.			Annual product.			Power used.		
	Number of.	Runs of Stone.	Water.	Steam.	Capital invested in real and personal estate in the business.	Bbls. flour made.	Value of.	Number of.	Water.	Steam.	Capital invested in real and personal estate in the business.
Bainbridge					. . . .	. . . .		1	1		$1,500
Berrien,					.		. .				. .
Benton,.					. .			1		1	5,000
Bertrand,	1		1		$6,000	6,000	33,000	2	1	1	9,000
Buchanan,	2		2		13,000	42,940	256370	8	5	3	20,050
Buchanan v						.	.				. . . . .
Chickaming						. .	.	6		6	60,600
Galien,						. . .	.	4	3	1	16,800
Hagar,						. .		1		1	1,800
Lake,					. . .	. .		3	1	2	104800
N. Buffalo,						. . .	.	1	1		1,000
Niles,	1		1		12,000	4,700	27,500	2	2		4,200
City, 1st w.,					.	. . .	. .				. . .
" 2d w.,										.	.
" 3d w.,					. .						. . .
" 4th w.,	*3	5	2	1	89,000	49,700	270500	2		2	15,400
Oronoco,					. . .	. . .	.	2		2	6,000
Pipestone,					. .	. .	. . .	3	3		8,800
Royalton,	1			1	3,000	1,500	5,000	4	1	3	11,000
Sodus,					.	. . .					. . .
St. Joseph,	1			1	20,500	6,379	37,471	3		3	24,000
Three Oaks,					. .	.		3		3	15,600
Watervliet,	1		1		5,000	175	1,225	3	2	1	29,500
Weesaw,					.	. .	. . . .	2	2		9,000
Total,	10	5	7	3	148500	111,394	631066	51	22	29	344050

* The whole city.

BERRIEN COUNTY—Continued.

Saw Mills.		Aggregate of all kinds of Manufactures, Mills included.				Estimated value of Real and Personal Estate.	
Annual product.			Hands employ'd				
Feet of Lumber Sawed.	Value of.	Capital invested in real and personal estate in the business.	Males.	Females.	Value of annual product.	By Assessors.	By assistant Marshals.
198,000	$1,188	$1,500	1		$1,188	145,990	218,985
.. ...	....	.			.	296,377	444,566
225,000	1,865	5,000	4		1,865	154,267	231,400
700,000	6,400	15,050	8		40,300	.	1,746,974
3,716,000	30,144	41,850	78		312,014	74,905	.
.					. ..		
3,113,600	37,500	62,600	54		39,500	83,601	
2,150,000	20,700	16,800	17		20,700	117,285	.
280,000	2,320	3,800	11		4,720	58,092	87,138
12,900,000	103000	105,150	60		103,000	138,242	
500.000	400	14,000	62		65,400	137,762	..
450,000	5,820	16,500	8	.	34,820	. . .	1,358,718
......		.			. ...		
. ..	......	..				..	
...	.	.			.	. .	.
520,000	4,960	232,007	198		509,275	... .	1,610,815
925,000	7,225	7,000	10	.	8,650	325,026	487,539
975,000	8,005	9,300	14		9,255	255,057	*382,585
2,984,000	27,440	14,000	17		32,440	154,965	. .
. ...	.. .	.. ...				..	.
2,840,000	28 740	58,200	70		79,437	191,604	287,406
2,145,000	59,200	15,600	25		59,200	127,716	.
1,790,000	9,350	34 500	18		10,575	129,375	194,062
1,200,000	.8,900	9,000	8		8,900	152,740	...
37,611,600	363157	661,857	663		1341239	4445503	† 6668255

* Includes Sodus.
† As given by Marshals.

[illegible] COUNTY (Continued).

BRANCH COUNTY.

TOWNSHIPS.	Dwelling Houses.		Number of Families.	Number of Inhabitants.				
	Whole number.	Number in Cities.		Whole number.	Colored.	Deaf and Dumb.	Blind.	Insane.
Algansee,	227		227	1,121				
Batavia,	235		236	1,189		1	2	1
Bethel,	236		235	1,185	5			
Bronson,	253		256	1,362	3			
Butler,	228		230	1,123		1		
California,	139		139	713		1		
Coldwater,	299		317	1,544	2	1		
Coldwater village,	550		563	2,905	15			2
Girard,	232		235	1,128				
Gilead,	115		114	683				
Kinderhook,	102		104	572				
Matteson,	193		193	1,005				
Noble,	118		118	797				
Ovid,	234		232	1,199	6	1		
Quincy,	262		281	1,362				
Quincy village,	128		123	573	1	1		
Sherwood,	198		198	1,051				1
Union,	343		343	1,685				
Total,	4,092		4,144	21,197	32	6	2	4

BRANCH COUNTY.—Continued.

TOWNSHIPS.	Value of Real Estate owned.	Occupied Farms. Whole number.	Acres improved.	Acres unimproved.	Cash value of.
Algansee,	$315,754	148	6,189	7,267	$300,910
Batavia,	385,804	160	7,472	7,264	347,125
Bethel,	293,707	155	6,507	7,529	275,457
Bronson,	332,338	98	5,049	6,226	265,910
Butler,	255,013	153	5,851	7,469	246,020
California,	182,773	94	4,704	4,584	166,300
Coldwater,	508,245	178	9,711	7,766	634,720
Coldwater vil.,	1,163,545			...	
Girard,	433,685	154	9,089	8,291	410,775
Gilead,	227,175	85	5,478	3,549	226,350
Kinderhook,	154,500	71	4,448	4,655	155,310
Matteson,	275,610	138	5,575	7,189	262,240
Noble,	175,490	80	4,317	4,535	153,890
Ovid,	387,725	149	6,258	7,439	310,053
Quincy,	552,814	199	9,449	8,780	560,029
Quincy village,	214,770				
Sherwood,	362,386	142	9,316	7,179	360,336
Union,	532,755	158	8,440	7,190	401,409
Total,	$6,754,089	2,162	107,853	106,912	$5,076,834

BRANCH COUNTY.—Continued.

Value of Farming Implements and Machinery.	Live Stock, June 1st, 1860.							
	Horses.	Asses and Mules.	Milch Cows.	Working Oxen.	Other Cattle.	Sheep.	Swine.	Value of Live Stock.
$8,883	291		413	136	547	2,489	1,560	$50,666
9,558	361	1	460	130	560	1,920	1,315	54,651
8,037	302		403	150	593	1,421	1,214	46,733
7,203	236		279	106	520	1,110	860	35,228
7,167	265		384	140	484	2,307	1,171	45,757
4,726	187		243	74	329	1,674	804	29,310
12,936	488		522	134	584	2,783	1,522	77,532
10,945	410		519	101	661	4,245	1,746	65,584
5,338	205		236	46	296	907	1,117	29,909
3,907	156		195	64	372	1,100	608	25,883
8,919	248		396	149	566	1,285	1,324	44,386
5,854	196		227	38	323	938	658	27,835
8,140	265		399	142	494	1,947	993	45,787
15,612	470		574	183	854	5,989	2,065	83,398
9,699	352	2	389	128	552	2,700	1,632	56,839
11,150	430		437	156	710	3,692	1,396	67,335
$138,064	4862	3	6076	1,877	8,445	36,507	19,985	$786,828

BRANCH COUNTY.—Continued.

TOWNSHIPS.	Produce, during the Year						
	Wheat, bushels of.	Rye, bushels of.	Indian corn, bushels of.	Oats, bushels of.	Barley, bushels of.	Buckwheat, bushels of.	Potatoes, bushels of.
Algansee,	14,114	288	32,554	4,731	458	1,173	10,969
Batavia,	15,063	291	39,544	3,363	208	1,124	20,585
Bethel,	14,020	272	23,472	3,028		1,122	11,174
Bronson,	15,245	1,056	24,416	3,046	115	478	11,969
Butler, ...	14,920	920	28,720	5,766	101	1,427	8,892
California, .	14,213	361	22,497	2,656	42	1,128	6,167
Coldwater, .	23,497	335	50,703	8,932	620	1,920	35,584
Coldwater vil	. .	.	.....	..			.. ..
Girard, ...	26,107	2,679	38,855	9,782	90	1,089	11,433
Gilead, ...	19,383	911	37,207	2,913	12	436	7,433
Kinderhook, .	10,589	105	17,345	2,242	45	1,383	8,009
Matteson, ..	14,080	35	27,810	4,342	150	895	15,445
Noble, ...	12,128	561	22,950	2,627	228	314	13,184
Ovid, ..	14,894	727	31,374	2,674	58	1,042	14,763
Quincy, ..	27,451	753	60,576	10,589	2,664	2,311	18,758
Quincy vil., .	..			....	.		....
Sherwood,	29,003	1,620	38,492	3,409	162	423	8,479
Union, . ..	23,469	360	38,617	6,545	738	444	8,408
Total,	288170	11218	545182	10,645	5,691	17709	211282

BRANCH COUNTY.—Continued.

Ending June 1st, 1860.							
Wool, pounds of.	Value of Orchard products.	Butter, pounds of.	Cheese, pounds of.	Hay, tons of.	Clover seed, bushels.	Maple Sugar, pounds.	Value of home-made manufactures.
5,806	$1,894	25,005	4,703	1,060	3	4,907	$5
5,211	1,572	32,104	2,206	1,557	248	9,826	152
3,319	1,459	28,150	3,039	1,330	44	3,065	109
8,516	1,182	13,545	2,260	1,323	176½	565	47
6,986	2,160	25,652	660	1,565	52	16,058	20
4,589	1,026	14,841	609	924	21	1,895	97
7,569	3,353	37,550	3,717	1,822	205	3,565	94
......	..	.	....	..	.	..	..
12,282	3,391	35,753	3,282	1,621	276	9,930	....
3,139	1,274	12,923	3,812	644	16½	917	23
2,340	845	11,352	825	1,198	13	35	.....
3,336	1,787	23,185	3,810	1,307	193	8,662	110
3,359	873	11,398	1,580	1,175	98	.....	....
4,760	2,230	24,631	2,372	1,216	12	4,320	204
17,200	6,176	42,597	4,355	2,429	116	6,965	127
......	..	..	....	..	.	..	....
7,666	1,657	22,396	2,145	1,415	476	11,100	40
10,295	2,267	28,310	10,426	1,410	4	28,670	10
101,373	33,136	389,392	49,801	21996	1996	110480	$1,038

BRANCH COUNTY.—Continued.

TOWNSHIPS.	Flouring Mills.							Saw Mills.			
	Number of.	Runs of Stone.	Power used.		Capital invested in real and personal estate in the business.	Annual product.		Number of.	Power used.		Capital invested in real and personal estate in the business.
			Water	Steam.		Bbls. flour made.	Value of.		Water.	Steam.	
Algansee,								4	2	2	$5,700
Batavia,								1		1	4,000
Bethel,								4		4	14,000
Bronson,	1	2		1	$7,000	2,000	11,000	4	2	2	8,000
Butler,								1		1	1,500
California,											
Coldwater,								4	3	1	14,800
Coldwater v.,											
Girard,								1	1		2,000
Gilead,											
Kinderhook,								1	1		3,000
Matteson,											
Noble,											
Ovid,								3	2	1	5,200
Quincy,	1			1	1,686	250	1,500	4		4	15,860
Quincy vil.,											
Sherwood,								1	1		3,000
Union,								2	2		5,000
Total,	2	2		2	$8,686	2,250	12,500	30	14	16	82,060

BRANCH COUNTY.—Continued.

Saw Mills.		Aggregate of all kinds of manufactures, Mills included.				Estimated value of Real and Personal Estate.	
Annual product.		Capital invested in real and personal estate in the business.	Hands employ'd		Value of annual products.	By Assessors.	By assistant Marshals.
Feet of Lumber Sawed.	Value of.		Males.	Females.			
1,370,000	11,700	$5,700	6		$11,700		
700,000	5,600	4,000	4		5,600		
1,875,000	14,700	14,000	9		14,700		
1,485,000	13,365	18,400	23		28,615		
450,000	3,150	2,100	4		4,650		
1,950,000	16,800	80,600	123	61	140,243		
400,000	2,800	2,000	2		2,800		
175,000	1,271	3,180	2		1,821		
410,000	3,080	5,200	7		3,080		
2,925,000	22,800	21,596	35		40,275		
300,000	2,400	3,000	1		2,400		
500,000	4,100	6,200	7		4,700		
12,540,000	101766	165,976	223	61	260,584	3738257	5,601,385

BRANCH COUNTY.—Continued.

Saw mills. Annual product. Feet of lumber sawed.	Value.	Aggregate of all other manufactures. Capital invested.	Hands employed. Male.	Female.	Value of annual products.	Estimated value of real and personal estate. Real estate.	Personal estate.
1,570,000	11,700	[illegible]	6		$11,700		
700,000	5,600	4,000	4		[illegible]		
1,475,000	14,700	14,000	9		14,700		
1,455,000	[illegible]	[illegible]	28		[illegible]		
450,000	[illegible]	2,100	1		[illegible]		
[illegible]	10,800	[illegible]	121	[illegible]	140,240		
400,000	2,800	2,000	[illegible]		[illegible]		
175,000	[illegible]	[illegible]	[illegible]		1,221		
410,000	3,080	[illegible]			3,080		
3,035,000	[illegible]	[illegible]	36		40,272		
[illegible]	[illegible]	[illegible]	1		2,400		
[illegible]	[illegible]	[illegible]	7		4,200		
[illegible]	[illegible]	[illegible]	[illegible]	[illegible]	280,584	[illegible]	[illegible]

CALHOUN COUNTY.

TOWNSHIPS.	Dwelling Houses.		Number of Families.	Number of Inhabitants.				
	Whole number.	Number in Cities.		Whole number.	Colored.	Deaf and Dumb.	Blind.	Insane.
Albion,	171		160	939				
Albion village,	336		329	1,720	22		1	
Athens,	204		161	980				
Battle Creek,	221		178	1,151	16			
City, 4 wards,	760	760	734	3,508	152		3	1
Bedford,	270		242	1,210	13	1		
Burlington,	189		182	941	4			
Burlington village,	30		30	150				
Clarence,	170		164	866		1	2	
Clarendon,	191		190	960				
Convis,	194		184	1,080				
Eckford,	201		198	1,023	1			1
Emmett,	272		207	1,223	11			
Eredonia,	174		163	900	8	1	3	1
Homer,	238		235	1,160	1		1	1
Lee,	178		174	878	16			
LeRoy,	239		223	1,174				
Marengo,	218		191	1,099	9		2	4
Marshall,	186		173	993	3		1	
City, 1st ward,	318	318	306	1,536	39	2		
" 2nd ward,	475	475	440	2,044	60			2
Newton,	187		168	882	2			
Penfield,	194		195	1,002	7			
Sheridan,	197		194	994				2
Tekonsha,	185		171	900	8			
Tekonsha village,	30		25	135				
Total,	6,028	1,555	5,623	29,398	372	5	13	12

CALHOUN COUNTY.—Continued.

TOWNSHIPS.	Value of Real Estate owned.	Occupied Farms.			
		Whole number.	Acres improved.	Acres unimproved.	Cash value of.
Albion,	$591,917	126	12,498	6,329	$526,486
Albion village,	537,600		...	...	..
Athens,	345,630	123	7,769	5,910	282,550
Battle Creek,	643,700	170	12,661	7,353	692,470
City, 4 wards,	1,466,416	1[illegible]	1,200	636	129,100
Bedford,	559,775	164	9,883	8,329	479,130
Burlington,	289,220	172	8,806	8,214	300,345
Burlington vil.,	47,310		..	..	
Clarence,	166,039	96	5,145	5,503	144,681
Clarendon,	309,885	109	7,093	6,484	285,315
Convis,	350.400	158	9,700	8,205	339,600
Eckford,	472,397	125	11,334	6,328	448,949
Emmett,	604,100	175	13 476	7,124	681,150
Fredonia,	438,000	158	9,818	9,559	419,200
Homer,	509,729	99	9,166	7,908	401,300
Lee,	172,565	82	3,723	3,893	118,600
LeRoy,	438,500	175	11,376	8,601	453,050
Marengo,	664,950	151	13,007	6,493	640,400
Marshall,	674,600	119	10,642	5,854	602,700
City, 1st ward,	822,540	..	...	.	..
" 2d ward,	656,450	*20	1,437	932	144,700
Newton,	338,750	156	9,254	9,088	360,780
Penfield,	408,530	142	10,130	8,697	506,100
Sheridan,	327,985	134	8,806	5,822	369,378
Tekonsha,	311,100	173	8,108	7,568	314,590
Tekonsha village,	43,900		...	..	
Total,	12,191,988	2,843	195,032	144,800	8,630,484

* The whole city.

CALHOUN COUNTY.—Continued.

Value of Farming Implements and Machinery.	Live Stock, June 1st, 1860.							
	Horses.	Asses and Mules.	Milch Cows.	Working Oxen.	Other Cattle.	Sheep.	Swine.	Value of Live Stock.
$16,469	433		422	73	496	7,291	1,074	$72,707
11,890	299		334	95	550	2,689	947	56,450
20,615	486	3	505	147	608	6,962	1,195	79,319
2,680	77	2	60	10	41	115	69	8,305
17,131	366		476	176	542	3,381	894	66,158
26,300	340		410	179	649	3,026	940	65,820
7,272	130		271	148	338	1,275	514	26,122
9,784	299		335	90	409	4,347	764	46,892
20,290	273		452	215	481	5,535	826	60,940
13,250	342		410	118	418	5,382	865	63,274
17,924	428		508	152	551	5,203	1,178	69,934
18,420	305		469	200	507	6,063	904	69,775
10,406	284		347	96	462	6,321	1,010	62,923
7,001	105	1	214	110	243	670	443	21,364
16,858	351		505	166	635	4,592	1,201	71,540
24,790	414		507	187	629	5,874	1,009	84,185
24,450	355	1	406	141	629	8,346	940	75,300
3,400	47		67	14	33	193	61	9,550
22,871	289		418	220	504	5,783	942	62,850
13,941	344	2	426	218	535	5,578	1,003	67,150
11,246	299		375	129	414	4,680	785	54,323
18,005	295		436	157	521	3,003	748	54,095
.....								
$334,993	6561	9	8353	3,041	10195	96,309	18,312	1,248,976

CALHOUN COUNTY.—Continued.

TOWNSHIPS.	Wheat, bushels of.	Rye, bushels of.	Indian corn, bushels of.	Oats, bushels of.	Barley, bushels of.	Buckwheat, bushels of.	Potatoes, bushels of.
	Produce during the Year						
Albion, ...	43,117	1,072	27,450	16,495	4,786	445	8,314
Albion village,		.		.. ..		.	......
Athens, ...	26,042	87	29,129	4,340	115	145	6,225
Battle Creek, ..	54,686	160	48,825	17,843	136	494	13,918
City, 4 wards,	1,830	87	3,270	925	40	5	1,465
Bedford, ...	30,003	542	31,015	4 350	510	201	12,313
Burlington, ..	38,028	220	30,755	7,200	282	298	11,634
Burlington v.,	.		. . .	.		.	.....
Clarence, ...	11,329	153	10,310	3,833	55	417	6,432
Clarendon, .	20,821	252	19,878	7,070	924	322	5,063
Convis, ...	34,961	608	30,875	9,343	945	216	11,835
Eckford, ...	40,036	604	29,541	14,953	1,117	183	8,390
Emmett, . .	47,897	1,800	49,925	7,128	1,012	76	19,132
Fredonia, . .	39,605	1,687	30,340	12,932	1,050	499	13,535
Homer, ...	29,885	462	28,601	9,821	1,183	1,038	6,311
Lee, ...	7,750	92	7,876	3,124	281	260	4,109
LeRoy, ...	38,048	6	33,080	8,225	664	750	11,622
Marengo, ...	54,972	935	46,325	14,620	1,825	324	13,242
Marshall, ...	41,663	297	30,770	14,182	753	506	12,985
City, 1st ward,	. ..		.. ..	......		.	......
" 2d ward,	4,880	.	3,265	300	690	110	2,160
Newton, ...	40,635	170	31,420	5,895	487	390	13,055
Penfield, ...	33,556	1,706	31,055	8,335	347	52	13,168
Sheridan, .	31,270	620	26,904	7,300	731	441	9,293
Tekonsha, ...	26,790	637	32,000	9,002	522	552	13,425
Tekonsha vil.	.	..	..	......	...	.	.....
Total, ...	692804	12197	612109	187816	18455	8,194	217658

CALHOUN COUNTY.—Continued.

ENDING JUNE 1ST, 1860.							
Wool, pounds of.	Value of Orchard products.	Butter, pounds of.	Cheese, pounds of.	Hay, tons of.	Clover seed, bushels.	Maple Sugar, pounds.	Value of home made manufactures.
22,000	$3,774	32,205	4,519	1,835	584	....	$523
.	.		.....			..	.
9,672	1,280	46,515	1,200	1,439	280	.. ..	.
23,411	5,945	58,114	3,610	2,644	471	.. .	240
200	95	3,800	300	261	13	.	.
9,274	2,095	49,065	3,790	1,993	326	.	35
9,807	3,038	40,675	3,860	2,229	184	.. .	10
...	....	.	.			.. ..	
3,073	1,463	21,175	150	1,571	35		444
12,341	4,121	31,120	2,143	1,855	137	1,285	648
18,177	2,533	45,900	5,120	2,373	379	....	284
16,409	2,658	29,720	5,024	2,150	281	.	402
15,437	3,108	69,996	2,430	2,340	540	.	150
18,700	3,712	41,820	4,429	2,732	481	.	189
19,640	4,706	21,625	2,380	2,146	515	. ..	709
1,948	946	18,827	810	969	5	2,840	831
16,581	2,886	69,660	1,900	2,321	429	.	.
21,484	7,331	48,350	8,510	2,587	436	.	579
21,432	2,877	36,925	3,305	1,930	497	600	754
. ..	... .					. ..	
650	405	6,500	200	222	35	. .	
17,399	2,662	37,165	3,285	2,235	145	. ..	174
16,689	2,501	59,840	279	1,884	173	......	120
16,799	2,839	28,273	4,565	1,968	144	. . ..	821
8,782	2,796	38,019	5,195	2,677	157	... ..	221
......	. ...		......	.	.	.....	. .
299,905	61,771	834,289	67,324	42361	6247	4,725	$7,134

CALHOUN COUNTY.—Continued.

TOWNSHIPS.	Flouring Mills.							Saw Mills.			
	Number of.	Runs of Stone.	Power used.		Capital invested in real and personal estate in the business.	Annual product.		Number of.	Power used.		Capital invested in real and personal estate in the business.
			Water.	Steam.		Bbls. flour made.	Value of.		Water.	Steam.	
Albion,	3		3		56,000	24,048	120240	1		1	15,000
Albion vil.,											
Athens,											
Battle Cr'k,											
City, 4 w'ds,	3		3		223000	42,000	260000				
Bedford,	1		1		6,000	1,600	11,640	2	2		5,000
Burlington,											
" vil.,											
Clarence,											
Clarendon,								2	1	1	5,000
Convis,								1		1	2,000
Eckford,											
Emmett,	1		1		10,000	5,000	28,250	1	1		3,000
Fredonia,								1		1	3,000
Homer,	1		1		5,000	1,600	8,000				
Lee,								1		1	3,500
LeRoy,											
Marengo,											
Marshall,											
City, 1st w.,											
" 2d w	5		4	1	114000	85,000	463000				
Newton,											
Penfield,								2		2	9,000
Sheridan,											
Tekonsha,	1		1		25,000	10,000	*9,000				
" vil.,											
Total,	15		14	1	439000	169,248	900130	11	4	7	45,500

* As returned, evidently a mistake.

CALHOUN COUNTY.—CONTINUED.

SAW MILLS.		AGGREGATE OF ALL KINDS OF MANUFACTURES, MILLS INCLUDED.				ESTIMATED VALUE OF REAL AND PERSONAL ESTATE.	
Annual product.			Hands employ'd				
Feet of Lumber Sawed.	Value of.	Capital invested in real and personal estate in the business.	Males.	Females.	Value of annual product.	By Assessors.	By assistant Marshals.
600,000	$6,000	$82,000	43		141,140	..	....
.	...	...		.	..	....	..
....	....				.	.	..
.	....	.				.	..
.....	.....	386,000	213		496,380	...	..
400,000	*1,300	12,100	11		17,240	.	..
......	...	.			.....	...	..
.		.			.....	..	....
..	....	..			.	....	.
450,000	3,700	5,000	6		3,700	....	...
....	3,000	2,500	11		6,600	...	..
.....	...	.....			.....	.	....
350,000	3,400	16,400	13		41,060	.	....
469,500	1,878	3,000	2		1,878	.....	.....
....	...	12,000	12		18,800	.	..
630,000	6,500	3,500	4		6,500	.	
.	.	...			..	......	.....
...	..	5,200	12		3,400	.	.....
.		..					....
..	.	...			..	.....	....
...	..	200,000	165		637,470	607,018	900,000
....		...				...	..
800,000	7,000	9,800	19		9,800	...	...
...	.				..		..
......	.	25,000	4		9,000	...	...
......	......	.		.	..	.....	..
3,699,500	32,778	762,600	515		1392968	5524740	†7900000

* As returned, evidently a mistake.
† As given by Marshals.

CASS COUNTY.

TOWNSHIPS.	Dwelling Houses.		Number of Families.	Number of Inhabitants.				
	Whole number.	Number in Cities.		Whole number.	Colored.	Deaf and Dumb.	Blind.	Insane.
Adamsville village,	20		20	105				
Calvin,	258		258	1,378	794			
Dowagiac village,	247		251	1,180	32			
Edwardsburg vil.,	52		53	241			1	
Howard,	218		222	1,140	80	1	1	
Jefferson,	209		211	1,232	4			2
LaGrange,	320		320	1,706	17	2	1	
Mason,	144		149	769	2			
Marcellus,	155		153	754	4	1		
Milton,	99		100	574	1			
Newburg,	167		169	861	51	1	1	2
Ontwa,	104		104	534				
Penn,	239		239	1,302	184		1	
Porter,	333		340	1,832	164	3		1
Pokagon,	190		191	1,000	1		1	
Pokagon village,	24		26	122				
Silver Creek,	212		222	1,102	2	1	1	
Summerville vil.,	34		34	130				
Volinia,	195		200	994	20	1		2
Wayne,	188		191	939				
Total,	3,408		3,453	17,895	1356	10	7	7

CHEBOYGAN COUNTY.

TOWNSHIPS.	Whole number.	Number in Cities.	Number of Families.	Whole number.	Colored.	Deaf and Dumb.	Blind.	Insane.
Burt,	31		20	170				
Duncan,	59		25	134				
Inverness,	81		61	295				
Total,	171		106	599				

CASS COUNTY.—CONTINUED.

TOWNSHIPS.	Value of Real Estate owned.	Occupied Farms.			
		Whole number.	Acres improved.	Acres unimproved.	Cash value of.
Adamsville vil.,	$18,600				
Calvin,	277,695	112	5,501	7,240	$243,100
Dowagiac vil.,	396,225				
Edwardsburg v.,	38,300				
Howard,	431,400	165	9,006	9,041	436,100
Jefferson,	416,800	148	11,929	7,893	439,600
LaGrange,	764,605	118	9,141	7,827	518,900
Mason,	334,272	86	6,184	3,544	285,050
Marcellus,	185,490	71	2,524	4,940	119,650
Milton,	330,050	90	7,100	4,101	359,250
Newburg,	240,245	89	4,136	6,924	173,680
Ontwa,	399,400	82	7,641	3,379	393,900
Penn,	633,095	99	7,380	8,936	515,435
Porter,	637,360	211	12,945	11,923	580,950
Pokagon,	619,220	137	8,742	9,229	556,275
Pokagon village,	32,600				
Silver Creek,	438,500	141	6,676	6,695	402,860
Summerville vil.,	31,700				
Volinia,	425,235	101	6,301	6,705	353,400
Wayne,	420,200	139	9,207	7,827	395,700
Total,	7,070,992	1,789	114,413	109,294	5,773,850

CHEBOYGAN COUNTY.—CONTINUED.

Burt,	$5,012	10	145	1,051	$3,241
Duncan,	6,151	7	257	692	3,958
Inverness,	19,592	13	171	617	5,778
Total,	$30,755	30	573	2,360	$12,977

CASS COUNTY.—Continued.

Value of Farming Implements and Machinery.	Live Stock, June 1st, 1860.							
	Horses.	Asses and Mules.	Milch Cows.	Working Oxen.	Other Cattle.	Sheep.	Swine.	Value of Live Stock.
$6,187	285		227	76	371	888	1,646	$37,075
12,000	389		421	130	456	1,103	1,266	52,500
11,535	409	2	380	83	579	2,693	1,526	58,255
14,867	364		379	81	602	1,880	2,088	62,260
6,975	235	2	276	50	389	839	490	36,450
3,522	122		172	60	172	270	674	20,028
10,700	253		291	29	450	952	1,016	35,750
5,604	171		205	70	275	911	782	27,050
10,532	286		288	49	373	1,042	845	40,330
10,497	315	2	316	49	656	3,362	1,086	66,425
16,742	514	1	588	181	686	3,854	1,778	80,209
12,119	420		387	80	572	1,603	1,234	57,508
9,859	268		353	137	420	950	1,177	43,542
9,435	289		284	62	385	1,051	1,078	44,615
13,701	313		361	118	406	1,660	1,129	50,690
$154,275	4633	7	4928	1,255	6,792	23,058	17,815	$712,687

CHEBOYGAN COUNTY.—Continued.

Value of Farming Implements and Machinery.	Horses.	Asses and Mules.	Milch Cows.	Working Oxen.	Other Cattle.	Sheep.	Swine.	Value of Live Stock.
$130	19		7	4	5	....	24	$1,225
198	6		13	10	27	14	45	1,803
210	10		16	11	20	....	35	2,078
$538	35		36	25	52	14	104	$5,106

CASS COUNTY.—CONTINUED.

TOWNSHIPS.	PRODUCE, DURING THE YEAR						
	Wheat, bushels of.	Rye, bushels of	Indian corn, bushels of.	Oats, bushels of.	Barley, bushels of.	Buckwheat, bushels of.	Potatoes, bushels of.
Adamsville v.,	.	..	..	..			.
Calvin, . ..	17,021	150	47,730	3,706	20	196	6,405
Dowagiac vil.,				. .			. . .
Edwardsb'g v.,	....	.	.. ..	. ...	.	..	.
Howard, ..	27,775	330	43,995	4,864	250	398	18,044
Jefferson,	35,333	50	71,330	6,963	.	517	12,537
LaGrange,	41,226	131	55,760	18,498	220	130	7,953
Mason, ...	23,058	105	34,045	3,147	.	357	9,665
Marcellus,	11,032	55	10,783	3,112	83	401	3,459
Milton, .	26,020	360	50,990	8,145		406	9,609
Newburg,	13,645	283	25,605	2,087	39	654	5,666
Ontwa, ...	28,979		52,090	10,970		56	13,763
Penn,. .	24,212	170	64,185	10,670	1,295	420	5,109
Porter, ..	59,914	1,331	82,110	7,274	400	1,078	14,854
Pokagon, .	31,082	150	38,700	15,900	50	493	8,217
Pokagon vil.,	. ...		.	. ..			. .. .
Silver Creek,	24,098		40,940	6,683	20	383	10,621
Summerville v.	....	.	. ..	..	.		. . ..
Volinia,..	28,710	25	24,755	15,613	450	115	3,878
Wayne,. . .	31,924	.	37,310	8,304	16	203	13,199
Total,	424029	3,140	680328	125936	2,843	5,807	142979

CHEBOYGAN COUNTY.—CONTINUED.

Burt, .	10	4½	299	210		.	1,284
Duncan, .	54	40		920	150	.	1,993
Inverness,	49	20	10	662		.	1,850
Total,	113	64½	309	1,792	150		5,127

CASS COUNTY.—CONTINUED.

[illegible]ENDING JUNE 1ST, 1860.							
Wool, pounds of	Value of Orchard products.	Butter, pounds of.	Cheese, pounds of.	Hay, tons of.	Clover seed, bushels.	Maple Sugar, pounds.	Value of home made manufactures.
3,056	$6,118	8,840	70	703	26½	14,825	$281
.	. .		.			....	
2,899	4,854	32,041	1,306	1,693	4	560	168
4,606	5,829	28,845	6,550	1,588	169	700	15
5,640	5,860	29,225	1,795	1,434	180	3,750	47
3,187	6,990	21,300	7,395	946	66	2,350	277
905	655	8,600	300	285	11	1,330	32
2,541	3,495	22,870	200	740	76	. . .	.....
1,130	2,595	11,280	250	768	37	4,172	171
4,221	4,498	23,400	3,150	852	241	1,000	.
10,088	4,750	17,650	555	1,125	94½	16,405	379
8,658	10,495	30,985	3,100	1,830	139	585	170
5,915	4,270	30,452	870	1,338	307	4,545	298
.. ..	. . .					... .	. ...
2,720	3,049	25,330	730	989	11	8,019	163
...	.		. .			.. ..	.. .
2,948	3,425	13,890	445	602	29	9,285	51
5,267	3,841	30,659	325	1,284	154	3,365	543
63,781	70,724	335,367	27,041	16177	1545	70,891	$2,595

CHEBOYGAN COUNTY.—CONTINUED.

Wool, pounds of	Value of Orchard products.	Butter, pounds of.	Cheese, pounds of.	Hay, tons of.	Clover seed, bushels.	Maple Sugar, pounds.	Value of home made manufactures.
	...	50	. . .	21½		5,500	.
.		1,000	. ...	50½		3,100	
..	.. .	900	..	41½	.	600	.....
. .	. ...	1,950	.....	113½		9,200	. .

CASS COUNTY.—Continued.

TOWNSHIPS.	Flouring Mills.							Saw Mills.			
	Number of.	Runs of Stone.	Power used.		Capital invested in real and personal estate in the business.	Annual product.		Number of.	Power used.		Capital invested in real and personal estate in the business.
			Water.	Steam.		Bbls. flour made.	Value of.		Water.	Steam.	
Adamsville v.,											
Calvin,								3	1	2	$9,000
Dowagiac vil.,	1	3	1		10,500	11125	70,000				
Edwardsb'g v											
Howard,								1	1		2,000
Jefferson,								2	2		2,200
LaGrange,	2		1	1	11,250	1,300	7,800	2	1	1	5,000
Mason,								1		1	2,000
Marcellus,								3	2	1	4,000
Milton,											
Newburg,								2	1	1	5,000
Ontwa,	2	6	1	1	19,000	9,175	41,375				
Penn,	1		1		5,000		5,000	2		2	19,000
Porter,											
Pokagon,	1	2	1		8,500	4,666	18,664	2	2		2,500
Pokagon vil.,											
Silver Creek,	1	2	1		4,000	300	13,300	5	3	2	11,600
Summ'rville v											
Volinia,								4	4		6,500
Wayne,											
Total,	8	13	6	2	58,250	26566	156139	27	17	10	68,800

CHEBOYGAN COUNTY.—Continued.

TOWNSHIPS.	Number of.	Runs of Stone.	Water.	Steam.	Capital.	Bbls. flour made.	Value of.	Number of.	Water.	Steam.	Capital.
Burt,											
Duncan,											
Inverness,								1		1	$2,300
Total,								1		1	$2,300

CASS COUNTY.—Continued.

Saw Mills. Annual product. Feet of Lumber Sawed.	Saw Mills. Annual product. Value of.	Aggregate of all kinds of Manufactures, Mills included. Capital invested in real and personal estate in the business.	Hands employ'd. Males.	Hands employ'd. Females.	Value of annual products.	Estimated value of Real and Personal Estate. By Assessors.	By assistant Marshals.
*250,000	$6,400	$9,000	7		$6,400	199,974	$259,000
	.	35,500	59		110,479	.. .	.
40,000	620	2,000	1		620	227,330	303,000
500,000	3,000	2,200	2		3,000	277,576	370,000
	2,600	35,050	36		64,800	439,947	596,000
	2,000	2,000	3		2,000	146,974	195,000
1,000,000	6,800	4,000	6		6,800	98,972	132,000
...	. .	.				215,754	287,000
1,000,000	7,500	5,000	5		7,500	137,518	185,357
.. .	.	20,700	8		45,725	270,055	360,000
*500,000	15,600	24,000	20		20,600	312,053	416,000
. .	. . .	. ..				291,730	388,000
140,000	1,820	11,850	7		22,779	409,513	546,000
2,310,000	18,700	15,600	10		32,000	199,858	266,000
. .	.				..	...	.
730,000	5,280	6,500	5		5,280	240,595	320,000
.	. .				..	237,664	316,000
6,470,000	70,320	173,400	169		327,983	2705513	4,939,357

CHEBOYGAN COUNTY.—Continued.

Feet of Lumber Sawed.	Value of.	Capital invested.	Males.	Females.	Value of annual products.	By Assessors.	By assistant Marshals.
	. ..				. ...	5,933	$9,850
	..	. .			. ...	36,670	13,744
300,000	$800	$6 200	22		$13,550	38,492	45,306
300,000	$800	$6,200	22		$13,550	$81,095	$68,900

* As returned, evidently a mistake.

CHIPPEWA COUNTY

TOWNSHIPS.	Dwelling Houses.		Number of Families.	Number of Inhabitants.				
	Whole number.	Number in Cities.		Whole number.	Colored.	Deaf and Dumb.	Blind.	Insane.
Saut Ste Marie,	294		294	1,304	8			
Sugar Island,	60		60	240				
Total,	354		354	1,544	8			

CLINTON COUNTY

TOWNSHIPS.	Dwelling Houses.		Number of Families.	Number of Inhabitants.				
	Whole number.	Number in Cities.		Whole number.	Colored.	Deaf and Dumb.	Blind.	Insane.
Bath,	126		110	577				
Bengal,	148		129	638				
Bingham,	303		273	1,460	6			
Dallas,	178		168	910				1
DeWitt,	254		220	1,139	7			2
Duplain,	193		181	915		1		
Eagle,	184		171	912				
Essex,	214		194	1,013		1	1	
Greenbush,	192		192	967				
Lebanon,	142		126	661				
Olive,	146		127	627				1
Ovid,	187		171	936				
Riley,	142		122	607				1
Victor,	148		139	662				
Watertown,	181		155	808				1
Westphalia,	208		191	1,091		1	3	2
Total,	2,946		2,669	13,923	13	3	4	8

CHIPPEWA COUNTY.—Continued.

TOWNSHIPS.	Value of Real Estate owned.	Occupied Farms.			
		Whole number.	Acres improved.	Acres unimproved.	Cash value of.
Saut Ste Marie,	$138,800	30	909	6,750	$37,230
Sugar Island,	26,750	13	570	2,471	33,300
Total,	$165,550	43	1,479	9,221	$70,530

CLINTON COUNTY.—Continued.

TOWNSHIPS.	Value of Real Estate owned.	Occupied Farms.			
		Whole number.	Acres improved.	Acres unimproved.	Cash value of.
Bath,	$131,600	92	3,509	4,940	$133,300
Bengal,	212,700	99	3,543	6,814	194,900
Bingham,	376,150	107	2,883	6,324	180,450
Dallas,	202,850	149	4,569	6,795	197,950
DeWitt,	367,805	133	7,629	8,576	308,750
Duplain,	279,575	152	4,306	9,417	228,975
Eagle,	331,640	142	6,944	8,217	305,840
Essex,	318,800	155	6,797	9,287	278,900
Greenbush,	193,875	172	4,719	7,861	194,215
Lebanon,	194,700	116	4,123	7,318	217,750
Olive,	180,950	100	3,702	6,711	178,300
Ovid,	226,970	132	3,900	7,301	192,550
Riley,	177,450	106	3,628	5,605	169,500
Victor,	247,650	108	5,475	8,507	238,500
Watertown,	261,650	139	5,159	8,984	260,200
Westphalia,	291,150	172	7,539	10,275	298,150
Total,	$3,993,515	2,074	78,425	112,932	$3,578,230

CHIPPEWA COUNTY.—CONTINUED.

Value of Farming Implements and Machinery.	Live Stock, June 1st, 1860. Horses.	Asses and Mules.	Milch Cows.	Working Oxen.	Other Cattle.	Sheep.	Swine.	Value of Live Stock.
$3,375	39	2	74	24	43		37	$6,505
1,610	17		21	21	24	18	8	2,789
$4,985	56	2	95	45	67	18	45	$9,294

CLINTON COUNTY.—CONTINUED.

Value of Farming Implements and Machinery.	Horses.	Asses and Mules.	Milch Cows.	Working Oxen.	Other Cattle.	Sheep.	Swine.	Value of Live Stock.
$6,560	75		218	142	280	1,093	320	$22,900
5,125	80		249	134	450	629	704	25,780
6,385	88		226	91	416	276	548	23,480
6,555	101		323	208	367	677	619	31,381
11,682	176		321	172	553	3,096	585	42,995
6,900	138		350	119	601	911	801	32,520
9,738	238		378	138	604	2,685	699	46,712
9,780	209		370	160	448	666	678	37,685
9,650	182		343	177	597	404	784	33,890
5,927	94		229	156	288	1,431	430	27,436
6,160	88		257	152	359	847	365	25,100
6,809	97		286	156	509	421	729	26,580
6,040	94	2	248	110	493	617	485	24,195
7,270	75		285	208	422	1,160	516	29,020
10,105	135		341	152	508	1,302	591	35,800
11,103	146		434	271	593	1,312	772	44,097
$125,969	2016	2	4858	2,546	7,488	17,527	9,626	$509,571

CHIPPEWA COUNTY—Continued.

TOWNSHIPS.	Produce, during the Year						
	Wheat, bushels of.	Rye, bushels of.	Indian corn, bushels of.	Oats, bushels of.	Barley, bushels of.	Buckwheat, bushels of.	Potatoes, bushels of.
Saut St. Marie,	50	240	. .	3,160	200		6,710
Sugar Island,	.	.		395		.	3,050
Total,	50	240	. .	3,555	200		9,760

CLINTON COUNTY—Continued.

TOWNSHIPS.	Wheat, bushels of.	Rye, bushels of.	Indian corn, bushels of.	Oats, bushels of.	Barley, bushels of.	Buckwheat, bushels of.	Potatoes, bushels of.
Bath,	9,053	411	7,080	2,830	166	663	4,342
Bengal,	4,348	30	8,595	5,033	216	208	2,048
Bingham,	2,278	145	7,002	2,123	80	291	2,959
Dallas,	9,120	394	6,983	4,619	43	80	2,743
DeWitt,	16,384	359	15,115	9,939	573	539	7,358
Duplain,	6,208	320	12,311	4,052	53	194	3,552
Eagle,	9,181	330	11,222	9,428	1,215	537	3,470
Essex,	19,025	805	20,345	10,605	210	338	4,069
Greenbush,	7,853	839	10,930	4,119	39	288	3,496
Lebanon,	11,181	87	8,006	4,492	229	124	2,024
Olive,	4,870	133	7,032	3,943	59	579	3,134
Ovid,	5,187	465	10,571	3,757	197	486	3,543
Riley,	3,653	151	7,536	4,367	270	461	2,758
Victor,	14,965	200	9,006	6,197	156	447	4,216
Watertown,	6,620	199	10,155	8,791	1,457	302	4,585
Westphalia,	19,356	863	9,216	5,828	174	426	5,483
Total,	149182	5,731	161105	90,123	4,146	5,963	59,780

CHIPPEWA COUNTY.—Continued.

Ending June 1st, 1860.							
Wool, pounds of.	Value of Orchard products.	Butter, pounds of.	Cheese, pounds of.	Hay, tons of.	Clover seed, bushels.	Maple Sugar, pounds.	Value of home made manufactures.
...		1,650		492	.	2,750	. ..
...		1,460		73		.	..
.. ..		3,110	.	565	.	2,750	..

CLINTON COUNTY.—Continued.

Wool, pounds of.	Value of Orchard products.	Butter, pounds of.	Cheese, pounds of.	Hay, tons of.	Clover seed, bushels.	Maple Sugar, pounds.	Value of home made manufactures.
3,347	420	20,650	2,070	1,288	2	725	$40
2,107	258	25,700	1,050	628	5	20,095	.
686	222	23,700	2,910	944	11	20,810	40
1,895	228	26 325	607	698		15,500	160
9,350	495	33,750	1,520	786	18	6,702	20
2,284	310	33,430	2,713	908		31,617	80
6,563	1,982	36,820	4,850	1,289	4	41,794	256
2,349	406	32,520	830	1,218		20,606	171
819	52	27,520	850	1,079	3	19,818	10
4,686	138	24,905	3,755	801	25	30,103	14
2,169	263	25,250	1,650	1,143	93	15,848	132
1,056	51	28,150	1,963	945	5	26,040	40
2,469	445	26,900	2,430	876	39	41,486	.
3,103	396	26,450	795	1,595	6	2,695	6
4,711	290	31,550	4,470	848	8	32,875	..
3,261	1,047	35,651	. . .	1,306	4	13,059	275
50,855	7,003	459,271	32,463	16352	223	339273	$1,244

CHIPPEWA COUNTY.—Continued.

TOWNSHIPS.	Flouring Mills.							Saw Mills.			
			Power used.			Annual product.			Power used.		
	Number of.	Runs of Stone.	Water.	Steam.	Capital invested in real and personal estate in the business.	Bbls. flour made.	Value of.	Number of.	Water.	Steam.	Capital invested in real and personal estate in the business.
Saut S. Marie,					.	.		1			12,000
Sugar Island,					. ..		. .				....
Total,					.	. .		1			12,000

CLINTON COUNTY.—Continued.

TOWNSHIPS.	Number of.	Runs of Stone.	Water.	Steam.	Capital invested in real and personal estate in the business.	Bbls. flour made.	Value of.	Number of.	Water.	Steam.	Capital invested in real and personal estate in the business.
Bath,					..						.
Bengal,							..	2		2	$6,000
Bingham,	1			1	$6,000	10500	64,000	2		2	8,000
Dallas,							.	1	1		1,500
DeWitt,	2		1	1	5,500	12700	73,200	2		2	4,500
Duplain,	1		1		6,000	10500	60,000	2	1	1	8,000
Eagle,					.. ..		.	3	2	1	7,500
Essex,	1		1		4,000		.	1	1		2,000
Greenbush,	1		.	1	4,000	5,400	32,400	1		1	2,000
Lebanon,					..						.
Olive,											
Ovid,	1			1	6,000	6,500	39,300	1		1	3,000
Riley,								.	.		
Victor,								1		1	2,000
Watertown,	1		1		10,000	4,500	27,500	1	1		2,000
Westphalia,	1			1	2,500			1		1	1,500
Total,	9		4	5	44,000	50100	296400	18	6	12	48,000

CHIPPEWA COUNTY.—Continued.

Saw Mills.		Aggregate of all kinds of Manufactures, Mills included.				Estimated value of Real and Personal Estate.	
Annual product.		Capital invested in real and personal estate in the business.	Hands employ'd		Value of annual product.	By Assessors.	By assistant Marshals.
Feet of Lumber Sawed.	Value of.		Males.	Females.			
		12,000				200,805	$200,805
....	.....	12,000				200,805	$200,805

CLINTON COUNTY.—Continued.

Feet of Lumber Sawed.	Value of.	Capital invested in real and personal estate in the business.	Males.	Females.	Value of annual product.	By Assessors.	By assistant Marshals.
1,100,000	66,000	$ 6,000	6		$66,000		
900,000	54,000	31,500	45		147,117		
9,000		1,500	2				
700 000	42,000	13,000	19		123,275		
900,000	54,000	15,000	14		116,000		
48,000		7,500	6				
		10,000	9		3,425		
200,000	10,000	7,000	10		45,600		
400,000	24,000	16,000	28		96,850		
300,000	18,000	2,000	3		18,000		
400,000	24,000	12,200	5		52,700		
9,000		6,000	6				
4,966,000	292000	137,900	153		668,967	2280159	2,280,159

DELTA COUNTY

TOWNSHIPS.	Dwelling Houses. Whole number.	Dwelling Houses. Number in Cities.	Number of Families.	Number of Inhabitants. Whole number.	Colored.	Deaf and Dumb.	Blind.	Insane.
Total,	244		215	1,172				

EATON COUNTY

TOWNSHIPS.	Dwelling Houses. Whole number.	Dwelling Houses. Number in Cities.	Number of Families.	Number of Inhabitants. Whole number.	Colored.	Deaf and Dumb.	Blind.	Insane.
Bellevue,	305		305	1,555				
Benton,	156		150	755				
Brookfield,	172		167	821		1	1	
Carmel,	297		287	1,411				
Chester,	137		143	798			1	
Delta,	142		133	618				
Eaton,	254		247	1,281	3			
Eaton Rapids,	478		454	2,318	1	4	3	1
Eaton Rapids vil.,	130		120	582	12			
Kalamo,	211		201	1,022				
Oneida,	268		276	1,382	2			1
Roxand,	157		153	807		1		
Sunfield,	105		101	500				
Vermontville,	169		176	878				
Walton,	214		209	1,025	2			
Windsor,	175		169	821				
Total,	3,370		3,291	16,574	20	6	5	2

EMMET COUNTY

TOWNSHIPS.	Dwelling Houses. Whole number.	Dwelling Houses. Number in Cities.	Number of Families.	Number of Inhabitants. Whole number.	Colored.	Deaf and Dumb.	Blind.	Insane.
Bear Creek,	54		47	213		1	1	
Charlevoix,	32		32	176				
La Croix,	287		113	485		2	1	
Little Traverse,	143		55	270		1	1	
Old Ft. Mackinaw,	6		1	11				
Total,	522		248	1,155		4	3	

DELTA COUNTY.—Continued.

TOWNSHIPS.	Value of Real Estate owned.	Occupied Farms. Whole number.	Acres improved.	Acres unimproved.	Cash value of.
Total,	$315,323	16	457	1,722	$12,170

EATON COUNTY.—Continued.

TOWNSHIPS.	Value of Real Estate owned.	Occupied Farms. Whole number.	Acres improved.	Acres unimproved.	Cash value of.
Bellevue,	$431,300	111	5,628	5,970	$235,610
Benton,	213,930	101	3,970	5,559	188,930
Brookfield,	164,910	79	2,752	4,568	157,500
Carmel,	450,165	115	5,570	6,502	238,550
Chester,	216,125	72	3,295	5,052	147,580
Delta,	177,340	71	2,821	4,181	140,790
Eaton,	330,620	143	6,449	8,680	256,610
Eaton Rapids,	717,595	285	14,160	15,193	645,250
Eaton Rapids vil.,	211,675				
Kalamo,	251,810	103	4,489	5,635	177,395
Oneida,	398,856	130	5,428	7,865	268,600
Roxand,	168,821	75	3,247	4,608	120,600
Sunfield,	100,164	43	1,843	3,361	66,464
Vermontville,	220,761	80	4,165	4,724	177,460
Walton,	293,795	105	4,459	6,573	193,005
Windsor,	198,325	93	3,607	4,495	160,675
Total,	$4,546,192	1,606	71,913	92,966	$3,175,019

EMMET COUNTY.—Continued.

TOWNSHIPS.	Value of Real Estate owned.	Occupied Farms. Whole number.	Acres improved.	Acres unimproved.	Cash value of.
Bear Creek,	$10,992	7	74	1,005	$1,954
Charlevoix,	5,886			....	
La Croix,	33,723	39	423	3,762	9,284
Little Traverse,	17,401	8	131	972	2,047
Old Ft. Mackinaw	50	1	40	600	8,000
Total,	$68,052	55	668	6,339	$21,285

DELTA COUNTY.—Continued.

Value of Farming Implements and Machinery.	Live Stock, June 1st, 1860. Horses.	Asses and Mules.	Milch Cows.	Working Oxen.	Other Cattle.	Sheep.	Swine.	Value of Live Stock.
$1,025	40		44	60	55	11	142	$5,300

EATON COUNTY.—Continued.

Value of Farming Implements and Machinery.	Horses.	Asses and Mules.	Milch Cows.	Working Oxen.	Other Cattle.	Sheep.	Swine.	Value of Live Stock.
$9,130	224		372	132	439	2,968	427	$43,809
9,058	181		300	123	631	1,589	730	35,376
6,045	64		188	96	372	937	594	22,110
6,681	181		349	124	446	2,404	635	35,806
6,210	143		284	85	384	1,172	423	28,086
6,595	125		191	84	35	504	485	21,074
5,421	240		384	140	474	1,609	734	34,879
27,051	423		762	322	1,485	6,345	1,768	102,231
6,932	147		348	119	416	1,752	501	33,688
12 060	230		430	142	982	1,392	1,086	44,682
4,853	112		266	88	384	839	399	23,518
3,804	86		123	54	219	608	191	14,084
7,320	185		291	96	484	2,251	534	37,573
7,995	181		278	113	366	1,379	429	30,727
6,160	147		256	114	503	1,174	605	30,376
$125,315	2669		4822	1,832	7,937	26,923	9,541	$538,019

EMMET COUNTY.—Continued.

Value of Farming Implements and Machinery.	Horses.	Asses and Mules.	Milch Cows.	Working Oxen.	Other Cattle.	Sheep.	Swine.	Value of Live Stock.
$98	12			2	3	...	46	$759
644	62		14	7	29	3	171	4,410
88	13		2	2	1	.	39	792
123	4		7	2	7		10	520
$953	91		23	13	40	3	266	$6,481

DELTA COUNTY.—Continued.

TOWNSHIPS.	Produce, during the Year						
	Wheat, bushels of.	Rye, bushels of.	Indian corn, bushels of.	Oats, bushels of.	Barley, bushels of.	Buckwheat, bushels of.	Potatoes, bushels of.
Total,	65		210	2,370	155		6,180

EATON COUNTY.—Continued.

TOWNSHIPS.	Wheat, bushels of.	Rye, bushels of.	Indian corn, bushels of.	Oats, bushels of.	Barley, bushels of.	Buckwheat, bushels of.	Potatoes, bushels of.
Bellevue,.	10,757	745	7,729	5,846	1,235	350	4,322
Benton, ...	3,839	155	14,142	6,224	966	266	3,952
Brookfield,...	3,574	390	10,115	2,599	166	391	3,097
Carmel,	4,134	248	6,716	8,479	908	568	2,885
Chester,. ..	1,803	136	5,214	4,126	592	236	2,776
Delta, .. .	1,612	197	8,580	3,824	214	502	3,172
Eaton,. .. .	5,912	484	9,877	7,288	578	848	4,468
Eaton Rapids,.	23,417	3,618	38,639	12,128	1,318	1,689	15,150
Eaton R. vil.,.	...						
Kalamo,	3,790	487	6,477	4,031	420	353	3,197
Oneida, ..	5,936	65	23,941	9,047	330	494	5,264
Roxand,	2,533	107	5,555	3,660	216	282	2,678
Sunfield,.	2,034	84	2,373	1,655		78	884
Vermontville,	2,898	42	9,743	6,743	856	404	3,444
Walton,.	4,982	111	4,297	4,896	1,094	456	2,921
Windsor,.	2,377	610	13 514	3,662	345	407	4,492
Total,	79,598	7,479	166312	84,208	8,938	7,384	62,702

EMMET COUNTY.—Continued.

TOWNSHIPS.	Wheat, bushels of.	Rye, bushels of.	Indian corn, bushels of.	Oats, bushels of.	Barley, bushels of.	Buckwheat, bushels of.	Potatoes, bushels of.
Bear Creek,.	100	15	337	80			1,184
Charlevoix,	..						
La Croix,.	...		1,341	1,053	.	37	4,285
Lit. Traverse,			318	360			1,090
O Ft. Mack.,				150			500
Total,	100	15	1,996	1,643		36	7,060

DELTA COUNTY.—Continued.

Ending June 1st, 1860.							
Wool, pounds of.	Value of Orchard products.	Butter, pounds of.	Cheese, pounds of.	Hay, tons of.	Clover seed, bushels.	Maple Sugar, pounds.	Value of home made manufactures.
. .		640		293		2,250	
EATON COUNTY.—Continued.							
10,256	$1,217	24,990	4,525	1,336		20,215	$665
4,689	1,038	32,830	5,601	828	49	42,842	458
3,230	807	18,025	4,815	640	7	21,304	116
8,673	275	26,647	1,344	1,012	2	20 198	370
4,070	386	20,075	11,753	873	4	43,485	351
1,488	202	20,865	2,541	723	3	23,437	294
5,402	637	29,785	2,034	862	6	29,159	426
20,690	6,528	75,900	17,229	3,465	199	20,498	1,936
. ..			...		.	..	.
6,086	836	27,080	1,695	1,054		48,425	749
3,420	1,401	46,510	8,321	1,429	10	52,713	516
3,133	157	21,395	3,345	567		37,527	370
2,258	40	9,850	880	448	5	23,122	249
8,846	375	22,395	3,174	1,245		36,226	272
4,694	556	24,603	3,436	917		11,722	383
3,199	398	27,400	3,825	685		20,775	503
90,134	14,853	428,350	74,519	16085	285	460645	7,658
EMMET COUNTY.—Continued.							
....	$80	.		.	.	5,190	
.. .	.		..	.		.	
...	25	187	. .	44		31,438	$50
.. ..	25	.	.	4		6,710	
.. .	20	.	. .			200	..
. ....	$150	187	. ...	48	..	43,538	$50

DELTA COUNTY.—Continued.

TOWNSHIPS.	Flouring Mills.							Saw Mills.			
	Number of.	Runs of Stone.	Power used. Water.	Power used. Steam.	Capital invested in real and personal estate in the business.	Annual product. Bbls. flour made.	Annual product. Value of.	Number of.	Power used. Water.	Power used. Steam.	Capital invested in real and personal estate in the business.
Total,								7	2	5	324000

EATON COUNTY.—Continued.

TOWNSHIPS.	Number of.	Runs of Stone.	Water.	Steam.	Capital.	Bbls. flour made.	Value of.	Number of.	Water.	Steam.	Capital.
Bellevue,	1	3	1		10,000	2,200	14,300	1	1		$400
Benton,											
Brookfield,											
Carmel,								1		1	3,000
Chester,											
Delta,											
Eaton,	1			1	6,800	2,666	23,200	1		1	2,000
Eaton Rapids,	1	2	1		6,000	800	6,600	5	4	1	17,000
Eaton R. vil.,	1	4	1		17,000	1,000	8,500	1	1		7,000
Kalamo,	1	3		1	7,000	10000	67,375	1		1	2,000
Oneida,											
Roxand,											
Sunfield,											
Vermontville,								1		1	3,500
Walton,	1	3	1	1	8,000	3,500	25,750	3	2	1	8,000
Windsor,	2	4	2		73,000	4,250	30,150	5	4	1	13,000
Total,	8	19	6	3	127800	24416	184875	19	12	7	56,700

EMMET COUNTY.—Continued.

TOWNSHIPS.	Number of.	Runs of Stone.	Water.	Steam.	Capital.	Bbls. flour made.	Value of.	Number of.	Water.	Steam.	Capital.
Bear Creek,											
Charlevoix,											
La Croix,	1				$2,000		$1,000				
Lit. Traverse,											
O. Ft. Mack.,											
Total,	1				$2,000		$1,000				

DELTA COUNTY.—Continued.

Saw Mills.		Aggregate of all kinds of Manufactures, Mills included.				Estimated value of Real and Personal Estate.	
Annual product.		Capital invested in real and personal estate in the business.	Hands employ'd		Value of annual products.	By Assessors.	By assistant Marshals.
Feet of Lumber Sawed.	Value of.		Males.	Females.			
30,500,000	170000	326,000	330	17	175,600	308,487	$499,521
EATON COUNTY.—Continued.							
300,000	$2,000	$14,725	19		$30 074		
360,000	2,880	5.385	7		9 647		
300,000	2,550	10,575	10		32,933		
*707,500	18,600	23,600	28		25 964		
500,000	4,000	40.000	28		30,170		
300,000	2,400	9.000	5		69,775		
175,000	1,225	4,660	5		4,194		
1,087,000	8,500	28,300	15		56,650		
2,493,000	18,571	87,000	21		59,196		
6,172,500	60,726	223,235	138		318,603	3111087	6,222,156
EMMET COUNTY.—Continued.							
						$647	$17,264
		$2,000	3		$1,000	3,631	63,107
						6,697	30,955
	....	$2,000	3		$1,000	10,975	111,686

* As returned, evidently a mistake.

GENESEE COUNTY

TOWNSHIPS.	Dwelling Houses.		Number of Families.	Number of Inhabitants.				
	Whole number.	Number in Cities.		Whole number.	Colored.	Deaf and Dumb.	Blind.	Insane.
Argentine,	163		175	860				1
Atlas,	292		290	1,441			1	2
Burton,	268		265	1,266	4	2		1
Clayton,	156		151	808		2		
Davison,	184		193	950		1		
Fenton,	271		273	1,395		1		
Flint,	299		286	1,585		84	1	
City, 1st ward,	158	158	158	807	5			2
" 2d "	195	195	195	1,125	7			
" 3d "	230	230	207	1,120	7			1
Forest,	116		117	633		1	1	1
Flushing,	172		175	867	1		1	
Flushing village,	86		82	406				
Gaines,	146		150	760				
Genesee,	239		239	1,211				1
Grand Blanc,	243		247	1,291			2	
Montrose,	78		78	389	11			
Mount Morris,	148		144	735				2
Mundy,	244		242	1,228		1		
Richfield,	206		205	963			4	
Thetford,	187		183	934				
Vienna,	212		210	1,050				
Fentonville village,	157		158	783		1		
Total,	4,451	583	4,423	22,607	35	93	10	11

GENESEE COUNTY.—CONTINUED.

TOWNSHIPS.	Value of Real Estate owned.	Occupied Farms.			
		Whole number.	Acres improved.	Acres unimproved.	Cash value of.
Argentine,	$249,100	63	4,026	5,209	$153,400
Atlas,	522,898	140	9,933	6,962	400,265
Burton,	517,360	141	7,819	5,393	466,550
Clayton,	238,610	93	4,938	3,824	182,790
Davison,	250,790	89	4,965	5,164	168,240
Fenton,	457,220	120	6,497	5,133	295,640
Flint,	595,355	166	9,933	5,696	453,140
City, 1st ward,	323,460	. .		.	
" 2d "	874,170		.		
" 3d "	699,025	*7	596	846	87,500
Forest,	113,215	44	1,581	2,784	74,300
Flushing,	251,810	113	4,371	7,163	198,140
Flushing village,	103,925		. .	. .	
Gaines,	159,848	45	2,218	3,208	89,500
Genesee,	514,492	138	8,585	5,553	455,750
Grand Blanc,	685,710	146	10,859	6,771	552,500
Montrose,	59,210	26	833	2,381	32,750
Mount Morris,	248,090	75	3,677	3,578	192,770
Mundy,	482,875	123	6,381	5,512	284,600
Richfield,	257,206	105	4,980	4,739	218,180
Thetford,	281,188	75	3,674	3,501	171,300
Vienna,	325,818	73	3,227	4,442	189,145
Fentonville vil.,	246,345		.	.	
Total,	8,451,720	178	99,093	87,859	4,666,460

* The whole city.

GENESEE COUNTY — Continued.

Value of Farming Implements and Machinery.	Live Stock, June 1st, 1860. Horses.	Asses and Mules.	Milch Cows.	Working Oxen.	Other Cattle.	Sheep.	Swine.	Value of Live Stock.
$6,415	162		223	112	392	2,073	286	$28,547
14,710	400		477	184	858	6,668	717	72,335
14,362	401		427	89	606	5,551	773	68,210
7,790	235		260	86	507	1,543	683	35,518
6,905	200		276	117	485	2,550	438	35,131
9,825	276		328	134	463	2,723	729	43,101
14,164	406		499	170	833	5,404	1,092	65,992
1,200	53		21	6	17	75	53	6,480
2,897	54		106	58	135	208	246	10,512
8,888	232		337	132	550	1,297	595	34,429
3,375	87		141	56	168	502	189	15,917
18,759	389	2	425	138	527	3,278	823	58,845
18,565	468	4	501	161	807	9,802	912	80,171
1,580	56		64	30	98	58	121	5,805
8,659	163		205	101	247	741	473	25,499
10,780	342		374	120	591	4,422	790	52,212
7,842	215		276	125	436	1,428	435	34,231
7,835	154		214	84	215	984	513	26,668
8,481	139		253	83	268	513	499	25,655
$173,032	4432	6	5407	1,986	8,103	49,820	10,266	$725,258

GENESEE COUNTY—CONTINUED.

TOWNSHIPS.	PRODUCE, DURING THE YEAR						
	Wheat, bushels of.	Rye, bushels of.	Indian corn, bushels of.	Oats, bushels of.	Barley, bushels of.	Buckwheat, bushels of.	Potatoes, bushels of.
Argentine,	9,828	218	11,101	3,270	246	498	4,942
Atlas,	18,923	2,650	16,155	10,509	4,195	1,261	8,038
Burton,	8,024	493	20,805	18,101	2,890	549	9,035
Clayton,	7,432	86	14,655	9,155	1,036	554	6,515
Davison,	7,779	478	7,620	5,930	1,450	236	3,211
Fenton,	18,518	147	15,360	8,770	608	1,050	7,761
Flint,	14,526	226	23,258	16,544	1,664	527	11,068
City, 1st ward,							
" 2d ward,			.	. ..			
" 3d ward,	1,042	.	1,802	605	140		982
Forest,	1,851	779	4,020	1,554	8	88	2,107
Flushing,	5,780	588	13,380	6,606	162	600	6,148
Flushing vil.,			. .				. ..
Gaines,	2,456	128	5,917	3,187	291	110	1,782
Genesee,	19,205	798	17,677	14,619	1,117	486	6,631
Grand Blanc,	19,632	2,221	25,140	19,019	7,007	1,648	9,882
Montrose,	764	43	2,803	1,658	6	53	1,147
Mount Morris,	6,896	389	9,660	8,893	571	294	4,615
Mundy,	6,177	737	18,015	13,817	3,188	701	7,076
Richfield,	7,323	1,025	10,241	5,675	955	109	5,141
Thetford,	5,653	1,061	7,270	6,692	253	168	4,363
Vienna,	4,499	447	10,085	4,876	62	390	4,865
Fentonville v.,				.			.
Total,	166308	12514	234969	159480	25849	9,352	105309

GENESEE COUNTY.—Continued.

Ending June 1st, 1860.							
Wool, pounds of.	Value of Orchard products.	Butter, pounds of.	Cheese, pounds of.	Hay, tons of.	Clover seed, bushels.	Maple Sugar, pounds.	Value of home made manufactures.
3,771	$978	20,025	645	1,243	39	300	$16
21,390	565	48,650	3,400	2,469	232	3,250	
14,728	765	39,998	6,345	1,626	100	11,312	41
3,844	1,102	24,800	300	929		16,990	
6,307		27,280	1,225	917		16,815	
7,597	2,370	32,250	450	1,609	62	2,180	60
13,259	1,377	45,187	7,365	1,560		13,355	45
350		1,800	30	103			10
620	9	8,805	280	279	19	5,746	74
3,774	972	27,154	3,514	1,122	7	16,238	160
1,978	249	11,800	1,450	425	2	11,035	65
11,053	1,374	33,474	3,991	1,434	75	8,101	703
31,747	1,978	51,450	7,640	2,815	53	3,790	33
432		5,320	100	192		1,385	
2,619	804	19,154	3,550	718		10,495	176
11,118	550	34,250	1,340	1,495	17	7,230	43
4,367	160	25,082	4,370	809		19,040	178
3,019	89	17,136	1,600	736	3	8,170	254
1,670	544	16,253	5,790	816		6,865	108
143,643	13,886	489,868	53,385	21297	612	163197	$1,966

GENESEE COUNTY.—Continued.

TOWNSHIPS.	Flouring Mills.							Saw Mills.			
			Power used.			Annual product.			Power used.		
	Number of.	Runs of Stone.	Water.	Steam.	Capital invested in real and personal estate in the business.	Bbls. flour made.	Value of.	Number of.	Water.	Steam.	Capital invested in real and personal estate in the business.
Argentine,	1		1		$9,000	4,000	26,050				
Atlas,											
Burton,											
Clayton,											
Davison,											
Fenton,											
Flint,											
City, 1st ward,											
" 2d ward,											
" 3d ward,	1		1	1	13,000	6,027	41,401	2	1	2	145000
Forest,	1			1	3,000	1,200	10,350	2		2	8,380
Flushing,								1		1	1,400
" vil.,	2	4	2		10,000	3,000	27,640	3	2	1	10,000
Gaines,											
Genesee,	2	3	2		8,000	2,400	15,370	4	4		13,000
Grand Blanc,											
Montrose,								2	2		4,000
Mount Morris,											
Mundy,											
Richfield,								2		2	13,500
Thetford,								4		4	19,500
Vienna,	1	2	1		2,000	2,000	14,000	6	4	2	24,500
Fentonville v.,	1		1		10,000	5,000	32,000				
Total,	9	9	8	2	55,000	23267	166811	26	13	14	239280

GENESEE COUNTY.—Continued.

Saw Mills.		Aggregate of all kinds of Manufactures, Mills included.				Estimated value of Real and Personal Estate.	
Annual product.			Hands employ'd				
Feet of Lumber Sawed.	Value of.	Capital invested in real and personal estate in the business.	Males.	Females.	Value of annual product.	By Assessors.	By assistant Marshals.
..	..	$9,000	3		$26,050		.
		4,500	13		9,180	..	
.	..				..	...	.
.		.			.	..	..
..	.	500	3		1,760	.	..
..		8,300	13		11,550	...	..
	.				...		.
....					.	..	.
..		..			.	..	...
7,500,000	70,000	229,000	148		218,052	...	.
1,250,000	8,500	11,380	18		18,850	.	...
260,000	1,900	1,400	3		1,900	...	
680,000	4,080	27,950	37		43,215	...	....
...	..				...	...	..
1,500,000	11,550	21,000	13		26,920	.....	....
..	.	....				.....	....
270,000	1,620	4,000	6		1,620	....	.....
.. ..	.....	.....			. ..	...	....
.....	.	....			...	...	....
1,936,000	13,552	13,500	9		13,552	.....	......
3,600,000	22,750	19,500	27		22,750	...	....
3,600,000	32,000	28,350	32		49,456	.....	..
....	..	13,600	11		14,475	...	....
20,796,000	165952	391,980	336		459,330	4618935	9,237,660

GRAND TRAVERSE COUNTY

TOWNSHIPS.	Dwelling Houses.		Number of Families.	Number of Inhabitants.				
	Whole number.	Number in Cities.		Whole number.	Colored.	Deaf and Dumb.	Blind.	Insane.
Meegezee,*	72		33	179				
Milton,	29		27	88				
Peninsula,	155		82	442				
Traverse,	115		91	495				
Whitewater,	76		60	263				
Total,	375	....	260	1,288				

GRATIOT COUNTY

TOWNSHIPS.	Dwelling Houses: Whole number.	Dwelling Houses: Number in Cities.	Number of Families.	Whole number.	Colored.	Deaf and Dumb.	Blind.	Insane.
Arcadia,	75		75	375				
Bethany,	17		17	93				
Elba,	16		16	78				
Emerson,	43		43	226				
Fulton,	126		126	600	5			1
Hamilton,	11		11	49				
LaFayette,	28		28	123				
Newark,	82		82	399				
New Haven,	39		39	216				
North Shade,	93		93	413				
North Star,	81		81	400				
Pine River,	81		81	400				
Seville,	31		31	169			1	
Sumner,	49		49	213				
Washington,	66		66	267				
Total,	838		838	4,027	5		1	1

*Belongs to the unorganized county of Antrim and not included in the total.

GRAND TRAVERSE COUNTY.—Continued.

TOWNSHIPS.	Value of Real Estate owned.	Occupied Farms. Whole number.	Acres improved.	Acres unimproved.	Cash value of.
Meegezee,	$45,850		. . .	. . .	. .
Milton,	4,100		. . . .	. . . . .	. .
Peninsula,	18,400	51	1,462	4,539	$39,430
Traverse,	98,100	5	215	1,265	11,000
Whitewater,	22,530	14	435	1,898	16,800
Total,	$143,130	70	2,102	7,702	$67,230

GRATIOT COUNTY.—Continued.

TOWNSHIPS.	Value of Real Estate owned.	Occupied Farms. Whole number.	Acres improved.	Acres unimproved.	Cash value of.
Arcadia,	$45,600	26	844	2,315	$24,800
Bethany,	8,850		. . . .	. . . . . .	. . . . .
Elba,	8,250	5	92	392	3,800
Emerson,	20,250		. . . .	.	. . . . . .
Fulton,	104,830	80	1,362	5,316	77,580
Hamilton,	5,950	.	. . . . .	. . . .	. . .
LaFayette,	13,050	1	50	280	1,000
Newark,	67,750	68	1,419	6,606	62,300
New Haven,	23,750	28	526	2,529	21,900
North Shade,	55,980	40	866	3,100	36,100
North Star,	57,950	20	639	2,288	25,000
Pine River,	74,825	27	1,006	5,430	48,200
Seville,	15,240	4	103	787	3,800
Sumner,	36,250	15	528	2,714	18,450
Washington,	31,035	19	423	1,670	15,300
Total,	$569,560	333	7,858	33,427	$338,230

GRAND TRAVERSE COUNTY.—Continued.

Value of Farming Implements and Machinery.	Live Stock, June 1st, 1860. Horses.	Asses and Mules.	Milch Cows.	Working Oxen.	Other Cattle.	Sheep.	Swine.	Value of Live Stock.
$1,630	42		68	48	82	21	146	$7,227
350	7	9	8	108	7		16	12,950
320			25	20	39		104	1,930
$2,300	49	9	101	176	128	21	266	$22,107

GRATIOT COUNTY.—Continued.

Value of Farming Implements and Machinery.	Horses.	Asses and Mules.	Milch Cows.	Working Oxen.	Other Cattle.	Sheep.	Swine.	Value of Live Stock.
$1,000	25		54	46	54	20	102	$4,575
170	6		14	8	21		27	975
2,958	71		162	109	226	172	346	12,307
50	2		4	2	4	25	2	450
1,861	18		120	100	147	26	238	7,118
645			51	54	58	29	98	3,598
1,443	16		97	60	108	112	151	6,232
800	14		50	34	79	44	70	4,000
960	12		60	46	61	123	85	4,653
95		..	9	8	6	8	9	604
855	14	..	32	28	34	8	47	3,080
507	5		60	38	65	19	94	3,250
$11,344	183	..	713	533	863	586	1,269	$50,842

GRAND TRAVERSE COUNTY.—Continued.

TOWNSHIPS.	Produce, during the Year						
	Wheat, bushels of.	Rye, bushels of.	Indian corn, bushels of.	Oats, bushels of.	Barley, bushels of.	Buckwheat, bushels of.	Potatoes, bushels of.
Meegezee,							
Milton,							
Peninsula,	4,172	346	2,480	935		163	4,650
Traverse,	390	35	120	3,180			770
Whitewater,	961	55	800	265	28	6	1,595
Total,	5,523	436	3,400	4,370	28	169	7,015

GRATIOT COUNTY.—Continued.

TOWNSHIPS.	Wheat, bushels of.	Rye, bushels of.	Indian corn, bushels of.	Oats, bushels of.	Barley, bushels of.	Buckwheat, bushels of.	Potatoes, bushels of.
Arcadia,	1,035	97	1,147	776	142	50	981
Bethany,							
Elba,	17		300	40		7	206
Emerson,							
Fulton,	5,201	32	4,575	3,511	68	40	1,461
Hamilton,							
LaFayette,	25		50			5	40
Newark,	1,852	353	3,583	930	34	226	1,466
New Haven,	563	77	1,131	310		121	745
North Shade,	1,758	20	2,335	859	23	183	677
North Star,	1,301	12	775	757	98	20	389
Pine River,	1,571	65	1,510	1,504	3	111	948
Seville,	147		290	35		14	177
Sumner,	260	138	1,120	385		48	595
Washington,	742	28	855	95	20	97	437
Total,	14,472	822	17,671	9,202	388	922	8,122

GRAND TRAVERSE COUNTY—Continued.

ENDING JUNE 1ST, 1860.

Wool, pounds of.	Value of Orchard products.	Butter, pounds of.	Cheese, pounds of.	Hay, tons of.	Clover seed, bushels.	Maple Sugar, pounds.	Value of home made manufactures.
		6,690		11	15	9,490	
		650				150	
		1,950		43		6,800	
....		9,290		54	15	16,440	

GRATIOT COUNTY—Continued.

Wool, pounds of.	Value of Orchard products.	Butter, pounds of.	Cheese, pounds of.	Hay, tons of.	Clover seed, bushels.	Maple Sugar, pounds.	Value of home made manufactures.
54		4,625		148		7,455	
		900		42		1,600	
541		11,025	200	392		17,275	
100		300		11		300	
50		8,710		275		20,138	
98		3,025		121		6,693	
398		7,525	125	227		18,185	
95		3,850	150	138		5,305	
419		5,314	700	179		6,530	
		625		10		1,500	
		2,150		89		3,870	
123		3,725		124		4,300	
1,878		51,775	1,175	1,756		93,150	....

GRAND TRAVERSE COUNTY.—Continued.

TOWNSHIPS.	Flouring Mills.							Saw Mills.			
			Power used.			Annual product.			Power used.		
	Number of.	Runs of Stone.	Water	Steam.	Capital invested in real and personal estate in the business.	Bbls. flour made.	Value of.	Number of.	Water.	Steam.	Capital invested in real and personal estate in the business.
Meegezee,								2	2		51,000
Milton,											
Peninsula,											
Traverse,	*1							*1			
Whitewater,								1	1		4,000
Total,	1							4	3		55,000

GRATIOT COUNTY.—Continued.

TOWNSHIPS.	Number of.	Runs of Stone.	Water	Steam.	Capital invested in real and personal estate in the business.	Bbls. flour made.	Value of.	Number of.	Water.	Steam.	Capital invested in real and personal estate in the business.
Arcadia,											
Bethany,											
Elba,											
Emerson,											
Fulton,											
Hamilton,											
LaFayette,											
Newark,											
New Haven,											
North Shade,											
North Star,											
Pine River,											
Seville,											
Sumner,											
Washington,											
Total,											

*No further returns.

GRAND TRAVERSE COUNTY.—Continued.

Saw Mills.		Aggregate of all kinds of Manufactures, Mills included.				Estimated value of Real and Personal Estate.	
Annual product.		Capital invested in real and personal estate in the business.	Hands employ'd		Value of annual products.	By Assessors.	By assistant Marshals.
Feet of Lumber Sawed.	Value of.		Males.	Females.			
3,200,000	26,000	$51,000	37	4	$26,000		
		300	2	1	770		
500,000	3,000	4,200	6		3,688		
3,700,000	29,000	$55,500	45	5	$30,458	435,649	$435,649

GRATIOT COUNTY.—Continued.

Feet of Lumber Sawed.	Value of.	Capital invested in real and personal estate in the business.	Males.	Females.	Value of annual products.	By Assessors.	By assistant Marshals.
						$59,607	$90,010
						37,765	11,540
						32,760	9,635
						52,470	24,095
						89,633	112,280
						46,882	8,120
						45,424	14,550
						59,921	84,880
						54,087	27,515
						62,172	71,060
						69,172	71,604
						74,199	90,010
						39,428	18,550
						44,772	34,447
						59,255	38,103
						827,547	$806,399

HILLSDALE COUNTY

TOWNSHIPS.	Dwelling Houses.		Number of Families.	Number of Inhabitants.				
	Whole number.	Number in Cities.		Whole number.	Colored.	Deaf and Dumb.	Blind.	Insane.
Adams,	322		312	1,559				
Allen,	298		298	1,590			2	1
Amboy,	145		146	777	5			1
Camden,	297		297	1,513		1		1
Cambria,	280		280	1,388				
Fayette,	92		90	467				
Hillsdale,	113		109	818				3
Hillsdale village,	412		416	2,173	3			
Jefferson,	274		287	1,455				1
Jonesville village,	200		202	1,008	5	1	1	
Litchfield,	369		369	1,855	1		1	
Moscow,	212		211	1,080				
Pittsford,	317		327	1,646		2		1
Ransom,	222		220	1,159			1	
Reading,	312		312	1,611				
Scipio,	201		202	1,038	9			
Somersett,	249		242	1,611	8	1		
Wheatland,	231		314	1,539				
Woodbridge,	184		184	875				
Wright,	222		231	1,139				
Total,	4,952		5,049	26,301	31	5	5	8

HILLSDALE COUNTY.—Continued.

TOWNSHIPS.	Value of Real Estate owned.	Occupied Farms.			
		Whole number.	Acres improved.	Acres unimproved.	Cash value of.
Adams,	$550,237	277	12,025	10,079	$552,866
Allen,	594,260	206	11,096	9,330	528,187
Amboy,	159,265	100	3,400	4,468	123,385
Camden,	333,090	191	7,214	10,554	328,650
Cambria,	471,045	195	8,544	8,003	423,860
Fayette,	256,326	69	5,478	3,546	259,651
Hillsdale,	284,395	111	7,514	5,234	391,305
Hillsdale village,	830,530	11	1,223	4,922	95,200
Jefferson,	323,080	170	6,514	6,609	279,156
Jonesville vil.,	356,920	10	590	228	45,500
Litchfield,	678,655	230	12,708	8,832	624,020
Moscow,	436,515	152	12,331	7,715	400,966
Pittsford,	591,688	233	11,057	8,248	560,237
Ransom,	242,470	153	6,293	6,307	246,705
Reading,	688,370	190	11,011	9,507	620,700
Scipio,	396,360	161	10,035	6,992	384,467
Somersett,	424,435	200	12,045	7,898	313,065
Wheatland,	702,105	231	13,193	9,101	653,520
Woodbridge,	231,980	118	4,523	6,952	207,150
Wright,	275,961	154	6,482	6,180	256,380
Total,	$8,827,687	3,162	163,276	140,705	$7,293,970

HILLSDALE COUNTY.—Continued.

Value of Farming Implements and Machinery.	Live Stock, June 1st, 1860.							
	Horses.	Asses and Mules.	Milch Cows.	Working Oxen.	Other Cattle.	Sheep.	Swine.	Value of Live Stock.
$19,618	462		732	195	981	4,332	856	$87,096
22,708	475	1	563	189	726	6,067	1,054	107,187
4,284	120		264	98	364	806	418	22,410
11,484	288	2	499	224	639	2,797	1,025	61,602
15,704	344		484	180	626	2,868	1,066	66,327
9,051	160		230	95	368	1,781	281	32,272
12,954	268		361	112	530	1,669	443	47,795
2,040	31		32	15	41	500	45	7,035
11,047	238		435	162	426	2,037	626	43,136
645	17		22	16	31	196	30	2,510
26,504	522		656	174	895	6,510	1,093	100,496
12,847	357		459	143	559	5,717	559	67,342
21,964	515		750	181	903	4,590	1,019	80,876
7,655	200		387	142	456	2,156	662	36,877
23,130	515	1	661	141	932	7,346	1,346	103,719
12,278	324		394	114	511	4,183	700	57,525
15,396	405		538	185	757	4,417	746	76,682
25,634	559	..	749	193	936	5,918	1,122	96,090
6,772	193	.	292	124	397	1,719	580	37,903
11,699	295		428	110	590	2,577	912	57,771
$273,514	6288	4	8936	2,793	11668	68,168	14,583	1,192,651

HILLSDALE COUNTY.—Continued.

TOWNSHIPS.	Produce, during the Year						
	Wheat, bushels of.	Rye, bushels of.	Indian corn, bushels of.	Oats, bushels of.	Barley, bushels of.	Buckwheat, bushels of.	Potatoes, bushels of.
Adams,	25,520	2,699	53,563	13,917	80	2,781	20,988
Allen,	28,692	518	69,936	9,742	504	1,995	18,712
Amboy,	4,109	830	13,287	1,548		1,546	6,358
Camden,	10,970	1,160	46,710	3,632	130	2,860	12,560
Cambria,	23,425	791	59,975	5,470	349	2,116	19,041
Fayette,	11,907	1,310	21,505	3,010		1,731	8 917
Hillsdale,.	19,151	1,732	37,682	3,310	386	1,452	10,217
Hillsdale vil.,	1,004	15	4,302	. .		49	580
Jefferson,.	13,736	2,764	30,479	3,082	422	2,568	11,999
Jonesville vil.,	1,410	20	2,500	225	20	205	960
Litchfield,	39,091	776	68,115	11,818	239	1,646	25,675
Moscow,	30,201	988	40,732	12,214	266	2,101	14,331
Pittsford,	20,799	1,294	51,034	7,153	797	3,260	19,977
Ransom,	7,771	715	29,777	3,000	12	3,154	10,899
Reading,	22,952	681	85,090	9,351	1,037	2,372	19,333
Scipio, ...	31,333	494	39,165	4,017	216	1,465	14,424
Somersett,	29,007	2,310	38,814	7,266	395	4,462	15,506
Wheatland,	45,038	1,568	66,030	12,165	1,488	2,056	16,094
Woodbridge,	4,961	707	25,345	3,017	91	1,399	9,496
Wright,.	7,339	1,066	29,953	3,138	101	2,052	7,980
Total,	378416	22438	813094	107075	6,623	41270	264047

HILLSDALE COUNTY.—Continued.

ENDING JUNE 1ST, 1860.							
Wool, pounds of.	Value of Orchard products.	Butter, pounds of.	Cheese, pounds of.	Hay, tons of.	Clover seed, bushels.	Maple Sugar, pounds.	Value of home made manufactures.
14,884	$6,867	100,392	3,751	2,825	192	9,451	$127
19,339	5,719	48,727	9,880	2,360	352	4 040	811
3,048	85	25,984	626	810	[illegible]	3,761	207
6,411	1,121	41,340	2,780	1,370	4	18,737	1,134
8,322	2,920	49 530	7,550	1,405	53	4,325	963
5,921	2,278	33,108	8,550	1,265	174	.	62
5,288	1 340	27,787	4,900	1,129	107	.	25
1,744	140	1,050	.. .	184	[illegible]	.	
7,375	2,032	45.148	2,670	1,240	60	2,694	505
1,076	120	2,080		164	11	. .	. . .
21,234	9,010	50,805	8,845	3,230	345	7,405	686
16,210	4 430	48,673	5,800	2,128	152	. .	102
14,551	4,633	73,298	18,429	2,159	11	5,530	950
7,198	662	43,147	3,547	1,172	5	3,341	349
23,781	5,980	58,881	23,361	2,252	101	38,300	649
14,521	3 550	41,115	2,787	1,607	21	..	12
13,783	5,162	71,860	2,815	2 589	129	841	573
22,447	6,950	68,080	4,910	2 811	120	7 668	892
4,887	689	28,595	600	1 035		10,492	294
8,280	524	43 899	3 518	1 307	21	5,429	604
220,301	64,230	903,517	110,319	33054	2067	122014	$8,945

HILLSDALE COUNTY.—Continued.

TOWNSHIPS.	Flouring Mills.							Saw Mills.			
	Number of.	Runs of Stone.	Power used. Water	Power used. Steam.	Capital invested in real and personal estate in the business.	Annual product. Bbls. flour made.	Annual product. Value of.	Number of.	Power used. Water.	Power used. Steam.	Capital invested in real and personal estate in the business.
Adams,..								3	1	2	$3,900
Allen,	1			1	$6,000		23,000	3	2	1	4,000
Amboy,	2	5	1	1	12,000		1,550				
Camden,	1		1		2,000		4,400	3	2	1	6,900
Cambria,	1		1		5,500	500	9,600	5	2	3	9,800
Fayette,											
Hillsdale,	1	2	1	1	4,400		4,000				......
Hillsdale vil.,.	1	3		1	8,000	2,650	15,900	1		1	
Jefferson,	1	2	1		4,000		1,500	3	2	1	4,700
Jonesville vil.,											......
Litchfield,	2		1	1	13,000	*5500	71,700	2		2	4,400
Moscow,	2	3	2		8,000	2,250	9,920	3	3		3,000
Pittsford,								2	1	1	4,000
Ransom,					....		...	4	1	3	6,600
Reading,	1			1	5,000		16,000	5	2	3	9,000
Scipio,. ...	2	4	2		16,000	4,000	26,100	1			1,800
Somersett,								1		1	1,500
Wheatland,.					...			4	1	3	7,800
Woodbridge,					....		..	2	1	1	2,200
Wright,					..		:.	1		1	2,000
Total, ..	15	19	10	6	83,900	14900	183670	43	18	24	71,600

*Only one returned.

HILLSDALE COUNTY.—Continued.

Saw-Mills.		Aggregate of all kinds of Manufactures, Mills included.				Estimated value of Real and Personal Estate.	
Annual product.			Hands employ'd				
Feet of Lumber Sawed.	Value of.	Capital invested in real and personal estate in the business.	Males.	Females.	Value of annual product.	By Assessors.	By assistant Marshals.
725,000	$7,060	$4,025	8		$7,060	. .	..
600,000	4,900	13,740	20		34,860	.. .	. ..
.. . .		12,000	3		1,550	...	
600,000	4,800	11,200	12		13,700	.	
2,075,000	23,600	15,300	10		32,200	. ..	. .
. . .	.	.	.		.	.. . .	.
.. .		6,800	22		11,128	.....	.. . .
200,000	1,800	75,845	91	23	114,211	.	.
650,000	5,900	8,700	8		7,400	.	... .
. .....	.. ...	48,100	46	4	44,534	......	
1,300,000	11,000	26,800	32		99,800	. . ..	.. .
940,000	6,590	14,000	7		19,110	.	..
500,000	4,000	4,000	4		4,000	..	... ..
810,000	6,780	6,600	10		6,780	. ...	....
1,200,000	9,600	25,800	41		44,660	......	. ..
20,000	.	21,300	10		36,100	......	.. ....
.. ... .	.	3,500	3		2,065	....	... ...
880,000	8,400	7,800	10		8,400	. ..	......
325,000	2,600	2,200	4		2,600	......	.. . ..
180,000	1,400	2,000	2		1,400	......	. .
11,005,000	98,430	309,710	349	27	488,558	5105417	5,106,467

HOUGHTON COUNTY.

TOWNSHIPS.	Dwelling Houses.		Number of Families.	Number of Inhabitants.				
	Whole number.	Number in Cities.		Whole number.	Colored.	Deaf and Dumb.	Blind.	Insane.
Copper Harbor,	48	..	30	194				
Eagle Harbor, .	207	....	210	1,309	3			.
Houghton, ..	319	. ..	329	2,150	18			.
Houghton village,	199	. ..	219	1 686	24			.
Hancock village,	193	..	202	1,618				.
L'Ance, . .	121	.	121	583	2			
Portage,	152	.	150	1 713	14			
Total, . .	1,239	... .	1,278	9,253	61		.	

HURON COUNTY

TOWNSHIPS.	Whole number.	Number in Cities.	Number of Families.	Whole number.	Colored.	Deaf and Dumb.	Blind.	Insane.
Bingham, .	74	..	76	326	.			.
Caseville, ...	42	.... .	39	191	1			
Dwight,. . ..	107	...	103	573	.			.
Huron,.	99	:.	98	525	.			.
Hume, ...	51	.. .	49	195				.
Rubicon,.	51	....	58	285	.			..
Sand Beach,... .	33	....	3	170	.			.
Sebawaing, ..	113	....	114	555	.			.
White Rock, .	75	...	75	343	..		1	.
Total, ...	645	. ..	641	3,167	1		1	.

HOUGHTON COUNTY.—CONTINUED.

TOWNSHIPS.	Value of Real Estate owned.	Occupied Farms. Whole number.	Acres improved.	Acres unimproved.	Cash value of.
Copper Harbor,	$44,800	2	54	400	$10,000
Eagle Harbor,.	27,100	3	300	4,680	14,900
Houghton, .	87,300	17	1,032	10,725	81,840
" village,	504,150		...	. .	
Hancock vil.,.	72,000		.	. ...	.
L'Ance, . .	13,200		.. .	. ....	....
Portage,.	8,900	3	155	476	10,000
Total,. ...	$757,450	25	1,541	16,272	$115,740

HURON COUNTY.—CONTINUED.

TOWNSHIPS.	Value of Real Estate owned.	Whole number.	Acres improved.	Acres unimproved.	Cash value of.
Bingham, ...	$37,300	9	168	1,517	$6,100
Caseville, ...	61,200	3	93	400	2,500
Dwight, ..	122,500	15	381	1,621	14,400
Huron, ...	105,650	16	522	2,898	17,000
Hume, .. .	35,250	4	53	395	2,700
Rubicon,	25,900	12	132	1,213	8,700
Sand Beach, ...	49,800	10	170	535	4,100
Sebawaing, . .	84,100	67	1,700	6,543	61,200
White rock, ..	47,300	12	252	1,232	8,100
Total, ...	$569,000	148	3,471	16,354	$124,800

HOUGHTON COUNTY.—Continued.

Value of Farming Implements and Machinery.	Live Stock, June 1st, 1860.							
	Horses.	Asses and Mules.	Milch Cows.	Working Oxen.	Other Cattle.	Sheep.	Swine.	Value of Live Stock.
$600	12		6		76			$2,500
275	14		3	5			9	550
1,245	38		14	16			4	6,340
50	3			10				600
$2,170	67		23	31	76		13	$9,950

HURON COUNTY.—Continued.

Value of Farming Implements and Machinery.	Horses.	Asses and Mules.	Milch Cows.	Working Oxen.	Other Cattle.	Sheep.	Swine.	Value of Live Stock.
			16	10	10		5	$1,057
	1			5			22	200
	10		14	17	1		2	1,775
	25	3	18	50	11		9	5,956
	5		4	4	2		3	780
300	5		6	15	1		8	1,440
	2		8	15			5	1,105
100	22		163	149	247	41	92	14,982
	1		15	19	8		9	1,362
$400	71	3	244	284	280	41	155	$28,657

HOUGHTON COUNTY.—Continued.

TOWNSHIPS.	PRODUCE, DURING THE YEAR						
	Wheat, bushels of.	Rye, bushels of.	Indian corn, bushels of.	Oats, bushels of.	Barley, bushels of.	Buckwheat, bushels of.	Potatoes, bushels of.
Copper Harb'r	50		. .	600			700
Eagle Harbor	. . .		.	1,000			1,480
Houghton,		20		1,630			3,270
" vil,	.		.			.	....
Hancock vil,	..		.	. .		.	.....
L'Ance,		. . .	.	. . :	.	.	. . . .
Portage,	50			800			2,600
Total,	100	20	. . . .	3,030	..		8,050

HURON COUNTY.—Continued.

TOWNSHIPS.	Wheat, bushels of.	Rye, bushels of.	Indian corn, bushels of.	Oats, bushels of.	Barley, bushels of.	Buckwheat, bushels of.	Potatoes, bushels of.
Bingham,	340		235	440		..	920
Caseville,	.		350	.			375
Dwight,	150	30	70	885			2.780
Huron,	.	.	40	965	.	.	2,615
Hume,	.		110	270			690
Rubicon,	.		30	800			550
Sand Beach,	90		50	195			630
Sebawaing,	4,319	732	1,758	1,844	.	.	3,690
White Rock,	244		113	545			2.200
Total,	5,143	762	2,756	5,944	. .	. .	14,450

HOUGHTON COUNTY.—Continued.

Ending June 1st, 1860.								
Wool, pounds of.	Value of Orchard products.	Butter, pounds of.	Cheese, pounds of.	Hay, tons of.	Clover seed, bushels.	Maple Sugar, pounds.	Value of home made manufactures.
				10		300	
				118			
				497			
				625		300	

HURON COUNTY.—Continued.

Wool, pounds of.	Value of Orchard products.	Butter, pounds of.	Cheese, pounds of.	Hay, tons of.	Clover seed, bushels.	Maple Sugar, pounds.	Value of home made manufactures.
				12			
				75			
				48			
				51			
				45			
				13			
				80			
		1,550		504			
				22			
		1,550		850			

HOUGHTON COUNTY.—Continued.

TOWNSHIPS.	Flouring Mills.							Saw Mills.			
	Number of.	Runs of Stone.	Power used. Water	Power used. Steam.	Capital invested in real and personal estate in the business.	Annual product. Bbls. flour made.	Annual product. Value of.	Number of.	Power used. Water.	Power used. Steam.	Capital invested in real and personal estate in the business.
Copper Harb'r											
Eagle Harbor,											
Houghton,											
" vil.,								2		2	29,000
Hancock vil.,											
L'Ance,.								1	1	1	38,000
Portage,											
Total,								3	1	3	77,000

HURON COUNTY.—Continued.

TOWNSHIPS.	Number of.	Runs of Stone.	Water	Steam.	Capital	Bbls. flour made.	Value of.	Number of.	Water.	Steam.	Capital
Bingham,.											
Caseville,								1		1	65,000
Dwight,								2		2	66,000
Huron,								2		2	99,000
Hume,								1		1	16,000
Rubicon,								3		3	44,000
Sand Beach,								2		2	53,000
Sebawaing,								2	1	1	8,000
White Rock,								1		1	20,000
Total,								14	1	13	371000

HOUGHTON COUNTY.—Continued.

Saw Mills.		Aggregate of all kinds of Manufactures, Mills included.				Estimated value of Real and Personal Estate.	
Annual product.			Hands employ'd				
Feet of Lumber Sawed.	Value of.	Capital invested in real and personal estate in the business.	Males.	Females.	Value of annual products.	By Assessors.	By assistant Marshals.
. .		..				117,487	$120,000
....		257,000	375		207,000	279,710	300,000
		289,500	639		584,800	430,323	500,000
2,500,000	28,500	361,600	296		163,000		
	. .	559,000	1078		481,780		
2,000,000	25,000	38,000	30		25,000	56,471	60,000
...	..	.				523,987	700,000
4,500,000	33,500	1505100	2418		1461580	1407978	1,680,000

HURON COUNTY.—Continued.

Feet of Lumber Sawed.	Value of.	Capital invested in real and personal estate in the business.	Males.	Females.	Value of annual products.	By Assessors.	By assistant Marshals.
3,000,000	30,000	$65,000	20		$30,000		
7,800,000	75,400		83				
6,500,000	65,800	99,000	104		65,800		
800,000	6,400	16,000	11		6,400		
5,200,000	46,800	44,000	74		46,800		
1,000,000	40,000	53,000	28		40,000		
550,000	4,150	8,000	16		4,150		
300,000	3,000	20,000	12		3,000		
25,150,000	271550	305,000	348		196,150	405,704	$405,704

INGHAM COUNTY.

TOWNSHIPS.	Dwelling Houses.		Number of Families.	Number of Inhabitants.				
	Whole number.	Number in Cities.		Whole number.	Colored.	Deaf and Dumb.	Blind.	Insane.
Alaiedon,.	178		170	894	.		1	1
Aurelius,	225	.	229	1,168			1	
Bunker Hill,	13		134	672	.			
Delhi, ...	170		175	928				.
Ingham..	234	.	230	1,163				
Kinneyville vil.,.	11		11	54				
Lansing,	101	..	99	497				
Lansing city, 1st w.	235	235	230	1,084	1		.	
" " 2d w	195	195	190	1,085	15	1		
" " 3d w	177	177	184	918	10			
Le Roy,.	119	. .	120	621				
Leslie, ...	252	..	254	1,248				
Locke, ...	165	. .	165	863			1	
Mason village, .	7	.... .	7	363	2			..
Meridian,. .	161	. ..	150	825	.			
Okemos village,.	18	..	17	75	..	.	.	
Onondaga, . .	219	....	219	1,135	.		1	
Stockbridge,	166	.	175	879	.	1		1
Vevay, ...	189	.	189	912	4	2	1	1
Wheatfield, ...	112	..	112	573		.		.
White Oak, ...	166	.	168	778	.	.	.	
Williamstown, .	143	.. .	148	693				.
Total,.	3,454	607	3,458	17,456	32	4	5	3

INGHAM COUNTY.—Continued.

TOWNSHIPS.	Value of Real Estate owned.	Occupied Farms.			
		Whole number.	Acres improved.	Acres unimproved.	Cash value of.
Alaiedon,	$308,420	78	3,670	4,136	$170,150
Aurelius,	309,008	117	4,926	6,261	231,250
Bunker Hill,	236,545	101	6,246	8,098	218,040
Delhi,	269,575	70	3,391	3,880	171,240
Ingham,	367,042	150	8,016	6,857	301,165
Kinneyville vil.,	18,150				
Lansing,	228,735	89	3,060	4,630	224,840
Lansing c., 1st w.	452,075	12	386	697	67,100
" 2d w.	611,125	1	80	230	21,700
" 3d w.	361,990	1	50	40	7,000
Le Roy,	161,170	73	2,738	4,598	127,579
Leslie,	379,025	128	5,865	7,083	276,250
Locke,	184,760	71	3,109	3,497	126,800
Mason village,	158,196				
Meridian,	293,510	90	4,435	6,297	344,610
Okemos village,	31,810				
Onondaga,	426,800	124	8,190	7,613	339,600
Stockbridge,	327,955	131	8,505	8,037	292,785
Vevay,	326,262	102	6,128	6,634	294,050
Wheatfield,	167,600	50	2,562	2,490	101,900
White Oak,	232,380	102	5,538	6,916	200,905
Williamstown,	256,725	86	4,421	5,148	173,200
Total,	$6,106,798	1,576	81,295	93,151	$3,690,164

INGHAM COUNTY.—Continued.

Value of Farming Implements and Machinery.	Live Stock, June 1st, 1860.							
	Horses.	Asses and Mules.	Milch Cows.	Working Oxen.	Other Cattle.	Sheep.	Swine.	Value of Live Stock.
$7,107	115		257	96	322	1,130	388	$27,933
9,163	177		309	111	359	1,700	519	33,763
6,998	191	5	267	130	406	2,375	499	37,765
5,551	118		217	56	273	1,234	272	23,088
12,373	247		385	146	555	4,420	589	58,690
4,850	117		217	89	276	746	384	22,629
1,340	13		22	4	30	86	31	2,592
100	2		6	2	8	18	8	343
125	3		2			65	3	325
4,326	114		170	78	208	600	303	19,086
8,888	205		327	160	431	3,086	618	44,978
4,316	103		221	82	334	1,602	324	22,826
344,610	145		268	148	282	1,151	375	29,827
11,150	270		336	145	437	3,197	577	45,403
8,936	294		365	168	470	3,484	635	50,363
9,860	243		324	113	530	3,391	488	46,098
3,535	90		134	59	214	1,334	287	18,212
7,274	162		289	136	474	2,270	539	37,218
5,945	112	6	207	135	352	1,351	399	26,151
$120,327	2721	11	4323	1,858	5,961	33,240	7,446	$547,280

INGHAM COUNTY.—Continued.

TOWNSHIPS.	Produce, during the Year						
	Wheat, bushels of.	Rye, bushels of.	Indian corn, bushels of.	Oats, bushels of.	Barley, bushels of.	Buckwheat, bushels of.	Potatoes, bushels of.
Alaiedon,..	4 028	182	7,315	7,042	485	412	2,757
Aurelius,	6,070	835	9,205	6,600	591	542	4,405
Bunker Hill,	16,234	667	20,389	5,098	167	590	7,835
Delhi,	2 242	46	7,290	5,202	103	408	3,144
Ingham,	11,654	753	35,103	13,364	213	1,743	0,082
Kinneyville v	.						...
Lansing,	2,616	403	6,440	3,684	417	437	3,473
" c., 1st w	422		870	520	.	47	980
" " 2d w	25		200	100			200
" " 3d w.	25		50	200			150
Le Roy, ..	3,230	697	11,665	5,649	26	218	3,007
Leslie,	11,749	354	23,290	7,330	385	759	6,346
Locke, ..	3,926	300	6,625	4,302	75	244	2,780
Mason village,	.	.	...	.			. ..
Meridian,. .	8,136	429	6,185	5,794	211	377	5,600
Okemos vil.,	.	.		.		. .	. ....
Onondaga,.	18,202	1,628	12,329	8,131	946	466	6,210
Stockbridge,	22,098	203	30,660	6,790	52	924	7,869
Vevay, .	5,621	449	12,988	7,832	610	690	5,679
Wheatfield,	2 118	232	6,600	4,612	88	416	1,703
White Oak,.	12,013	370	24,071	7,203	50	870	9,341
Williamstown.	9.628	135	11,845	4,298	238	328	4,146
Total,	140043	7,683	233426	103757	4,657	9,472	85,607

INGHAM COUNTY.—Continued.

Ending June 1st, 1860.							
Wool, pounds of.	Value of Orchard products.	Butter, pounds of.	Cheese, pounds of.	Hay, tons of.	Clover seed, bushels.	Maple Sugar, pounds.	Value of home made manufactures.
2,867	850	25,275	2,855	707	13	23,845	$1,875
4,491	1,428	28,715	3,900	906	8	26,100	3,336
5,653	1,428	23,650	1,110	1,973	39	...	11
8,404	417	20,900	3,720	710	6	14,765	2,177
12,323	2,214	39,065	1,090	2,080	34	12,155	26
...	....	.					...
1,850	280	14,360	3,440	622	11	9,286	1,051
357	45	1,700	330	95		1,095	120
60	.	200	50	10		225	.
200		200	....	10		....	30
1,701	466	17,850	2,030	758		22,956	.
6,952	2,150	35,910	1,543	1,300	12	12,405	15
2,893	829	24,350	3,470	861		18,335	191
......	.	.	..		.	...	...
2,374	486	20,745	1,680	1,094		8,880	1,141
....	.....	.	....		..	..	......
10,506	2,827	28,440	3,075	1,705	256	3,730	3,377
10,318	2,661	28,560	2,360	2,635	111	...	121
11,006	2,141	28,245	4,525	1,112	2	20,480	3,122
3,176	43	13,475	1,280	347		9,520	52
6,818	1,929	26,130	680	1,639		5,427	99
2,854	695	22,285	650	918		2,310	......
89,803	20,895	400,055	37,788	19485	492	190514	$16,744

INGHAM COUNTY.—Continued.

TOWNSHIPS.	Flouring Mills.							Saw Mills.			
	Number of.	Runs of Stone.	Power used. Water.	Power used. Steam.	Capital invested in real and personal estate in the business.	Annual product. Bbls. flour made.	Annual product. Value of.	Number of.	Power used. Water.	Power used. Steam.	Capital invested in real and personal estate in the business.
Alaiedon,					..		.	1		1	$3,000
Aurelius,		.			. .		.	2		2	4,000
Bunker Hill,					..		.....	1		1	1,500
Delhi,						.	.	2		2	5,500
Ingham,	1	1		1	$4,000	6,100	$37300	1		1	3,000
Kinneyville v.					. .	.					..
Lansing,		.			.		.	1		1	2,000
" c., 1st w.,	2	5	2		19,500	5,900	31,800	2	2		10,000
" " 2d w.,						.	.				..
" " 3d w.,					.	. .	...	1		1	3,000
Le Roy,					.. .		.....	1		1	2,500
Leslie,	1	1		1	2,000	1,224	8,550	3	.	3	8,700
Locke,					... ..	.	.	1		1	3,000
Mason vil.,	1	2	.	1	6,000	4,500	29,500	1		1	2,500
Meridian,			.			..	.			.	. ..
Okemos vil.,	1	2		1	6,000	6,000	30,000	1		1	3,000
Onondaga,	1	3	1		8,000	1,500	8,475	3	1	2	5,900
Stockbridge,					...	. .	.	..		..	.
Vevay,					...		. ...	1		1	4,000
Wheatfield,				.	.. .	.	. .	2	1	1	3,000
White Oak,			.	.	.	.	.	1		1	3,000
Williamst'wn,	1	2	1		5,000	6,100	37,000	..			. ...
Total,	8	18	4	4	50,500	31324	182625	25	4	21	67,600

INGHAM COUNTY.—Continued.

Saw Mills.		Aggregate of all kinds of Manufactures, Mills included.				Estimated value of Real and Personal Estate.	
Annual product.			Hands employ'd				
Feet of Lumber Sawed.	Value of.	Capital invested in real and personal estate in the business.	Males.	Females.	Value of annual product.	By Assessors.	By assistant Marshals.
875,000	7,875	$3,000	3		$7,875	*	*
600,000	4,400	4,200	8		5,000	*	*
240,000	1,920	1,650	3		2,720	$111439	$286,340
768,000	6,612	5,500	5		6.612	*	*
500,000	4,500	9,000	10		49,570	191,621	422,112
.						*	*
400,000	3,200	2,000	3		3,200	*	*
2,000,000	12,000	55,400	72	7	109,905	*	*
. . ..	. ..	41,000	137	14	98,020	*	*
250,000	2,500	11,800	29		30,716	*	*
500,000	4,000	2,500	3		4,000	124,660	162,489
1,250,000	8,150	13,300	21		21,121	181,543	339,967
600,000	4,800	3,000	4		4,800	121,703	182,038
500,000	4,000	12,475	35		54,561	*	*
......	.. .	.				*	*
1,000,000	10,000	9,800	9		41,600	*	*
515,000	2,520	14,750	18		16,355	*	*
.. ...	.	1,025	8		3,855	171,665	385,157
520,000	4,160	4,000	4		4,160	*	*
400,000	3,080	3,000	5		3,080	113,745	148,622
500,000	4,000	6,060	8		12,050	125,311	265,547
.. .	. .	11,700	8		41,925	148,836	251,010
11,418,000	87,717	215,165	394	21	521,325	3039939	†9000,000

* Not reported.
† The footings of the two last columns are as given by Marshals.

IONIA COUNTY

TOWNSHIPS.	Dwelling Houses.		Number of Families.	Number of Inhabitants.				
	Whole number.	Number in Cities.		Whole number.	Colored.	Deaf and Dumb.	Blind.	Insane.
Berlin,	201		203	1,026				
Boston,	256		256	1,244		3		1
Campbell,	116		115	518				
Danby,	149		149	727			1	
Easton,	184		161	837		2		
Ionia,	374		367	1,926		1	2	
Keene,	198		192	1,150				
Lyons,	400		381	1,949		4	1	
North Plains,	207		189	921		3	3	
Odessa,	116		117	488				
Orange,	165		153	801		1		
Orleans,	172		170	857		3	3	2
Otisco,	280		262	1,349				
Portland,	296		282	1,381		7		
Ronald,	161		158	893	1	1	1	
Sebewa,	236		230	598				
Total,	3,499		3,385	16,665	1	27	11	3

IOSCO COUNTY

TOWNSHIPS.	Whole number.	Number in Cities.	Number of Families.	Whole number.	Colored.	Deaf and Dumb.	Blind.	Insane.
Aux Sauble,	55		20	73				
Tawas City,	58		27	102				
Total,	113		47	175				

ISABELLA COUNTY

TOWNSHIPS.	Whole number.	Number in Cities.	Number of Families.	Whole number.	Colored.	Deaf and Dumb.	Blind.	Insane.
Chippewa,	36		24	128				
Coe,	82		63	323				
Isabella,	210		217	994				
Total,	328		304	1,445				

IONIA COUNTY.—Continued.

TOWNSHIPS.	Value of Real Estate owned.	Occupied Farms. Whole number.	Acres improved.	Acres unimproved.	Cash value of.
Berlin,	$292,910	120	3,630	4,661	$250,450
Boston,	394,805	129	4,724	6,419	269,850
Campbell,	140,544	80	1,827	3,966	89,810
Danby,	221,360	125	4,072	7,557	228,985
Easton,	317,225	112	4,451	7,082	279,550
Ionia,	662,985	97	5,740	4,605	348,700
Keene,	298,750	165	8,190	5,451	344,850
Lyons,	627,950	142	6,705	5,173	361,060
North Plains,	239,650	139	6,036	7,341	234,450
Odessa,	160,165	127	2,690	5,778	126,585
Orange,	221,100	112	3,145	5,268	208,350
Orleans,	240,930	125	3,923	6,101	211,750
Otisco,	477,215	160	8,062	7,446	384,660
Portland,	543,720	151	6,627	7,819	346,850
Ronald,	255,100	131	6,171	7,673	231,100
Sebewa,	179,775	112	2,819	7,138	134,276
Total,	$5,274,184	2,027	79,712	97,478	$4,051,276

IOSCO COUNTY.—Continued.

TOWNSHIPS.	Value of Real Estate owned.	Whole number.	Acres improved.	Acres unimproved.	Cash value of.
Aux Sauble,	$1,400				
Tawas City,	11,550				
Total,	$12,950				

ISABELLA COUNTY.—Continued.

TOWNSHIPS.	Value of Real Estate owned.	Whole number.	Acres improved.	Acres unimproved.	Cash value of.
Chippewa,	$24,300	32	489	4,019	$28,000
Coe,	55,045	59	1,391	6,292	57,100
Isabella,	14,750	8	195	1,705	12,500
Total,	$94,095	99	2,075	12,016	$97,600

IONIA COUNTY.—Continued.

Value of Farming Implements and Machinery.	Live Stock, June 1st, 1860.							
	Horses.	Asses and Mules.	Milch Cows.	Working Oxen.	Other Cattle.	Sheep.	Swine.	Value of Live Stock.
$8,640	187		365	162	446	1,455	470	$36,865
10,645	192	2	327	162	383	1,720	316	23,055
3,621	39	2	142	90	243	400	240	18,903
8,520	209		283	162	279	1,024	1,672	32,195
10,090	163		345	757	520	1,372	410	40,187
10,225	212		258	144	399	1,994	384	22,368
11,371	286		421	172	474	1,608	613	36,205
13,775	315		398	145	575	2,569	540	59,517
9,827	210	2	306	172	1,220	1,638	652	28,302
6,556	98	30	192	155	383	547	3,367	17,658
7,116	184		316	126	294	973	535	25,890
9,736	164		286	152	280	1,660	305	33,030
15,490	261		426	182	476	2,271	425	42,224
15,015	285		406	174	517	3,119	686	48,620
12,230	248		249	190	367	2,418	496	36,544
4,883	126		250	119	399	657	381	23,187
$157,740	3179	36	5070	3,064	7,259	25,425	11,492	$533,750

IOSCO COUNTY.—Continued.

. .				. .	.	. . .	. . . .	
. . ...				. .			.....	

ISABELLA COUNTY.—Continued.

$1,797	9		29	34	39	9	61	$3,005
3,185	2		97	84	118	66	194	7,191
794	5		15	13	27	.	21	1,295
$5,776	16	.	141	131	184	75	276	$11,491

IONIA COUNTY.—Continued.

TOWNSHIPS.	Produce, during the Year						
	Wheat, bushels of.	Rye, bushels of.	Indian corn, bushels of.	Oats, bushels of.	Barley, bushels of.	Buckwheat, bushels of.	Potatoes, bushels of.
Berlin,	12,033	641	15,165	10,204	462	445	5,207
Boston,	13,137	1,018	13,477	5,161	78	546	7.373
Campbell,	3,269	237	5,534	2,262	219	225	1,730
Danby,	7,148	619	8,795	5.432	178	734	4,292
Easton,	12,638	194	7,839	5,403	324	355	4,003
Ionia,	10,738	804	8,855	5,941	929	160	4,473
Keene,	27,455	1,199	10,970	11,462	445	570	7,895
Lyons,	24,507	1,049	11,639	13,913	1,053	24[illegible]	4,992
North Plains,	14,322	209	5.115	5,505	145	214	3,679
Odessa,	3,856	599	8,816	1 159	168	584	3,447
Orange,	9,561	440	11,053	5,087	394	361	3 531
Orleans,	15,902	701	6,552	4 631	24	180	1,107
Otisco,	22,630	2,273	11,079	8,087	55	356	5,535
Portland,	20,513	1,377	16,010	10,382	212	487	5,596
Ronald,	26 370	1,474	8,063	8,344	248	180	4,908
Sebewa,	3,827	195	7,867	2,625	36	471	2,206
Total,	227906	13049	156829	105597	4,970	6,122	69,876

IOSCO COUNTY.—Continued.

Aux Sauble,	.		..				
Tawas City,	..			.			. .
Total,	..						.

ISABELLA COUNTY.—Continued.

Chippewa,	369	327	204	268	13	21	388
Coe,	1,597	409	1,451	565	15	69	1.299
Isabella,	199		122	104		45	287
Total,	2,165	736	1,777	937	28	135	1,974

IONIA COUNTY.—Continued.

Ending June 1st, 1860.							
Wool, pounds of.	Value of Orchard products.	Butter, pounds of.	Cheese, pounds of.	Hay, tons of.	Clover seed, bushels.	Maple Sugar, pounds.	Value of home made manufactures.
3,977	$1,505	34,030	1,470	1,291	64	45,425	$245
4,910	600	13,700	5,035	1,896	239	19,470	311
1,167	170	8,571	280	740	65	12,000	1,047
2,384	359	20,073	1,149	770		27,427	441
3,348	788	31,820	6,780	1,498	11	16,370	317
5,758	1,065	22,275	3,095	1,376	75	3,715	434
4,275	1,949	42,250	2,970	2,134	173	24,485	1,327
6,923	630	37,150	4,085	1,598	35	15,310	218
4,523	107	28,540	2,975	950	49	25,327	347
1,333	658	13,965	4,850	741	50	24,512	291
2,470	945	20,320	880	873		31,950	758
4,061	396	8,700	500	415	10	4,790	37
6,447	1,127	37,300	3,800	1,996	64	2,986	394
7,012	1,388	38,650	3,400	1,142	59	17,985	750
6,693	697	28,900	5,804	1,823	157	7,161	167
1,627	215	22,994	1,806	656		35,910	1,122
66,908	12,599	408,248	44,879	19893	1051	315323	$7,906

IOSCO COUNTY.—Continued

.....	...		.	..		.	
.....	..		.	.			.
.....	. .		.			.	. .

ISABELLA COUNTY.—Continued.

.....	...	610	.	25	2	3,343	
143	.	1,353	200	156		18,140	
....	.	80	. .	5		2,323	.
143	. .	2,043	200	186	.	23,806	..

IONIA COUNTY.—Continued.

TOWNSHIPS.	Flouring Mills.							Saw Mills.			
			Power used.			Annual product.			Power used.		
	Number of.	Runs of Stone.	Water.	Steam.	Capital invested in real and personal estate in the business.	Bbls. flour made.	Value of.	Number of.	Water.	Steam.	Capital invested in real and personal estate in the business.
Berlin,								1	1		$600
Boston,								4	3	1	11,900
Campbell,											
Danby,											
Easton,	1		1		$4,000	450	$3,075				
Ionia,	4		3	1	18,500	21550	111800	1		1	11,000
Keene,											
Lyons,	2		2		22,000	9,125	47,213	4	2	2	24,500
North Plains,	1		1		8,000	7,000	35,000				
Odessa,	1			1	2,500		100	2		2	
Orange,											
Orleans,											
Otisco,	2		2			3,533	20,109	2	2		20,000
Portland,	2		2		40,000	16666	85,930	2	2		5,000
Ronald,											
Sebewa,											
Total,	13		11	2	94,000	58324	303227	16	10	6	73,000

IOSCO COUNTY.—Continued.

TOWNSHIPS.	Number of.	Runs of Stone.	Water.	Steam.	Capital invested in real and personal estate in the business.	Bbls. flour made.	Value of.	Number of.	Water.	Steam.	Capital invested in real and personal estate in the business.
Aux Sauble,											
Tawas City,								1		1	20,000
Total,								1		1	20,000

ISABELLA COUNTY.—Continued.

TOWNSHIPS.	Number of.	Runs of Stone.	Water.	Steam.	Capital invested in real and personal estate in the business.	Bbls. flour made.	Value of.	Number of.	Water.	Steam.	Capital invested in real and personal estate in the business.
Chippewa,											
Coe,											
Isabella,											
Total,											

IONIA COUNTY.—Continued.

Saw Mills. Annual product. Feet of Lumber Sawed.	Value of.	Aggregate of all kinds of manufactures, Mills included. Capital invested in real and personal estate in the business.	Hands employ'd Males.	Females.	Value of annual products.	Estimated value of Real and Personal Estate. By Assessors.	By assistant Marshals.
100,000	$600		1			*	*
1,000,000	8,200	26,000	15		26,200	*	*
	.. .				..	†198442	†$265,022
						*	*
.. .			1			*	*
350,000	3,500	46,350	50		149,200	*	*
						*	*
1,630,000	12,860	48,000	26		65,073	*	*
		42,100	20		61,025	*	*
520,000	6,120	2,500	6		7,120	*	*
. ...	. ...					*	*
					. .	*	*
2,200,000	11,000	20,000	24		31,649	*	*
390,000	2,730	56,650	23		109,410	*	*
	. ..	.			.. ..	*	*
.	. ...				.	‡229108	‡305,477
6,190,000	55,010	241,600	166		449,677	3341933	4,455,000

IOSCO COUNTY.—Continued.

250,000	10,000	20,000	20		10,000	$78,000	
250,000	10,000	20,000	20		10,000	$78,000	. .

ISABELLA COUNTY.—Continued.

						$29,132	$29,132
		.				133,843	133,843
		.				301,000	301,000
		..			.	463,975	$463,975

*Not returned. †Includes Odessa. ‡Includes Danby.

JACKSON COUNTY

TOWNSHIPS.	Dwelling Houses. Whole number.	Dwelling Houses. Number in Cities.	Number of Families.	Number of Inhabitants. Whole number.	Colored.	Deaf and Dumb.	Blind.	Insane.
Blackman,	244	.	242	1,268	3			
Brooklyn,	188	. .	187	1,003	8			
Brooklyn village,	71	..	71	331	1			
Columbia,..	168	.	172	883	1			
Concord,	238	.	227	1,164	1	1		
Grass Lake,	223	...	222	1,230				
Grass Lake village,	98	....	96	479				
Hanover,	214	.	197	969				
Henrietta,	178	...	178	889				
Jackson city, 1st w.,	193	193	201	1,111	36			
" " 2d w.,	203	203	208	1,047				
" " 3d w.,	177	177	188	961	36		1	1
" " 4th w.,	209	209	223	1,680	59		1	
Leoni,	282	.. ..	277	1,396	9	1	1	.
Liberty,	200	. ..	195	1,020				
Napoleon,.	160	.. .	157	802	1			1
Parma,	243	....	232	1,350	5		2	1
Pulaski,	201	. ..	198	1,103	. .		.	.
Rives,	224	.....	229	1,154		1		
Sandstone,	266	...	266	1,393	1	4	1	..
Spring Arbor,	217	...	208	1,023	.		1	.
Springport,	211	.....	212	1,114		1		..
Summit,	164	......	162	890	6		2	
Tompkins,.	211	.. .	206	952	.	1		1
Waterloo,	277	......	279	1,452	1			..
Total,	5,060	782	5,033	26,664	167	9	9	4

JACKSON COUNTY.—Continued.

TOWNSHIPS.	Value of Real Estate owned.	Occupied Farms.			
		Whole number.	Acres improved.	Acres unimproved.	Cash value of.
Blackman,	$566,260	135	9,181	7,732	$485,666
Brooklyn,	478,739	127	11,464	8,609	445,120
Brooklyn village,	180,605				
Columbia,	344,085	123	8,853	7,377	354,980
Concord,	649,500	140	13,399	9,450	573,600
Grass Lake,	729,719	153	15,750	10,152	708,529
Grass Lake vil.,	142,450				
Hanover,	409,525	142	11,596	7,173	498,135
Henrietta,	319,100	116	7,854	8,899	297,950
Jackson c., 1st w.,	1,126,310				
" " 2d w.,	501,580				
" " 3d w.,	243,843				
" " 4th w.,	349,920				
Leoni,	465,139	137	10,136	7,967	371,919
Liberty,	404,830	140	11,678	8,155	366,280
Napoleon,	352,803	100	6,913	6,457	304,705
Parma,	516,520	147	13,099	7,277	530,900
Pulaski,	546,230	147	10,927	7,318	428,550
Rives,	379,765	130	9,199	6,771	359,365
Sandstone,	536,295	138	11,018	8,238	484,090
Spring Arbor,	618,348	120	12,449	8,728	558,195
Springport,	475,920	143	11,636	8,508	441,600
Summit,	551,730	98	10,046	7,785	537,620
Tompkins,	346,275	127	8,353	7,077	319,890
Waterloo,	476,780	233	14,832	14,832	470,925
Total,	11,712,271	2,596	209,023	158,504	$8,448,019

JACKSON COUNTY.—CONTINUED.

Value of Farming Implements and Machinery.	Live Stock, June 1st, 1860.							
	Horses.	Asses and Mules.	Milch Cows.	Working Oxen.	Other Cattle.	Sheep.	Swine.	Value of Live Stock.
$12,237	352	1	429	185	480	5,480	505	$58,735
16,011	367		380	98	447	8,047	441	71,311
11,095	331		374	111	550	3,933	521	57,873
11,965	376		407	196	526	8,120	820	87,815
18,055	425		471	172	542	7,143	835	78,405
13,460	378		408	147	479	4,230	700	71,981
9,847	233		338	157	453	3,246	508	45,563
12,550	324	2	387	126	517	4,148	530	57,515
13,870	385		465	158	558	3,845	713	71,100
10,175	263	2	282	49	335	4,292	343	42,459
17,150	415		438	198	478	7,624	752	88,700
11,626	320		361	149	467	5,223	957	70,067
10,396	281		393	223	473	3,258	536	52,651
13,071	326	4	444	223	553	7,424	645	66,276
15,910	430		418	229	545	8,415	678	96,745
13,779	306		448	216	564	7,684	681	67,975
13,424	338	5	393	137	648	5,502	686	68,585
9,777	250		327	169	393	3,575	634	47,135
16,893	417		609	330	860	6,742	1,064	78,422
$251,321	6507	14	7782	3,273	9,868	107931	12,549	1,279,313

JACKSON COUNTY.—Continued.

TOWNSHIPS.	Produce, during the Year						
	Wheat, bushels of.	Rye, bushels of.	Indian corn, bushels of.	Oats, bushels of.	Barley, bushels of.	Buckwheat, bushels of.	Potatoes, bushels of.
Blackman,	24,123	1,011	18,370	6,899	445	1,366	12,174
Brooklyn,	28,446	333	37,730	4,875	665	834	11,605
Brooklyn vil.,							
Columbia,	20,743	812	31,160	2,096	469	2,388	12,723
Concord,	52,502	365	37,805	15,043	5,309	478	8,784
Grass Lake,	61,483	1,672	45,645	5,071	988	1,778	21,661
Grass Lake v.,							
Hanover,	40,603	736	50,170	8,867	425	1,495	11,045
Henrietta,	22,331	440	14,386	5,482	162	713	9,715
Jackson, 1st w							
" 2d w							
" 3d w							
" 4th w							
Leoni,	30,097	2,261	28,276	2,611	285	2,482	14,394
Liberty,	30,766	1,203	43,895	3,484	200	2,973	11,764
Napoleon,	19,152	888	24,995	1,966	7	982	10,871
Parma,	49,121	970	42,355	11,546	2,196	433	9,408
Pulaski,	45,446	432	51,904	7,879	842	1,435	8,912
Rives,	26,056	1,092	16,925	8,261	866	386	7,595
Sandstone,	31,933	480	23,356	14,510	696	1,199	10 360
Spring Arbor,	44,671	779	37,170	11,817	1,447	424	8,655
Springport,	38,646	1,042	23,958	13,505	15	947	7,822
Summit,	31,674	1,593	28,775	7,967	1,457	892	13,317
Tompkins,	24,625	1,780	15,121	6,374	580	1,025	5,317
Waterloo,	45,274	1,702	28,272	7,388	433	1,592	20,040
Total,	667691	19591	600268	145641	17487	23822	216152

JACKSON COUNTY.—CONTINUED.

ENDING JUNE 1ST, 1860.							
Wool, pounds of.	Value of Orchard products.	Butter, pounds of.	Cheese, pounds of.	Hay, tons of.	Clover seed, bushels.	Maple Sugar, pounds.	Value of home made manufactures.
20,004	3,718	36,035	2,950	3,229	46		907
27,347	3,055	35,008	4,859	2,664	202		
11,964	4,550	33,816	760	2,542	190		
27,644	5,312	38,800	3,300	2,248	216		
26,427	5,613	40,015	3,235	2,814	217		
12,045	7,020	37,040	1,360	2,135	158		
10,733	1,862	24,460	900	2,609	83		921
11,818	4,830	34,855	500	2,557	141		
11,628	5'473	42'440	2,960	2,390	160		
13,775	2,878	26,455	250	1,965	213		
27,215	8,000	40,750	1,340	2,460	147		20
15,224	5,780	34,400	1,310	2,019	249		10
10,135	2,759	29,125	1,860	2,615	163		937
23,141	4,798	34,186	16,930	3,057	81		880
28,816	6,272	36,790	3,200	3,475	152		
27,356	3,330	28,666	8,385	2,892	84	200	722
14,202	3,331	37,350	1,300	3,266	161		
10,629	2,486	23,200	2,150	1,855	41	200	675
21,329	4,462	49.168	730	4,915	420		1,516
352,304	85,579	662,559	58,279	51707	3124	400	6,588

JACKSON COUNTY.—Continued.

TOWNSHIPS.	Flouring Mills.							Saw Mills.			
			Power used.			Annual product.			Power used.		
	Number of.	Runs of Stone.	Water.	Steam.	Capital invested in real and personal estate in the business.	Bbls. flour made.	Value of.	Number of.	Water.	Steam.	Capital invested in real and personal estate in the business.
Blackman,								1		1	$2,000
Brooklyn,..	1		1		$15000	10000	57,750				
Brooklyn vil.,.	1		1		15,000	1,000	6,268				
Columbia,	1		1		7,000	500	2,645				
Concord,	1		1		40,000	9,000	50,000				
Grass Lake,.											
" " vil.,											
Hanover,	1		1		6,000	1,000	5,000				
Henrietta,.											
Jacks'n, 1st w.											
" 2d w.											
" 3d w.	1		1		40,000	14800	85,000				
" 4th w.	1			1	33,000	21700	130000				
Leoni, . ..	2		2		11,000	1,700	9,193				
Liberty,	1		1		11,000	4,000	20,000				
Napoleon,											
Parma,. . .											
Pulaski,											
Rives,.... .											
Sandstone, .								2		2	3,000
Spring Arbor,											
Springport,								1		1	3,000
Summit,	1		1		6,000	1,000	6,200				
Tompkins,	1				3,000			2		2	5,000
Waterloo,	2		2		9 000		37.500	3	3		1,600
Total,	14		12	1	196000	64700	409555	9	3	6	14,600

JACKSON COUNTY—Continued.

Saw Mills.		Aggregate of all kinds of Manufactures, Mills included.				Estimated value of Real and Personal Estate.	
Annual product.			Hands employ'd				
Feet of Lumber Sawed.	Value of.	Capital invested in real and personal estate in the business.	Males.	Females.	Value of annual product.	By Assessors.	By assistant Marshals.
90,000	$800	$5,000	23		$9,700	*	*
.....	......	15,000	3		57,750	$331456	$360,955
....	.....	27,000	16		18,890	*	*
....		12,000	4		6,792	187,938	225,777
....	.	52,000	16		59,000	271,918	321,509
......	..	..			.	423,540	443,905
.	...	10,500	13		9,000	*	*
....	....	8,000	5		8,600	211,023	246,995
.....	..	1,200	2		900	*	*
......	..	68,100	39	13	73,945	334,865	407,510
.....	.	21,700	22		29,823	285,895	344,945
......	.	58,500	32	1	105,159	181,850	223,911
..	...	308,000	433	6	501,439	194,269	236,275
...	..	11,000	4		9,193	335,012	349,831
......	.	11,000	4		20,000	188,564	226,832
....	...	2,500	2		2,550	178,131	209,885
......	.	11,100	21		20,400	282,661	314,568
....	......	..				217,469	248,177
...	.	800	4		1,400	*	*
320,000	3,200	7,000	11		6,500	*	*
......	.	...				253,554	276,436
150,000	1,500	5,150	10		5,750	*	*
....	.	6,000	2		6,200	260,356	310,996
266,000	2,550	8,000	6		2,550	*	*
238,000	2,380	11,150	9		40,605	*	*
1,654,000	10,430	660,700	681	20	996,148	5679352	†6685,568

*Not reported.
†The footings of the two last columns are as reported by Marshals.

KALAMAZOO COUNTY

TOWNSHIPS.	Dwelling Houses.		Number of Families.	Number of Inhabitants.				
	Whole number.	Number in Cities.		Whole number.	Colored.	Deaf and Dumb.	Blind.	Insane.
Alamo,	187	.....	184	943	3			1
Brady,	194	. .	195	1,012	11		1	
Charleston,	263	.	263	1,309		2	1	
Climax,	220	. .	220	1,160	1	1	1	.
Comstock,	401	....	401	2,012	6	1	2	8
Cooper,	236	......	231	1,231	7			
Kalamazoo,	158	.	148	875	9			1
Kalamazoo village,	1,094		1,09[illegible]	6,075	205	2	1	79
Oshtemo,	244	..	247	1,240	18	1		
Pavilion,	194	. ..	194	964				
Portage,	187	. ..	187	974	12		2	
Prairie Ronde,	188		184	1,036	2			
Richland,	257	. .	257	1,331			.	
Ross,	293	.. ..	299	1,514	3			
Schoolcraft,	276	.	268	1,500	19	2		
Texas,	165	..	165	829	1	.		
Waukeshma,	130	.	132	658				
Total,	4,787	. ...	4,668	24,663	297	9	8	89

KALAMAZOO COUNTY.—Continued.

TOWNSHIPS.	Value of Real Estate owned.	Occupied Farms.			
		Whole number.	Acres improved.	Acres unimproved.	Cash value of.
Alamo, ...	$339,450	81	5,271	8,523	$44,400
Brady,	342,280	146	7,493	17,008	345,190
Charleston, ...	562,470	154	10,557	5,916	494,100
Climax,	484,786	105	9,212	8,171	437,970
Comstock, ...	805,810	160	11,243	8,216	583,065
Cooper,.	601,140	83	9,025	8,846	610,530
Kalamazoo,	592,950	134	8,784	5,730	1,502,340
Kalamazoo vil.,.	3,860,425		......	. ....	.. .. .
Oshtemo, .. .	618,400	163	10,000	5,686	568,420
Pavilion,.	398,751	89	2,829	3,161	213,240
Portage,.	593,215	139	11,447	5,509	598,695
Prairie Ronde,. .	647,785	89	9,958	9,810	635,115
Richland,.. ...	706,263	148	12,850	15,345	620,013
Ross, ...	451,048	138	5,885	6,029	351,920
Schoolcraft, .	977,645	88	13,150	7,063	657,890
Texas, ...	426,950	136	8,611	8,324	453,495
Waukeshma, .	165,575	87	1,342	5,939	36,430
Total, . . .	12,574,943	1,940	137,663	129,276	$8,152,813

KALAMAZOO COUNTY.—Continued.

Value of Farming Implements and Machinery.	Live Stock, June 1st, 1860.							
	Horses.	Asses and Mules.	Milch Cows.	Working Oxen.	Other Cattle.	Sheep.	Swine.	Value of Live Stock.
$20,773	271	2	332	120	411	1,390	567	$53,434
9,700	280		351	114	331	2,333	916	50,494
13,053	382	4	463	94	414	6,521	927	72,614
14,747	202		349	84	498	6,213	1,022	55,895
17,492	373		372	122	531	3,082	754	62,054
28,010	350	2	382	114	513	3,253	948	63,828
22,618	456	4	399	108	580	3,817	969	50,242
					.	.	.....	. ..
17,880	332		424	104	551	3,269	1,160	59,914
5,287	121		119	58	218	1,339	263	22,654
20,355	429	:	466	92	438	4,303	882	79,992
19,689	419	4	423	80	625	1,939	1,467	71,340
21,885	438		421	62	625	9,232	741	75,619
9,279	253		333	171	335	2,296	566	43,536
23,841	490		400	40	643	3,118	994	77,130
15,477	317		345	117	441	2,369	898	50,167
4,150	132	1	195	97	229	103	623	23,252
$264,335	5345	17	5774	1,577	7,383	54,576	13,697	912,165

KALAMAZOO COUNTY.—Continued.

TOWNSHIPS.	Produce, during the Year						
	Wheat, bushels of.	Rye, bushels of.	Indian corn, bushels of.	Oats, bushels of.	Barley, bushels of.	Buckwheat, bushels of.	Potatoes, bushels of.
Alamo,	23,845	60	31,402	3,703	458	1,818	9,865
Brady,	26,059	850	30,037	2,262	421	192	7,323
Charleston,	50,243	196	26,225	9,815	680	70	2,557
Climax,	44,968	157	28,017	15 799	273	139	7,166
Comstock,	39,907	371	31,905	10,075	579	112	10,144
Cooper,	32,177	225	50,750	8,342	103	212	10,707
Kalamazoo,	30,672	75	27,360	9,503	550	97	12,601
Kalamazoo vil:							
Oshtemo,	39,014	342	42,255	10,122	1,050	264	11,379
Pavilion,	14,115	120	9,215	4,175	150	220	4,650
Portage,	49,571	883	48,055	7,283	998	171	11,867
Prairie Ronde,	36,186	504	41,940	12,957	5,918	415	5,687
Richland,	64,387	540	44,585	28,037	832	18	8,312
Ross,	28,380	425	20,155	4,543	337	168	6,398
Schoolcraft,	60,674	1,218	66,705	14,354	3,575	351	6,453
Texas,	38,754	402	35,210	5,840	20	364	9,436
Waukeshma,	6,283		14,875	718		257	3,508
Total,	585235	6,368	548691	147529	15944	4,868	128053

KALAMAZOO COUNTY.—Continued.

ENDING JUNE 1ST, 1860.

Wool, pounds of.	Value of Orchard products.	Butter, pounds of.	Cheese, pounds of.	Hay, tons of.	Clover seed, bushels.	Maple Sugar, pounds.	Value of home made manufactures.
4,739	$1,835	15,890	2,479	869	46	5,087	$149
7,561	1,648	25,420	2,172	1,554	74	1,585	211
22,449	675	10,200	4,210	666	77	200	120
23,183	1,500	27,675	4,005	2,030	129	15,750	222
10,824	3,659	39,585	9,435	1,723	281	10,730	126
9,868	7,121	48,740	5,120	1,768	61	6,490	175
11,619	4,334	50,722	10,246	2,510	237	72,960	110
11,759	3,231	40,175	1,160	1,733	106	.	166
4,254	550	11,050	1,175	843	157	1,720	86
14,791	2,855	42,980	6,335	2,380	307	1,800	381
7,617	2,715	37,675	4,737	1,326	165	897	372
31,832	3,125	39,950	7,976	2,747	7		114
6,972	1,304	22,165	1,930	1,464	104	600	280
12,585	2,015	32,916	4,207	1,504	377	..	217
6,822	1,933	32,400	2,300	950	133	.	161
285	370	18,615	750	375		23,671	
187,160	39,920	496,158	68,237	24442	2263	141490	$2,890

KALAMAZOO COUNTY.—Continued.

TOWNSHIPS.	Flouring Mills.							Saw Mills.			
	Number of.	Runs of Stone.	Power used.		Capital invested in real and personal estate in the business.	Annual product.		Number of.	Power used.		Capital invested in real and personal estate in the business.
			Water.	Steam.		Bbls. flour made.	Value of.		Water.	Steam.	
Alamo, . . .	.			. .	. . . . .	. . . . . .	. . . .	1	1	.	$2,000
Brady,		.			. . . .	. . . . . .	. .	4	2	2	7,700
Charleston,					. . .	. . .	. . . .	1	1		1,500
Climax,.					. . .	. . . . .	. . .	2	1	1	2,200
Comstock,	3		2	1	22,000	39,500	230100	2	1	1	5,500
Cooper,.	.					. . . . .	. . . . .	2	2	.	2,500
Kalamazoo,						.	. . .				. . . . .
Kal. vil.,	1		1		23,000	20,000	107800	4	2	2	11,500
Oshtemo,					.	. .	. .				. . .
Pavilion,.	1		1		6,000	8,000	49,000	3	3		4,200
Portage,					.	.	. .	1	1		1,000
Pr. Ronde,					. .		. . . . .	3	2	1	5,500
Richland,		:	.		. . . .	. .					. . . .
Ross,.	2		2		12,500	78,250	398100	4	4		6,500
Schoolcraft,	1		1		6,000	4,500	27,000	1	1		4,000
Texas,					.	. . . .	. .				. . .
W'uk'shma	1		1		10,000	7,000	28,125	2	1	1	9,500
Total,.	9		8	1	79,500	157,250	840125	30	22	8	63,600

KALAMAZOO COUNTY—Continued.

Saw Mills.		Aggregate of all kinds of Manufactures, Mills included.				Estimated value of Real and Personal Estate.	
Annual product.			Hands employ'd				
Feet of Lumber Sawed.	Value of.	Capital invested in real and personal estate in the business.	Males.	Females.	Value of annual products.	By Assessors.	By assistant Marshals.
350,000	$2,800	$2,800	5		$3,450	155,998	...
1,325	10,600	8,425	22		12,810	143,734	. .
20,000	1,800	4,450	13		8,775	286,686	. ...
500,000	4,000	4,200	16		11,320	230,237	..
600,000	8,400	34,300	30		267,965	391,224	..
450,000	3,600	3,500	11		6,200	269,488	
. .. .	. . .				. .		
1,800,000	22,000	167,500	204	9	374,840	1311485	2,622,970
. .....	...	. ..				258,825	
460,000	9,500	11,550	17		63,940	162,268	
50,000	500	1,000	1		500	233,010	
1,130,000	9,870	15,600	14		38,995	305,104	
.. . .	.. . .	2,850	11		7,470	303,319	
1,539,000	12,360	59,750	62		452,784	206,115	
250,000	2,500	24,100	27	:	56,000	465,876	
. ..		. .			..	182,905	
350,000	2,800	10,250	13		6,110	83,137	
7,590,325	89,730	350,275	446	9	1311159	4989411	2,622,970

KENT COUNTY

TOWNSHIPS.	Dwelling Houses.		Number of Families.	Number of Inhabitants.				
	Whole number.	Number in Cities.		Whole number.	Colored.	Deaf and Dumb.	Blind.	Insane.
Ada,	238		212	1,116				
Algoma,	224		195	993				
Alpine,	271		246	1,248				
Bowne,	439		405	745				
Byron,	210		196	1,042	5	3		
Cannon,	210		206	1,061		1	1	1
Caledonia,	159		145	762				
Cascade,	178		171	893				
Courtland,	204		185	937				
Gaines,	180		167	868	11			
Gratton,	228		219	1,127		1		
Grand Rapids,	193		174	1,021				
G. R. city, 1st w.,	356	356	322	1,668	22			1
" " 2d w.,	490	490	421	2,132				
" " 3d w.,	503	503	447	2,299	25			3
" " 4th w.,	315	315	273	1,368	13			
" " 5th w.,	152	152	233	623				
Lowell,	275		254	1,200	24			
Nelson,	105		93	461				
Oakfield,	234		211	1,079		1		1
Paris,	289		255	1,327	14	2		1
Plainfield,	264		235	1,240				1
Sparta,	206		188	941				
Solon,	97		82	393				
Tyrone,	38		37	173		3		
Vergennes,	258		237	1,347				
Walker,	266		259	1,430				
Wyoming,	287		242	1,239				
Total,	6,894	1,816	6,310	30,743	114	11	1	8

KENT COUNTY.—Continued.

TOWNSHIPS.	Value of Real Estate owned.	Occupied Farms. Whole number.	Acres improved.	Acres unimproved.	Cash value of.
Ada, ...	$418,680	142	7,266	8,834	$334,600
Algoma, ...	200,590	48	1,834	3,859	80,500
Alpine, ..	487,340	184	7,782	9,404	430,480
Bowne,	197,080	104	4,606	7,739	82,500
Byron, .	268,140	116	3,971	6,039	201,850
Cannon,	393,800	155	7,791	8,984	316,400
Caledonia, ...	157,975	84	2,879	4,258	129,100
Cascade, ...	300,000	128	5,528	6,111	284,190
Courtland,	256,851	108	5,587	7,064	228,100
Gaines, .. .	366,030	124	5,786	7,620	296,700
Gratton, . .	350,640	172	7,121	10,058	342,810
Grand Rapids,.	485,050	139	4,725	4,645	331,250
G. R. city, 1st w.,	1,004,420	.	. .	. .	
" " 2d w.,	1,096,700			. .	
" " 3d w.,	2,216,640	..	..	......	.
" " 4th w.,	471,350		..	.	. .
" " 5th w.,	153,475	*69	1,189	807	375,040
Lowell, . ..	336,685	71	3,581	4,483	152,900
Nelson, .	48,830	31	758	3,418	32,940
Oakfield,. . .	308,785	113	5,984	8,282	145,200
Paris, . .	529,175	165	5,574	7 858	489,950
Plainfield, ...	344,155	76	3,581	4,060	73,100
Sparta,	314,620	122	4,824	9,021	262,500
Solon,	54,304	7	150	705	9,000
Tyrone, ..	36,450	21	516	1,274	24,400
Vergennes,	517,210	130	8,658	7,906	441,850
Walker, ...	635,950	196	7,054	7,191	605,300
Wyoming, .	468,510	117	4,633	6,243	350,660
Total,.. ...	11,409,435	2,634	111,558	143,866	6,453,320

*This includes the whole city.

KENT COUNTY.—Continued.

Value of Farming Implements and Machinery.	Live Stock, June 1st, 1860.							
	Horses.	Asses and Mules.	Milch Cows.	Working Oxen.	Other Cattle.	Sheep.	Swine.	Value of Live Stock.
$8,460	214		395	150	517	2,616	718	$42,529
3,467	63		112	52	93	176	210	11,201
14,867	261		475	166	474	1,588	693	50,349
6,292	119		237	182	401	1,112	769	28,730
5,624	124		309	139	408	401	563	27,697
13,032	220		352	178	347	1,746	462	42,046
2,639	43		182	147	197	275	568	16,004
7 645	163		353	153	533	1,248	795	28,962
9 849	182		273	132	233	1,124	367	31,092
7,902	142		344	164	554	1,024	911	37,544
12,093	220		429	207	451	2,162	562	45,776
11,996	233		328	112	286	814	422	36,141
6,188	110		128	10	73	54	112	14,207
4,342	89		172	117	196	292	491	18,323
1,355	10		63	41	60	13	102	5,007
8,562	158		279	165	318	1,382	325	31,276
11,315	269	3	435	113	556	1,601	963	42,977
6,815	130		190	66	161	265	241	18,380
8,673	163		332	156	331	635	421	32,310
440	3		10	12	8		15	1,135
770	6		33	28	41	138	62	3,399
14,690	292		513	172	786	1,854	849	57,546
30,200	394		529	132	504	1,626	712	53,381
8.682	194		335	135	372	591	686	33,732
205,898	3893	3	6808	2,929	7,900	22,737	12,019	709,744

KENT COUNTY.—Continued.

TOWNSHIPS.	Produce, during the Year						
	Wheat, bushels of.	Rye, bushels of.	Indian corn, bushels of.	Oats, bushels of.	Barley, bushels of.	Buckwheat, bushels of.	Potatoes, bushels of.
Ada,	21,461	2,771	11,178	4,713	127	656	7,804
Algomá,	3,542	353	2,426	1,123	22	88	1,570
Alpine,	13,428	3,714	16,222	13,350	318	519	6,565
Bowne,	16,082	248	9,255	7,690	354	270	5,850
Byron,	5,550	605	13,936	5,962	138	481	7,675
Cannon,	21,469	1,381	10,867	5,164		273	6,753
Caledonia,	6,809	658	6,651	3,395	30	585	5,208
Cascade,	16,984	2,568	12,710	7,620	33	628	9,669
Courtland,	16,677	933	9,286	6,655	73	113	4,977
Gaines,	9,943	2,799	14,437	9,160	121	546	4,942
Gratton,	30,978	974	11,232	8,412	91	423	7,394
Grand Rapids,	10,544	2,092	9,985	5,712	12	99	7,360
G R. c., 1st w.,							
" " 2d w.,							
" " 3d w,							
" " 4th w.,							
" " 5th w.,	1,629	470	2,921	890	18	23	3,742
Lowell,	11,001	96	6,590	4,412	43	240	4,038
Nelson,	1,508	90	1,551	358		52	1,194
Oakfield,	20,428	1,509	11,0[illegible]0	7,121		506	6,758
Paris,	7,794	3,761	14,680	9,130	226	203	9,418
Plainfield,	8,228	2,165	7,860	1,570		114	3,237
Sparta,	6,282	1,960	9,131	5,899	746	448	5,267
Solon,	242		265			9	270
Tyrone,	519	89	960	950		49	707
Vergennes,	32,928	2,045	14,272	8,734	137	626	6,794
Walker,	13,847	1,480	17,361	13,568	299	345	8,766
Wyoming,	9,253	1,695	12,826	3,091	258	71	5,726
Total,	287121	34456	227682	134774	3,046	7,367	131684

KENT COUNTY.—Continued.

ENDING JUNE 1ST, 1860.							
Wool, pounds of.	Value of Orchard products.	Butter, pounds of.	Cheese, pounds of.	Hay, tons of.	Clover seed, bushels.	Maple Sugar, pounds.	Value of home made manufactures.
8,330	1,459	31,810	1,210	1,969	.	1,330	$710
513	29	11,650	400	378	. .	1,901	619
4,769	1,873	41,545	11,884	2,086	1	27,047	799
2,923	516	18,005	1,970	1,068	10	16,755	208
1,215	296	26,660	3,240	1,237		33,645	191
4,663	2,144	35,960	1,435	1,911	19	...	438
1,280	......	14,490	150	800	..	9,055	64
4,271	130	31,460	1,600	1,645	.	14,909	275
2,881	791	23,980	1,641	1,410	.	580	1,790
3,374	1,065	30,852	820	1,571	.. .	39,720	205
7,036	1,916	43,587	3,583	2,128	11	1,210	656
2,044	1,810	34,013	1,560	2,050	10	4,495	229
....	......	......	...	.	.	.. .	...
....	......	......	...	.	.	.	...
......	......	......	..	.	.	......	...
....	......	......	......	.	.	....	...
135	1,575	12,604	240	400	..	.....	90
860	147	12,925	250	578	9	4,285	88
......	...	5,170	25	136	.	3,712	2,227
4,504	315	19,950	2,040	1,397	..	1,500	528
4,340	1,091	42,170	6,100	2,646	.	33,887	935
931	250	20,540	467	861	.. .	300	144
1,807	576	27,130	2,125	1,088	..	51,737	726
......	...	1,100	....	42	.	100	475
70	21	3,580	140	107		7,767	20
6,345	1,704	38,315	3,925	2,544	172	3,700	989
5,114	4,955	59,001	990	2,956	.	14,398	680
1,697	851	16,925	1,275	1,273	2	10,345	107
69,102	23,914	603,422	47,070	32281	234	282378	$13,193

KENT COUNTY.—Continued.

TOWNSHIPS.	Flouring Mills.							Saw Mills.			
			Power used.			Annual product.			Power used.		
	Number of.	Runs of Stone.	Water.	Steam.	Capital invested in real and personal estate in the business.	Bbls. flour made.	Value of.	Number of.	Water.	Steam.	Capital invested in real and personal estate in the business.
Ada,	1		1		$15000	5,000	$29900	1	1		$2,000
Algoma,	2		2		7,500	3,333	36,032	7	7		18,000
Alpine,	1		1		3,000	1,000	10,125	5	5		11,000
Bowne,											
Byron,								1		1	5,000
Cannon,	2		2		12,000	10400	61,950	2	2		2,500
Caledonia,	1		1		5,000	1,500	12,000	1	1		1,000
Cascade,								1	1		2,500
Courtland,											
Gaines,											
Gratton,	1		1		5,000	2,000	16,700				
Grand Rapids,											
G. R. c., 1st w.,											
" " 2d w.,											
" " 3d w.,											
" " 4th w.,											
" " 5th w.,	4		4		59,500	22958	193588	6	5	1	21,650
Lowell,	1		1		28,000	11000	56,900				
Nelson,								1	1		4,000
Oakfield,								3	1	2	10,000
Paris,	1		1		7,500	1,000	11,000	1		1	4,500
Plainfield,								6	6		26,800
Sparta,	1			1	3,000	1,200	10 800	4	3	1	9,000
Solon,											
Tyrone,											
Vergennes,	1		1		6,000						
Walker,											
Wyoming,	1		1		17,000	5,553	31,000	5	4	1	53,000
Total,	17	[illegible]	16	1	168500	65541	469995	44	37	7	170950

KENT COUNTY.—Continued.

Saw Mills.		Aggregate of all kinds of Manufactures, Mills included.				Estimated value of Real and Personal Estate.	
Annual product.			Hands employ'd				
Feet of Lumber Sawed.	Value of.	Capital invested in real and personal estate in the business.	Males.	Females.	Value of annual product.	By Assessors.	By assistant Marshals.
200,000	1,500	$18,000	5		$33,240	..	.
3,100,000	14,160	28,150	27		48,646	.	...
1,750,000	8,750	14,000	18		18,875	...	.
.		..			......	.....	.
300,000	2,500	5,000	5		2,500		.
400,000	2,600	16,500	19		62,075	..	..
150,000	900	7,200	5		14,900	...	...
300,000	2,400	2,500	3		2,400	.	...
..	.	..				...	.
	.....	.			...	....	..
....	..	5,000	2		16,700	...	...
.	.	..		.	..	...	.
.					..	..	....
....	...	....			.....		....
.	...	.			.....	.....	.....
..	.	....	.		..	.....	......
3,600,000	26,000	812,230	721	190	1139360	.	.....
		40,400	24		75,800	.....	...
200,000	1,000	4,000	4		1,000	.	.
2,400,000	9,500	10,000	19		9,500	...	..
2,000,000	10,000	12,500	7		22,100	.....	....
3,400 000	17,420	27,050	39		19,381	.	...
1,150,000	6,150	12,350	11		18,062	..	.
.	...	50	4		650	....	...
..	...				..	...	...
..	....	7,000	5		19,900	...	...
.	.	.			...	...	...
6,800 000	42,600	160,000	86		108,100	...	.
25750000	145480	1,183,930	1004	190	1620164	....	.....

LAPEER COUNTY

TOWNSHIPS.	Dwelling Houses.		Number of Families.	Number of Inhabitants.				
	Whole number.	Number in Cities.		Whole number.	Colored.	Deaf and Dumb.	Blind.	Insane.
Allison, ...	64	...	62	345				
Almont, ...	462		438	2,297	13		2	
Arcadia,...	40	......	37	200	.			
Attica,.	200	...	189	862				
Burlington, .	81	..	81	452				1
Deerfield, . .	23	....	23	109	.	.		
Dryden, ...	355	...	340	1,752		2		1
Elba, ...	162	....	153	809			1	..
Goodland, ...	83	. ....	82	448	1	.		.
Hadley, ..	296	. . .	275	1,354	.	1	1	1
Imlay,.......	113	...	112	654	.	1		
Lapeer, . .	556	. .	514	2,735	29	5	1	2
Marathon, ...	122	. ..	120	788	.			.
Metamora, ...	244	.. .	233	1,155	..	2		
North Branch, .	53	......	50	244	9			1
Oregon,.	115	......	102	518	. .	.	1	.
Rich, ...	36	..	36	153	.			.
Total, ...	3,005	......	2,847	14,875	52	11	6	6

LEELENAW COUNTY

TOWNSHIPS.	Whole number.	Number in Cities.	Number of Families.	Whole number.	Colored.	Deaf and Dumb.	Blind.	Insane.
Centerville,..	128	... .	133	938	.			..
Crystal Lake, .	41	......	42	216	3	.	..	..
Glen Arbor, ...	64	......	58	252	.	.	..	.
Leelenaw,........	204	......	203	1,039	..	1	.	..
Total,. . . .	437	.....	436	2,445	3	1	.	.

LAPEER COUNTY.—CONTINUED.

TOWNSHIPS.	Value of Real Estate owned.	OCCUPIED FARMS. Whole number.	Acres improved.	Acres unimproved.	Cash value of.
Allison,	$48,855	32	807	5,499	$35,000
Almont,	956,670	198	13,699	7,251	601,300
Arcadia,	33,350	19	622	2,470	30,000
Attica,	227,600	107	4,747	6,012	183,000
Burlington,	75,160	43	1,304	5,944	54,410
Deerfield,	23,380	17	369	1,396	13,950
Dryden,	600,305	198	12,240	7,111	483,900
Elba,	251,450	96	5,899	5,156	213,400
Goodland,	62,730	43	1,473	5,230	51,550
Hadley,	399,360	166	9,447	7,046	343,460
Imlay,	102,030	62	1,971	4,231	90,200
Lapeer,	1,162,815	236	13,487	13,668	659,300
Marathon,	179,240	78	3,058	5,225	149,990
Metamora,	420,445	160	10,983	6,299	371,171
North Branch,	59,470	29	932	3,190	42,050
Oregon,	95,250	44	1,985	1,182	63,800
Rich,	27,450	16	360	2,031	19,000
Total,	$4,765,560	1,544	83,383	88,941	$3,405,481

LEELENAW COUNTY.—CONTINUED.

TOWNSHIPS.	Value of Real Estate owned.	OCCUPIED FARMS. Whole number.	Acres improved.	Acres unimproved.	Cash value of.
Centerville,	$56,286	33	782	3,159	$24,609
Crystal Lake,	20,596	3	42	767	2,800
Glen Arbor,	24,900	6	110	1,621	5,200
Leelenaw,	137,351	12	439	2,825	34,204
Total,	$239,133	54	1,373	8,372	$66,813

LAPEER COUNTY—Continued.

Value of Farming Implements and Machinery.	Live Stock, June 1st, 1860. Horses.	Asses and Mules.	Milch Cows.	Working Oxen.	Other Cattle.	Sheep.	Swine.	Value of Live Stock.
$1,012	19		73	54	61	72	108	$5,496
31,725	725	2	626	111	974	5,850	829	93,282
981	31		47	16	40	36	62	4,240
6,939	169		241	102	198	964	445	26,486
1,601	36		118	56	98	83	177	8,554
369	4		36	32	31	....	36	2,609
24,046	520	2	547	124	660	3,858	819	76,217
8,925	171		263	134	323	2,228	272	36,388
2,378	48		93	64	93	54	135	9,770
17,543	339		366	195	437	2,918	438	56,792
3,419	83		154	79	155	375	215	14,944
30,680	552		700	296	1,036	5,198	802	100,639
4,530	107		191	93	262	433	299	20,977
17,505	419	2	413	192	598	4,173	624	68,274
1,548	31		64	32	79	66	92	5,802
4,915	97		114	38	127	658	127	15,737
421	5		32	27	29	....	37	2,429
$158,537	3356	6	4078	1,645	5,201	26,966	5,517	$548,636

LEELENAW COUNTY—Continued.

Value of Farming Implements and Machinery.	Horses.	Asses and Mules.	Milch Cows.	Working Oxen.	Other Cattle.	Sheep.	Swine.	Value of Live Stock.
$970	19		20	29	26	10	124	$3,358
125	1		7		3		16	453
360			9	12	2	....	12	710
1,700	14		17	24	16	....	56	2,649
$3,155	34		53	65	47	10	208	7,170

LAPEER COUNTY.—Continued.

TOWNSHIPS.	Produce, during the Year						
	Wheat, bushels of.	Rye, bushels of.	Indian corn, bushels of.	Oats, bushels of.	Barley, bushels of.	Buckwheat, bushels of.	Potatoes, bushels of.
Allison,	720	66	1,357	950	8	104	1,695
Almont, .	20,463	3,021	35,926	33,078	976	1,833	21,811
Arcadia, .	660	139	1,225	325	26	116	1,161
Attica,. ..	6,448	1,183	12,037	6,529	373	826	8,054
Burlington,	2,946	72	1,678	. .	100	24	1,928
Deerfield, ...	177	130	495	399	17	36	748
Dryden, ...	21,910	4,547	30,179	18,989	1,174	2,812	16,579
Elba,	11,769	455	3,933	4,644	561	392	3,659
Goodland,	817	118	2,402	685	15	134	5,294
Hadley, . .	23,352	2,130	17,036	6,053	1,842	917	7,928
Imlay, . .	3,054	126	5,290	3,856	25	675	5,505
Lapeer, .	38,780	2,786	29,964	13,284	3,429	923	16,901
Marathon,	4,555	105	5,158	6,795	47	359	3,517
Metamora,	29,162	3,120	25,048	11,379	2,285	2,516	12,834
North Branch,	748	10	1,243	857	37	157	1,426
Oregon,. ...	3,575	602	2,632	2,688	146	597	2,140
Rich, ...	533	20	865	390		9	775
Total, .	169668	18630	177468	110880	11061	12430	111955

LEELENAW COUNTY.—Continued.

Centerville,. .	765	328	3,441	805	3	177	5,636
Crystal Lake,	....		170	150	.	. .	912
Glen Arbor,	35	170	510	240	.	.	1,100
Leelenaw,	440	120	1,250	585	.	35	2,996
Total,...	1,240	618	5,371	1,770	3	212	10,644

LAPEER COUNTY.—Continued.

...ending June 1st, 1860.							
Wool, pounds of.	Value of Orchard products.	Butter, pounds of.	Cheese, pounds of.	Hay, tons of.	Clover seed, bushels.	Maple Sugar, pounds.	Value of home made manufactures.
.. ..	....	7,107		74		10,000	$10
20,442	$3,288	65,800	8,080	2,340	48	25,695	1,728
190		4,740	265	165	.	2,650	43
2,018	..	23,700	1,050	801	.	18,865	195
158	.	9,533	1,078	127	.	14,553	40
. . .	...	3,635	450	80		2,780	
12,228	2,138	57,285	4,471	1,541	56	16,011	1,848
7,445	206	28,229	4,460	1,179	37	7,930	65
24		9,605	412	416		9,484	44
9,479	1,233	49,040	5,630	1,869	249	3,940	399
873	..	14,210	4,500	430		16,915	102
19,225	1,965	73,320	8,236	3,216	43	19,068	1,219
949	. ..	20,665	1,010	470		10,264	136
13,019	1,654	46,276	2,118	1,880	228	2,970	741
124		7,098	440	72		9,526	3
1,794	90	15,575	470	438	.	1,640	280
......		3,395	100	30		3,116	10
87,968	10,572	439,313	42,770	15134	661	175397	$6,863

LEELENAW COUNTY.—Continued.

Wool, pounds of.	Value of Orchard products.	Butter, pounds of.	Cheese, pounds of.	Hay, tons of.	Clover seed, bushels.	Maple Sugar, pounds.	Value of home made manufactures.
30	......	825	....	45	.	16,148	.. ..
. ....	.... .	450	... .	13		2,500	. .
... ..	...	390	.....	24	.	680	. ...
... ..	....	750	.. .	73	.	3,300	... .
30	... ..	2,415	......	155		22,628	....

LAPEER COUNTY.—Continued.

TOWNSHIPS.	Flouring Mills.							Saw Mills.			
	Number of.	Runs of Stone.	Power used. Water.	Power used. Steam.	Capital invested in real and personal estate in the business.	Annual product. Bbls. flour made.	Annual product. Value of.	Number of.	Power used. Water.	Power used. Steam.	Capital invested in real and personal estate in the business.
Allison,											
Almont,	3	†2		*2	12,100	*8000	*60800	3		*2	*2,500
Arcadia,								1		1	5,000
Attica,								5	2	3	15,100
Burlington,											
Deerfield,											
Dryden,	1		1		2,000	800	5,750	1			1,000
Elba,								1	1		1,000
Goodland,											
Hadley,								4	4		3,800
Imlay,								2		2	6,200
Lapeer,	2	*3	2		12,000	3,150	23,750	13	10	2	37,900
Marathon,								2	1	1	3,200
Metamora,	1		1		5,000	3,000	19,000	1		1	2,000
North Branch,								1		1	2,000
Oregon,	1		1		2,500	300	1,500	3	3		3,300
Rich,	1							1	1		3,000
Total,	9	5	5	2	33,600	15250	110800	38	22	13	86,000

LEELENAW COUNTY.—Continued.

TOWNSHIPS.	Number of.	Runs of Stone.	Water.	Steam.	Capital invested in real and personal estate in the business.	Bbls. flour made.	Value of.	Number of.	Water.	Steam.	Capital invested in real and personal estate in the business.
Centerville,								1	1		$1,000
Crystal Lake,											
Glen Arbor,								1	1		1,000
Leelenaw,								1	1		2,000
Total,								3	3		$4,000

* But one returned. † One not returned.

LAPEER COUNTY.—Continued.

Saw Mills.		Aggregate of all kinds of manufactures, Mills included.				Estimated value of Real and Personal Estate.	
Annual product.		Capital invested in real and personal estate in the business.	Hands employ'd		Value of annual products.	By Assessors.	By assistant Marshals.
Feet of Lumber Sawed.	Value of.		Males.	Females.			
....	..	.				..	..
600,000	$3,200	$37,400	36	2	$94,950	......	..
1,000,000	6,000	5,000	6		6,000	†	†
2,100,000	14,700	15,100	23		14,700		....
....	..	..				...	.
...	....					.	...
80,000	480	3,300	5		8,130	†	†
200,000	1,200	1,000	1		1,200	†	†
.....					.	...	..
550,000	3,000	5,800	7		6,200	†	†
1,500,000	7,030	6,200	15		7,030		...
10,700,000	81,750	75,300	93	3	174,610	†	†
900,000	6,600	2,200	7		6,600	.	...
400,000	2,500	7,000	5		21,500	†	†
125,000	750	2,000	3		750	.	..
500,000	3,500	5,800	6		5,000	†	†
150,000	1,250	3,000	1		1,250	.	..
18,805,000	131960	170,100	208	5	317,920	2253251	*4506502

LEELENAW COUNTY.—Continued.

Feet of Lumber Sawed.	Value of.	Capital invested	Males.	Females.	Value of annual products.	By Assessors.	By assistant Marshals.
250,000	$1,500	$3,500	20		$3,052	....	....
......	...	3,250	16		7,560	.	...
70,000	525	1,000	3		525	...	.
300,000	1,800	2,800	9		4,848		....
620,000	$3,825	$10,550	48		$15,985	.....	..

*Of towns marked thus, †, balance not returned.

LENAWEE COUNTY

TOWNSHIPS.	Dwelling Houses.		Number of Families.	Number of Inhabitants.				
	Whole number.	Number in Cities.		Whole number.	Colored.	Deaf and Dumb.	Blind.	Insane.
Adrian,	289		289	1,587	1			
City, 1st ward,	275	275	289	1,440	16			
" 2d ward,	441	441	447	2,243	68	1		1
" 3d ward,	154	154	157	958	12			
" 4th ward,	318	318	325	1,553	20			1
Blissfield,	357		359	1,857				
Cambridge,	218		222	1,150			1	
Canandaigua vil.,	29		31	139				
Clinton village,	130		135	680		2		1
Dover,	282		282	1,377		1		1
Fairfield,	330		343	1,595		1		
Franklin,	274		276	1,457	10			
Hudson,	284		289	1,441	2	1		
Hudson village,	297		310	1,489	18	1		
Macon,	251		255	1,410		1		
Madison,	272		272	1,610	16	1	2	16
Medina,	316		327	1,615				
Medina village,	50		52	211				
Morenci village,	98		100	459	1			
Ogden,	198		196	1,034			1	
Palmyra,	296		296	1,656		1		1
Raisin,	292		299	1,585	18		2	1
Ridgeway,	184		187	880				1
Riga,	127		127	664	5	1	1	
Rollin,	273		286	1,636	8		1	
Rome,	313		316	1,613	1			2
Seneca,	234		259	1,286		1		
Tecumseh,	189		194	1,102	1	1		
Tecumseh village,	315		320	1,640	11	2		
Woodstock,	227		227	1,159	11			2
Total,	7,313	1,188	7,476	38,497	219	15	8	27

LENAWEE COUNTY.—Continued.

TOWNSHIPS.	Value of Real Estate owned.	Occupied Farms.			
		Whole number.	Acres improved.	Acres unimproved.	Cash value of.
Adrian,	$778,810	183	12,562	6,841	$716,550
City, 1st ward,	476,400		...	.	.
" 2d ward,	908,446	..	.	.	.
" 3d ward,	421,700		.	...	.
" 4th ward,	693,100	..	..	.	.
Blissfield,	480,565	84	5,112	3,686	224,495
Cambridge,	435,100	193	10,901	8,795	412,270
Canandaigua vil.,	26,450		..	...	...
Clinton village,	229,750		..	.	
Dover,	501,025	202	12,497	8,246	473,110
Fairfield,	666,535	217	11,351	8,912	582,615
Franklin,	605,310	224	14,035	8,006	578,350
Hudson,	426,270	193	9,633	7,912	444,000
Hudson village,	426,340		...	.	.
Macon,	509,735	158	8,910	7,064	457,710
Madison,	748,640	138	10,456	7,450	634,710
Medina,	573,500	251	14,351	10,436	600,750
Medina village,	77,700	.			..
Morenci village,	148,150		..	...	...
Ogden,	268,686	111	4,754	5,048	232,977
Palmyra,	616,935	117	7,627	7,664	460,280
Raisin,	718,710	164	13,199	8,937	672,904
Ridgeway,	304,658	66	4,571	3,138	227,000
Riga,	105,900	21	866	1,232	45,700
Rollin,	399,170	163	8,174	6,663	359,470
Rome,	641,680	217	14,029	8,546	606,200
Seneca,	418,825	185	11,399	8,730	464,480
Tecumseh,	527,625	201	15,201	10,710	825,880
Tecumseh village	686,825	.	...	.	.
Woodstock,	368,055	170	9,327	8,630	332,490
Total, ...	14,190,592	3,258	198,955	147,241	9,348,941

LENAWEE COUNTY—Continued.

Value of Farming Implements and Machinery.	Live Stock, June 1st, 1860.							
	Horses.	Asses and Mules.	Milch Cows.	Working Oxen.	Other Cattle.	Sheep.	Swine.	Value of Live Stock.
20,575	620	6	696	76	859	7,023	1,308	$95,287
9,114	264		329	66	607	1,534	742	43,799
11,323	421		506	177	745	6,607	1,041	73,140
21,016	593		691	116	882	5,443	853	77,021
24,663	693	2	823	176	1,747	4,625	2,913	118,038
18,029	590		760	146	1,041	9,915	1,467	116,018
16,430	438		574	102	629	4,475	1,118	64,779
13,130	494		534	86	833	4,070	1,051	84,219
25,885	557	4	532	112	927	2,649	1,619	71,790
22,696	662	2	889	185	1,258	7,811	1,702	100,136
11,870	329		409	90	985	1,324	1,182	49,088
19,280	445		506	112	954	2,576	997	62,830
20,284	614	2	640	64	925	4,930	1,770	95,415
7,285	262		309	38	534	1,328	622	40,615
1,845	51		59	30	103	95	119	8,210
14,291	409		464	110	641	3,392	761	57,256
23,853	604		701	116	1,074	8,673	1,162	103,859
17,412	483		634	134	1,122	4,086	1,537	72,666
22,350	659		703	132	1,106	7,646	1,738	120,347
8,841	373		491	151	777	2,336	1,152	56,791
329,372	9561	16	11256	2219	17749	90,538	24,854	1,511,304

LENAWEE COUNTY.—Continued.

TOWNSHIPS.	Produce, during the Year						
	Wheat, bushels of.	Rye, bushels of.	Indian corn, bushels of.	Oats, bushels of.	Barley, bushels of.	Buckwheat, bushels of.	Potatoes, bushels of.
Adrian,	26,478	74	48,065	18,626	2,036	1,954	15,212
City, 1st w'rd,							
" 2d ward,							
" 3d ward,							
" 4th ward,							
Blissfield,	9,023	262	31,653	3,158	70	1,658	15,037
Cambridge,	21,748	1,349	58,319	8,309	859	2,560	10,549
Can'd'gua v.,							
Clinton vil.,							
Dover,	23,116		57,150	21,183	1,645	3,121	21,008
Fairfield,	21,690	700	105,722	10,698	893	3,522	20,687
Franklin,	33,150	1,272	86,194	12,666	1,929	3,445	12,727
Hudson,	16,960	606	44,317	15,049	1,083	2,282	19,133
Hudson vil.,							
Macon,	27,875	2,022	92,975	7,999	1,216	3,270	10,659
Madison,	25,565	400	90,454	10,928	1,154	1,656	17,912
Medina,	24,915	646	60,058	12,865	603	3,521	17,982
Medina vil.,							
Morenci vil.,							
Ogden,	7,466	25	61,518	1,946	80	1,248	13,326
Palmyra,	11,048	201	61,441	5,540	107	2,388	19,923
Raisin,	35,542	452	61,700	9,231	989	2,527	23,890
Ridgeway,	10,613	72	31,870	10,027	572	624	5,920
Riga,	557	60	5,525	360		572	4,267
Rollin,	13,335	712	32,999	8,025	281	2,186	11,039
Rome,	22,918	170	58,556	23,898	1,356	2,061	12,587
Seneca,	18,810	[illegible]	51,575	4,026	76	3,564	13,567
Tecumseh,	47,467	650	130,300	15,045	3,089	3,514	19,290
Tecumseh v.,							
Woodstock,	26,026	3,444	54,977	4,692	109	2,658	11,967
Total,	424302	13119	1225371	204271	18147	48330	296682

LENAWEE COUNTY.—Continued.

ENDING JUNE 1ST, 1860.							
Wool, pounds of.	Value of Orchard products.	Butter, pounds of.	Cheese, pounds of.	Hay, tons of.	Clover seed, bushels.	Maple Sugar, pounds.	Value of home made manufactures.
22,984	8,234	56,950	7,634	2,974	64	3,495	$130
......							
......							
......							
......							
5,597	5,753	35,400	2,125	1,803		510	
22,499	3,172	37,455	1,770	2,771	168	190	18
......							
......							
16,810	7,277	67,425	6,980	2,739	34	2,637	22
11,939	6,175	74,150	34,455	3,724	48	7,116	790
33,610	6,228	61,715	4,825	3,445	152	2,406	
12,134	1,135	49,645	2,520	1,565	1[illegible]	2,661	32
......							
12,277	4,732	47,380	7,085	2,422	433	1,050	
8,034	6,492	47,640	6,163	2,267	150	637	163
20,218	1,558	69,685	9,620	2,877	268	4,495	35
......							
......							
3,045	2,497	39,219	3,780	1,378		5,167	377
8,025	4,196	45,200	6,438	1 933	13	2,605	485
18,065	6,627	70,730	5,457	3,249	253	..	20
4,068	2,436	30,090	960	1,012	174		
172	590	6,100	.	241		620	
9,734	4,044	38,599	600	1,717	379	255	
25,406	5,634	63,104	5,788	3,290	15	4,355	73
10,076	2,231	53,540	20,100	2,547	134	2,167	
27,395	5,483	59,525	3,125	3,661	475	200	
......							
7,124	4,040	29,313	1,808	2,620	157	.	10
279,193	88,534	982,855	131,233	48241	2927	40,566	$2,155

LENAWEE COUNTY.—Continued.

TOWNSHIPS.	Flouring Mills.							Saw Mills.			
	Number of.	Runs of Stone.	Power used.		Capital invested in real and personal estate in the business.	Annual product.		Number of.	Power used.		Capital invested in real and personal estate in the business.
			Water.	Steam.		Bbls. flour made.	Value of.		Water.	Steam.	
Adrian,	2		2		$6,600	18,500	120500	2	2		$6,200
City, 1st w.,											
" 2d w.,											
" 3d w.,	2		2	1	6,700	7,600	48,037				
" 4th w.,											
Blissfield,								5	2	3	26,500
Cambridge,								2		2	6,215
Can'd'gua v	*										
Clinton vil.,											
Dover,	*										
Fairfield,								1		1	3,000
Franklin,								4	1	3	11,000
Hudson,	*										
Hudson vil.,	*										
Macon,											
Madison,											
Medina,	*										
Medina vil.,	*										
Morenci vil.	*										
Ogden,	1			1	2,000		1,000	2		2	5,500
Palmyra,	1		1		12,000	4,333	26,000	4	1	3	15,000
Raisin,	1		1		16,000	7,000	42,681	3	1	2	11,000
Ridgeway,								1		1	5,000
Riga,								2		2	9,000
Rollin,.	*										
Rome,	*										
Seneca,	*										
Tecumseh,	3		3		47,000	44,189	216707	1	1		3,000
Tecums'h v.											
Woodst'ck,											
**	5		2	3	17,800	21,830	208380	10	2	8	19,200
Total,	15		11	5	108100	103,452	663305	37	10	27	120615

** Aggregate of towns marked thus *.

LENAWEE COUNTY.—Continued.

Saw Mills.		Aggregate of all kinds of Manufactures, Mills included.				Estimated value of Real and Personal Estate.	
Annual product.		Capital invested in real and personal estate in the business.	Hands employ'd		Value of annual product.	By Assessors.	By assistant Marshals.
Feet of Lumber Sawed.	Value of.		Males.	Females.			
450,000	$7,600	$12,800	11	.	$128100	. ..	..
	...	*				...	.
..		30,500	66	3	45,070		
.	.	95,000	77	34	142,418		.
.	...	13598941	684	181	2260577	.	.
2,380,000	20,000	33,050	41		26,180	...	....
316,727	3,900	7,715	7		4,508	..	. .
	. . .	.			...	..	.. . .
.	.	.					..
						.	. ...
150,000	1,550	3,000	3		1,550	..	.
1,330,000	11,540	11,000	11		11,540	.....	.
...	..					..	..
...	..						. .
	.. .				. .	....	. ...
..	.	.				... .	.
	.....				.		.
.... .	. . .	.			... .	.	.
. . .	.					.	..
1,000,000	7,100	7,500	8		8,100	.	.
1,612,000	14,900	27,000	30	7	40,900	.. ..	. .
1,980,000	16,800	28,500	14		60,881	.	. ... .
1,200,000	9,600	5,000	5		9,600	.	...
1,700,000	16,000	9,000	8		16,000		.
.. .						..	. .
....	.	.			.	. ..	.....
. .	.				. ....	.	. .
300,000	2,400	117,800	82		301,687	.	. .
					..	. .	. . .
.	.... .	.			.	....	. ..
2,410,000	20,680	78,100	125		319,310	. ..	.
14828727	132070	14064906	1172	225	3376421	†	10328323

* Included in the 4th ward.

† Not returned.

LIVINGSTON COUNTY

TOWNSHIPS.	Dwelling Houses.		Number of Families.	Number of Inhabitants.				
	Whole number.	Number in Cities.		Whole number.	Colored.	Deaf and Dumb.	Blind.	Insane.
Brighton,	222		223	1,186	2	1	1	
Cohoctah,	167		166	857				1
Conway,	150		148	764				
Deerfield,	189		192	1,017		1	1	
Genoa,	162		160	878			1	
Green Oak,	174		175	944	1			1
Hamburgh,	182		183	996	1			
Handy,	191		188	905	4			
Hartland,	235		234	1,206			2	
Howell,	219		199	1,063				1
Howell village,	151		142	757				
Iosco,	150		150	770				
Marion,	181		179	682				
Osceola,	202		213	1,128			1	
Putnam,	204		209	1,215	9		1	2
Tyrone,	198		203	1,144				
Unadilla,	205		210	1,117	13		2	1
Total,	3,182		3,174	16,629	30	2	9	6

MACKINAW COUNTY

TOWNSHIPS.	Whole number.	Number in Cities.	Number of Families.	Whole number.	Colored.	Deaf and Dumb.	Blind.	Insane.
Holmes,	285		238	1,296	6			
Moran,	48		42	244				
St. Ignace,	82		76	399		1	1	
Total,	415		356	1,939	6	1	1	

LIVINGSTON COUNTY.—Continued.

TOWNSHIPS.	Value of Real Estate owned.	Occupied Farms.			
		Whole number.	Acres improved.	Acres unimproved.	Cash value of.
Brighton,.. ...	$485,620	153	12,066	11,413	$431,830
Cohoctah,..	210,475	56	3,972	4,152	131,275
Conway,. ...	192,445	42	3,355	2,407	106,575
Deerfield, . ..	379,004	80	6,766	6,361	268,090
Genoa,....... ..	353,168	88	6,819	7,040	274,338
Green Oak,	384,620	120	10,309	7,528	350,800
Hamburgh, .	393,100	132	10,386	16,997	349,610
Handy,.. .	189,025	45	2,679	2,985	100,010
Hartland, ...	442,165	185	11,183	9,838	381,940
Howell, ...	336,230	179	8,750	9,834	333,490
Howell village,	252,655		. .	. .	.
Iosco, ...	206,730	70	5,281	4,851	162,020
Marion,.......	371,139	100	8,753	7,580	316,049
Osceola,... .	383,540	185	11,538	10,042	385,410
Putnam, .	512,220	127	11,625	8,321	343,300
Tyrone, ...	325,458	77	6,123	3,802	218,358
Unadilla, ..	408,600	140	11,172	10,041	382,020
Total,	$5,826,194	1,779	130,777	122,192	$4,535,115

MACKINAW COUNTY.—Continued.

Holmes,.. .	$111,815	3	390	1,414	$12,000
Moran,.	8,575	5	256	909	4,350
St. Ignace,	11,817		.... .	...	.
Total, .	$132,207	8	646	2,323	$16,350

LIVINGSTON COUNTY.—Continued.

Value of Farming Implements and Machinery.	Live Stock, June 1st, 1860. Horses.	Asses and Mules.	Milch Cows.	Working Oxen.	Other Cattle.	Sheep.	Swine.	Value of Live Stock.
$18,325	400	4	446	154	561	3,916	714	$64,845
4,458	118		198	104	407	1,407	271	24,345
4,070	120		175	78	278	1,789	201	21,695
7,038	218		265	116	456	2,819	383	39,744
10,447	249		292	137	467	3,357	518	41,097
13,161	337		442	86	515	6,092	681	57,394
11,568	340	1	344	169	653	4,979	685	64,161
3,337	104		140	49	174	1,303	190	18,072
16,084	340		476	203	572	4,223	794	60,370
12,021	259		393	216	491	2,607	681	56,470
.	. .		.	. .	.	. . .	. . .	. . . .
5,518	182		259	72	422	2,535	356	31,651
12,145	292		378	114	545	4,066	576	54,983
13,800	347		477	233	657	6,020	838	64,523
9,827	298		484	162	596	3,603	892	50,615
7,554	208		266	92	423	2,378	374	37,339
13,153	387	1	526	173	810	5,587	768	62,393
$162,506	4199	6	5561	2,158	8,027	56,681	8,922	$749,699

MACKINAW COUNTY.—Continued.

Value of Farming Implements and Machinery.	Horses.	Asses and Mules.	Milch Cows.	Working Oxen.	Other Cattle.	Sheep.	Swine.	Value of Live Stock.
$65	10		23	6	26	......	40	$1,590
90	13		27	4	22	.....	20	1,580
. .					.	. ...	.	. .
$155	23		50	10	48	...	60	$3,170

LIVINGSTON COUNTY.—Continued.

TOWNSHIPS.	Produce, during the Year						
	Wheat, bushels of.	Rye, bushels of.	Indian corn, bushels of.	Oats, bushels of.	Barley, bushels of.	Buckwheat, bushels of.	Potatoes, bushels of.
Brighton,	22,092	5,498	24,860	6,716	1,656	1,436	18,067
Cohoctah,	7,067	1,687	5,769	3,901	370	631	3,881
Conway,	3,920	647	3,385	3,843	119	546	2,860
Deerfield,	20,404	1,934	13,700	6,502	442	846	8,309
Genoa,	19,852	4,022	16,464	7,120	487	1,857	8,470
Green Oak,	16,005	4,213	30,043	9,435	904	847	16,146
Hamburgh,	24,754	1,718	27,085	5,737	490	1,720	12,388
Handy,	2,152	670	3,995	2,615	66	264	2,302
Hartland,	24,341	5,451	18,560	6,013	1,128	1,246	13,861
Howell,	13,752	2,727	15,500	7,082	254	2,116	10,584
Howell vil.,	....		...	....	.		...
Iosco,	10,310	994	10,030	6,541	465	606	4,958
Marion,	19,608	1,303	20,765	7,464	1,254	1,236	8,391
Osceola,	25,451	4,866	15,902	8,174	297	1,743	12,519
Putnam,	21,022	1,625	25,295	6,472	679	870	14,185
Tyrone,	16,006	1,889	12,165	5,746	427	1,001	5,998
Unadilla,	26,809	290	24,955	12,010	1,029	920	18,303
Total,	273545	39534	268473	105371	10067	17885	161222

MACKINAW COUNTY.—Continued.

TOWNSHIPS.	Wheat	Rye	Indian corn	Oats	Barley	Buckwheat	Potatoes
Holmes,	...		..	290	25		800
Moran,	2	.	10	310	35	2	782
St. Ignace,	......	.	...	...	.	.	..
Total,	2		10	600	60	2	1,582

LIVINGSTON COUNTY —Continued.

...ending June 1st, 1860.

Wool, pounds of.	Value of Orchard products.	Butter, pounds of.	Cheese, pounds of.	Hay, tons of.	Clover seed, bushels.	Maple Sugar, pounds.	Value of home made manufactures.
10,464	755	36,999	3,935	2,459	95	350	$121
3,524	225	12,090	1,064	1,198	8	460	45
4,778	736	11,940	1,243	970	.	2,805	20
9,532	667	19,500	1,200	1,548	54	...	7
11,463	1,374	26,412	1,785	1,803	300		233
19,698	1,591	34,560	2,599	2,402	397	.. .	46
14 541	2,036	34,020	2,060	2,842	676		948
4,602	230	10,988	550	681	.	5,255	. .
4,820	1,257	38,500	697	2,420	71	956	176
7,626	660	34,395	2,070	1,936	52	2,045	117
....	. .			.		.	.. .
6,158	918	19,700	3,365	1,820	79	1,750	75
12,957	2,126	30,580	2,778	2,595	235	.. .	1,263
19,552	1,074	41,580	2,515	2,792	53	657	177
11,547	1,693	32,910	5,520	2,693	294	...	38
8,073	943	22,650	1,290	1,433	96	..	204
17,793	2,104	34,030	3,408	3,445	480	...	165
167,028	18,389	440,874	36,065	33037	2890	14,378	3,635

MACKINAW COUNTY.—Continued.

Wool, pounds of.	Value of Orchard products.	Butter, pounds of.	Cheese, pounds of.	Hay, tons of.	Clover seed, bushels.	Maple Sugar, pounds.	Value of home made manufactures.
...	30	150	...	111	.	.	......
... .	......	500	.	95		1,600	....
......	..	.	..	...	.	..	.. ..
......	30	650	. ....	206	. .	1,600	. .

LIVINGSTON COUNTY.—Continued.

TOWNSHIPS.	Flouring Mills.							Saw Mills.			
			Power used.			Annual product.			Power used.		
	Number of.	Runs of Stone.	Water.	Steam.	Capital invested in real and personal estate in the business.	Bbls. flour made.	Value of.	Number of.	Water.	Steam.	Capital invested in real and personal estate in the business.
Brighton,	2		2		$20500	4,650	$46100				......
Cohoctah,	1	.	1		4,800	1,700	8,000	1	1		$700
Conway,					..		. ..				.....
Deerfield,	1		1		4,800	2,500	10,000	1	1		700
Genoa,				.	. .	..	.. .	1	1		400
Green Oak,	1		1	..	7,000	500	2,600				. .
Hamburgh,	3		3	1	9,000	1,540	19,500	1	1		1,000
Handy,	1			1	4,000	1,462	7,000	1		1	700
Hartland,	2		2		13,000	1,610	43,900	3	3		5,000
Howell,	2		2	1	10,500	2,749	28,500	3	3	2	8,500
Howell vil.,					....		. ..				..
Iosco,					.		.	1		1	800
Marion,					. .		..	1	1		300
Osceola,							..				..
Putnam,	2		2		16,000	1,800	19,100	1	1		1,000
Tyrone,					. .		.....				..
Unadilla,	1		1	1	3,000		12,000	1	1		1,000
Total,	16		15	4	92,600	18511	196700	17	13	4	$20100

MACKINAW COUNTY.—Continued

Holmes,											
Moran,	..						.				.
St. Ignace,							. .				.
Total,											

LIVINGSTON COUNTY.—Continued.

Saw Mills.		Aggregate of all kinds of Manufactures, Mills included.				Estimated value of Real and Personal Estate.	
Annual product.			Hands employ'd				
Feet of Lumber Sawed.	Value of.	Capital invested in real and personal estate in the business.	Males.	Females.	Value of annual products.	By Assessors.	By assistant Marshals.
....		$26,300	17		$57,160	.	....
100,000	700	5,500	2		8,700	. .	
. ..	.	.. .					.
150,000	1,200	5,500	4		11,200	.. .	.
65,000	520	400	1		520		.
	.	7,000	2		2,600	..	...
60,000	600	20,500	13	1	45,317	. ..	... .
150,000	1,200	6,500	8		8,880	.	.
448,000	3,750	32,150	20		53 730		
780,000	6,890	46,400	55		60,398	. .	
.. .					. :	..	
480,000	3,860	800	3		3,860	..	
75,000	600	300	1		600		
... .	... .	.			. .	...	
120,000	960	21,000	13		27,360		....
..	..	. .			.		
.	. ..	4,500	4		13,500	...	
2,428,000	20,280	176,850	144	1	293,825	3190816	6,181,631

MACKINAW COUNTY.—Continued.

Feet of Lumber Sawed.	Value of.	Capital invested in real and personal estate in the business.	Males.	Females.	Value of annual products.	By Assessors.	By assistant Marshals.
.	......	$2,800	10		$5,300	$145712	$350,247
..		800	6		1,400	40,999	22,290
	.	. .			..	15,904	31,205
	. ..	*$3,600	*16		*$6,700	$202615	$403,742

*Fisheries not included.

MACOMB COUNTY

TOWNSHIPS.	Dwelling Houses.		Number of Families.	Number of Inhabitants.				
	Whole number.	Number in Cities.		Whole number.	Colored.	Deaf and Dumb.	Blind.	Insane.
Armada,	275	...	293	1,489	8	1	1	
Bruce,	348		379	1,808	1	2	2	1
Chesterfield,	350		350	2,164	1	3		
Clinton,	259	......	279	1,587	7	2		1
Erin,	389	....	383	1,975				
Harrison,	88	...	88	549	1	1		
Lenox,	300	....	306	1,454		1	1	
Macomb,	311	..	276	1,370			2	
Mt. Clemens vil.,	272	...	282	1,428	10	1		
Ray,	289	.	324	1,543		1	3	
Richmond,	328	.	338	1,704	1	1	1	
Shelby,	349	...	336	1,800	7	1		1
Sterling,	231	...	216	1,159	5	1		
Warren,	278	.	269	1,235	2			
Washington,	383	.	377	1,847	8		2	3
Total,	4,448	....	4,498	23,112	51	15	12	[illegible]

MANISTEE COUNTY

TOWNSHIPS.	Whole number.	Number in Cities.	Number of Families.	Whole number.	Colored.	Deaf and Dumb.	Blind.	Insane.
Brown,	74	...	56	219				
Manistee,	138	.	10[illegible]	549	4			
Stronach,	35		28	106				
Total,	247	...	191	874	4			

MANITOU COUNTY

TOWNSHIPS.	Whole number.	Number in Cities.	Number of Families.	Whole number.	Colored.	Deaf and Dumb.	Blind.	Insane.
Beaver Island,	115	...	109	493				
Garden Island,	44	...	47	198			1	
Little Fox Island,		...		9				
North Manitou Isl.,	54	...	51	270				
South Manitou Isl.,	18	..	18	73				
Total,	231	.....	225	1,043	...	.	1	..

MACOMB COUNTY.—Continued.

TOWNSHIPS.	Value of Real Estate owned.	Occupied Farms.			
		Whole number.	Acres improved.	Acres unimproved.	Cash value of.
Armada,	$670,530	195	12,480	9,869	$636,450
Bruce,	1,021,607	165	16,692	6,880	753,895
Chesterfield, ..	528,870	206	7,677	7,589	361,650
Clinton,..	386,944	214	7,124	7,173	397,899
Erin,......	525,130	193	4,799	6,094	441,700
Harrison, ...	153,880	61	2,854	3,843	128,730
Lenox, ...	331,310	211	7,284	9,411	345,580
Macomb,	348,535	151	6,508	7,281	309,080
Mt. Clemens vil.,	393,715	.	.		.....
Ray, ..	610,100	234	10,534	9,795	538,780
Richmond,	592,686	213	9,567	9,020	444,675
Shelby,	715,454	183	14,340	8,327	615,795
Sterling, .	377,735	135	6,972	6,687	339,345
Warren, ...	434,055	141	4,327	5,134	311,300
Washington,	1,053,695	182	16,771	8,949	786,970
Total, ..	8,144,516	2,484	127,929	106,052	6,411,849

MANISTEE COUNTY.—Continued.

Brown, ..	$6,020		. .		
Manistee, ..	38,560		....	.	..
Stronach, ...	2,100	.			. .
Total,....	$46,680		.		

MANITOU COUNTY.—Continued.

Beaver Island,	$17,827	2	120	150	$1,000
Garden Island,	1,860		....		.
Little Fox Island,			...	..	.
N. Manitou Isl'nd,	160	1	200	200	5,000
S. Manitou Isl'nd,	3,950	.	......	.....	. .
Total,......	$23,797	3	320	350	$6,000

MACOMB COUNTY.—Continued.

Value of Farming Implements and Machinery.	Live Stock, June 1st, 1860.							
	Horses.	Asses and Mules.	Milch Cows.	Working Oxen.	Other Cattle.	Sheep.	Swine.	Value of Live Stock.
$31,345	682		654	85	834	6,349	731	$95,439
34,653	623		544	80	797	9,497	789	107,940
14,908	495		558	174	704	2,115	700	53,865
17,926	487		572	90	519	1,724	1,011	55,113
19,330	460		482	43	365	495	1,040	51,305
3,976	279		189	60	754	743	338	17,221
15,326	377		581	145	575	1,683	602	49,987
15,331	355		457	85	440	1,718	348	43,083
. .						... .	... .	. .
27,572	602	2	746	92	776	4,110	758	82,315
20,484	531		585	147	641	2,464	518	71,203
25,440	552		582	75	601	5,988	673	85,281
13,005	314		431	91	439	2,421	626	50,579
15,295	364		413	27	434	715	638	43,178
39,360	758		668	52	882	9,143	1,014	113,419
293,941	6879	2	7467	1,246	8,316	49,176	9,785	919,928

MANISTEE COUNTY.—Continued.

...						. .	.	
. ..						.	..	
......								..

MANITOU COUNTY.—Continued.

$180	7		9	2	15	. .	15	$750
.							..	
... ..						..	..	
1,000	6		7	24	20	40	5	1,661
......				. .			......	
$1,180	13		16	26	35	40	20	$2,411

MACOMB COUNTY.—Continued.

TOWNSHIPS.	Produce, during the Year						
	Wheat, bushels of.	Rye, bushels of.	Indian corn, bushels of.	Oats, bushels of.	Barley, bushels of.	Buckwheat, bushels of.	Potatoes, bushels of.
Armada,	8,692	886	25,358	45,996	2,169	2,076	15,529
Bruce,	22,808	2,743	31,309	38,529	2,500	2,475	14,842
Chesterfield,	1,810	2,950	17,274	19,563	250	4,021	23,629
Clinton,	1,695	1,877	19,768	14,512	147	3,367	24,729
Erin,	857	2,571	20,034	18,743	1,156	2,951	22,257
Harrison,	701	1,573	9,614	9,751	845	2,301	5,500
Lenox,	1,760	915	13,426	19,760	162	2,604	16,651
Macomb,	876	2,044	15,011	12,661	319	1,486	15,614
Mt. Clemens v.,							.. ...
Ray,	3,957	1,517	22,718	21,568	536	2,136	14,827
Richmond,	5,648	1,733	27,158	28,673	648	1,951	20,056
Shelby,	9,344	2,425	51,470	26,568	940	2,486	29,330
Sterling,	730	295	20,220	23,394	348	2,581	24,347
Warren,	300	846	10,402	11,887	94	2,699	20,107
Washington,	15,745	2,549	45,476	28,388	2,324	3,265	17,900
Total,	74,923	24914	329238	319993	12438	36399	265318

MANISTEE COUNTY.—Continued.

TOWNSHIPS.	Wheat	Rye	Indian corn	Oats	Barley	Buckwheat	Potatoes
Brown,							
Manistee,							
Stronach,							...
Total,							..

MANITOU COUNTY.—Continued.

TOWNSHIPS.	Wheat	Rye	Indian corn	Oats	Barley	Buckwheat	Potatoes
Beaver Island,	..		130	.		130	
Garden Island,	.					.	.. .
Little Fox Isl.			.			.	......
N. Manitou Isl.		200	1,500		.	800	50
S. Manitou Isl.,						....	. ...
Total,		200	1,630	..		930	50

MACOMB COUNTY.—CONTINUED.

ENDING JUNE 1ST, 1860.

Wool, pounds of.	Value of Orchard products.	Butter, pounds of.	Cheese, pounds of.	Hay, tons of.	Clover seed, bushels.	Maple Sugar, pounds.	Value of home made manufactures.
24,935	2,735	58,104	10,440	1,428	15	10,195	1,062
32,834	5,452	47,701	3,781	2,204	171	2,931	279
6,143	334	44,094	7,008	1,041	16	1,288	601
8,470	1,023	48,769	2,500	1,505			283
957	299	44,205	140	1,338		.	123
1,918	601	9,499	400	611	3	.	
4,396	16	49,004	3,044	734		4,587	651
6,230	473	40,335	2,085	1,042		2,851	740
16,434	1,667	65,816	6,091	1,562	5	13,433	749
8,126	468	54,744	6,829	1,129	11	7,605	759
22,899	3,330	53,073	2,991	1,445	98	2,452	668
8,600	1,338	41,350	1,492	1,276		2,621	206
2,215	559	33,121	2,300	1,164		260	55
30,483	7,549	62,694	13,300	2,166	100	3,385	484
177,640	25,544	652,509	62,411	18645	413	51,608	6,660

MANISTEE COUNTY.—CONTINUED.

Wool, pounds of.	Value of Orchard products.	Butter, pounds of.	Cheese, pounds of.	Hay, tons of.	Clover seed, bushels.	Maple Sugar, pounds.	Value of home made manufactures.
....	.		. .		.	.	.
.....	..	.	. .	...	.	.. .	.

MANITOU COUNTY.—CONTINUED.

Wool, pounds of.	Value of Orchard products.	Butter, pounds of.	Cheese, pounds of.	Hay, tons of.	Clover seed, bushels.	Maple Sugar, pounds.	Value of home made manufactures.
. .	.	450		28	.	500	... ..
.....	. ..		. .			.	. .
.....	...					.. .	.. ..
50	.	300	..	..			.... .
.....			.			..	. .. .
50	...	750	. ...	28		500	. . ...

MACOMB COUNTY.—CONTINUED.

TOWNSHIPS.	Flouring Mills. Number of.	Runs of Stone.	Power used. Water.	Steam.	Capital invested in real and personal estate in the business.	Annual product. Bbls. flour made.	Value of.	Saw Mills. Number of.	Power used. Water.	Steam.	Capital invested in real and personal estate in the business.
Armada,											
Bruce,											
Chesterfield,								2		1	$4,500
Clinton,	1			1	$2,000	450	$2,875	2	1	1	6,200
Erin,								1		1	4,000
Harrison,											
Lenox,								1		1	2,500
Macomb,	1		1		2,500	600	11,600	1	1		1,000
Mt. Clemens v.											
Ray,	2		2		11,000	3,050	18,450	2	1	1	2,400
Richmond,								2	2		3,000
Shelby,	1		1		9,000	700	19,550	1		1	2,000
Sterling,								3	2	1	5,700
Warren,								1		1	2,000
Washington,	1		1		10,000	3,200	23,500				
Total,	6		5	1	$34500	8,000	$75975	16	7	8	33,300

MANISTEE COUNTY.—CONTINUED.

TOWNSHIPS.	Flouring Mills. Number of.	Runs of Stone.	Water.	Steam.	Capital.	Bbls. flour made.	Value of.	Saw Mills. Number of.	Water.	Steam.	Capital.
Brown,											
Manistee,								7	2	5	455000
Stronach,								2	2		100000
Total,								9	4	5	555000

MANITOU COUNTY.—CONTINUED.

TOWNSHIPS.	Flouring Mills. Number of.	Runs of Stone.	Water.	Steam.	Capital.	Bbls. flour made.	Value of.	Saw Mills. Number of.	Water.	Steam.	Capital.
Beaver Island											
Garden "											
Little Fox "											
N Manitou "											
S. Manitou "											
Total,											

MACOMB COUNTY.—CONTINUED.

SAW MILLS. Annual product. Feet of Lumber Sawed.	SAW MILLS. Annual product. Value of.	AGGREGATE OF ALL KINDS OF MANUFACTURES, MILLS INCLUDED. Capital invested in real and personal estate in the business.	Hands employ'd. Males.	Hands employ'd. Females.	Value of annual product.	ESTIMATED VALUE OF REAL AND PERSONAL ESTATE. By Assessors.	By assistant Marshals.
.. ...	..	$1,000	6		$3,661	..	.. ..
....		9,800	20		20,442	. .	
1,200.000	10,000	13,575	41		29,464	.	
357,000	8,400	69,725	97		108,906	.	.
300,000	2,700	4,250	5		3,100	..	
....	.. .				. .		. .
500.000	3,500	2,500	4		3,500	. ..	..
125,000	1,000	4,000	4		13,400	. .	.. ..
.... .	.....	...				....	.
750,000	5,600	13,600	9		25,400	. .. .	.. .
660,000	4,700	7,450	15		13,740	..	.. ..
200,000	1,400	20,200	21	1	44,210	....	.. ..
905,000	6,700	11,500	17		25,867	. .	...
540,000	3,840	2,500	8		4,540	.....	. ....
..... .		29.000	39		66,405	.	. .
5,537,000	47,840	189,100	286	1	361,641	5074767	7,699,220

MANISTEE COUNTY.—CONTINUED.

Feet of Lumber Sawed.	Value of.	Capital invested.	Males.	Females.	Value of annual product.	By Assessors.	By assistant Marshals.
......	.. .	$4,300	78		$14,800	. .	.
$1,000,000	192500	464,600	301	37	225,069	. ..	....
4 000.000	26,000	100,950	123	5	38,420	...	.. ...
$5,000,000	218500	$569850	502	42	$278289	$605943	$605,943

MANITOU COUNTY.—CONTINUED.

Feet of Lumber Sawed.	Value of.	Capital invested.	Males.	Females.	Value of annual product.	By Assessors.	By assistant Marshals.
....:		$7,000			$42,000	. ..	..
.. .. .		. .			... ..	.	. . .
......	....	. ..			. ..	...	.
. .... .	....	...				.. ..	.....
....	...	. .			..	...	. ...
....	. ..	$7,000			$42,000	$73,771	$73,771

MARQUETTE COUNTY

TOWNSHIPS.	Dwelling Houses.		Number of Families.	Number of Inhabitants.				
	Whole number.	Number in Cities.		Whole number.	Colored.	Deaf and Dumb.	Blind.	Insane.
Chocolay,	44		41	213	1			
Marquette,	303		297	1,664	57			
Negawnee,	177		144	944	1			
Total,	524	....	482	2,821	59			

MASON COUNTY

TOWNSHIPS.	Whole number.	Number in Cities.	Number of Families.	Whole number.	Colored.	Deaf and Dumb.	Blind.	Insane.
Free Soil,			.....	60				
Little Sauble,	104		104	300				
Pere Marquette,	108	....	106	356				
Summit,	29		28	11[illegible]				
Total,	241		238	831				

MECOSTA COUNTY

TOWNSHIPS.	Whole number.	Number in Cities.	Number of Families.	Whole number.	Colored.	Deaf and Dumb.	Blind.	Insane.
Green,	49		44	246				
Hinton,	33		32	153	1			
Leonard,	72		71	317	3			
Pearson,	69	....	62	301				
Total,	223		209	1,017	4			

MIDLAND COUNTY

TOWNSHIPS.	Whole number.	Number in Cities.	Number of Families.	Whole number.	Colored.	Deaf and Dumb.	Blind.	Insane.
Ingersoll,	18		20	111				
Jerome,	29		27	114				
Midland,	126		126	557	1			
Total,	173		173	782	1			

MARQUETTE COUNTY.—Continued.

TOWNSHIPS.	Value of Real Estate owned.	Occupied Farms. Whole number.	Acres improved.	Acres unimproved.	Cash value of.
Chocolay, .	$20,380	2	18	72	$440
Marquette,. .	35,240	25	969	1,244	58,245
Negawnee,. .	80,710	3	95	257	5,500
Total,. . .	$136,330	30	1,082	1,573	$64,185

MASON COUNTY.—Continued.

TOWNSHIPS.	Value of Real Estate owned.	Occupied Farms. Whole number.	Acres improved.	Acres unimproved.	Cash value of.
Free Soil, ..		.	.	.	
Little Sauble, ..	$10,000		..	. . .	...
Père Marquette,	12,100		. . .	.. .	
Summit, .	7,850		.. .	.	. ...
Total, .	$29,950	*43	1,214	28,600	$165,250

MECOSTA COUNTY.—Continued.

TOWNSHIPS.	Value of Real Estate owned.	Occupied Farms. Whole number.	Acres improved.	Acres unimproved.	Cash value of.
Green,	$29,400	10	267	1,232	$11,000
Hinton, .	6,100	6	140	683	3,400
Leonard,. .	37,550	10	370	1,290	9,900
Pearson, .	28.450	4	130	640	5 100
Total,	$101,500	30	907	3,845	$29,400

MIDLAND COUNTY.—Continued.

TOWNSHIPS.	Value of Real Estate owned.	Occupied Farms. Whole number.	Acres improved.	Acres unimproved.	Cash value of.
Ingersoll,..	$23,000	24	555	1,514	$24,100
Jerome,. .	16,000	9	270	877	10,200
Midland,. . ..	107.450	38	835	13.853	58.000
Total, . .	$146,450	71	1,660	26,244	$92,300

*Agricultural products not returned by townships.

MARQUETTE COUNTY.—Continued.

Value of Farming Implements and Machinery.	Live Stock, June 1st, 1860.							
	Horses.	Asses and Mules.	Milch Cows.	Working Oxen.	Other Cattle.	Sheep.	Swine.	Value of Live Stock.
$20				2		.	.	$180
1,447	23		20	10	14	.	6	4,376
155	7		7	3	9		..	1,390
$1,622	30		27	15	23	.	6	$5,946
MASON COUNTY.—Continued.								
$8,460	50		5[illegible]	129	54	..	464	$13,615
MECOSTA COUNTY.—Continued.								
...	6		17	14	12		47	$1,565
165	3		15	6	30	13	23	972
450	13		22	13	15	..	14	2,055
95			12	8	11	..	7	685
$710	22		66	41	68	13	91	$5,277
MIDLAND COUNTY.—Continued.								
$684	14		47	50	53	....	104	$4,250
425	2		16	18	26		22	1,740
2,004	3[illegible]		78	69	76	.	164	7,377
$3,113	48	.	141	137	155	.	290	$13,360

MARQUETTE COUNTY.—CONTINUED.

TOWNSHIPS.	PRODUCE, DURING THE YEAR						
	Wheat, bushels of.	Rye, bushels of.	Indian corn, bushels of.	Oats, bushels of.	Barley, bushels of.	Buckwheat, bushels of.	Potatoes, bushels of.
Chocolay,		20	..	230			300
Marquette,	.	10		2,167			9,545
Negawnee,			.	500			
Total,	...	30	.	2,897			9,845
MASON COUNTY.—CONTINUED.							
Free Soil, ...			..	.			
Little Sauble,	..						. . .
P Marquette,	..						. ..
Summit, .	..		.	...			...
Total,	555	27	8,360	810	5	81	7,920
MECOSTA COUNTY.—CONTINUED.							
Green, .	395	55	175	1,085	27		645
Hinton, ..	397	125	35	. . .	20	32	495
Leonard, :	234	226	272	840			575
Pearson,	286		205	95		12	268
Total,	1,312	406	687	2,020	47	44	1,983
MIDLAND COUNTY.—CONTINUED.							
Ingersoll,	932	531	3,385	114	335	112	1,231
Jerome, .	550	250	1,115	.	210	99	690
Midland,	2,479	245	5,065	..	99	260	2,873
Total,	3,961	1,026	9,565	114	644	471	4,794

MARQUETTE COUNTY.—Continued.

Ending June 1st, 1860.							
Wool, pounds of.	Value of Orchard products.	Butter, pounds of.	Cheese, pounds of.	Hay, tons of.	Clover seed, bushels.	Maple Sugar, pounds.	Value of home made manufactures.
				243		400	
				243		400	

MASON COUNTY.—Continued.

Wool, pounds of.	Value of Orchard products.	Butter, pounds of.	Cheese, pounds of.	Hay, tons of.	Clover seed, bushels.	Maple Sugar, pounds.	Value of home made manufactures.
	620	2,765		85		4,024	

MECOSTA COUNTY.—Continued.

Wool, pounds of.	Value of Orchard products.	Butter, pounds of.	Cheese, pounds of.	Hay, tons of.	Clover seed, bushels.	Maple Sugar, pounds.	Value of home made manufactures.
		700		29		2,800	
35		1,050		31		2,800	
		700		88		4,010	
		600		17		2,450	
35		3,050		165		12,060	

MIDLAND COUNTY.—Continued.

Wool, pounds of.	Value of Orchard products.	Butter, pounds of.	Cheese, pounds of.	Hay, tons of.	Clover seed, bushels.	Maple Sugar, pounds.	Value of home made manufactures.
		3,200		99		6,400	
		1,750		28		1,150	
		3,880		166		3,100	
		8,830		293		10,650	

24

MARQUETTE COUNTY.—Continued.

TOWNSHIPS.	Flouring Mills. Number of.	Runs of Stone.	Power used. Water.	Power used. Steam.	Capital invested in real and personal estate in the business.	Annual product. Bbls. flour made.	Annual product. Value of.	Saw Mills. Number of.	Power used. Water.	Power used. Steam.	Capital invested in real and personal estate in the business.
Chocolay,								1		1	10,000
Marquette,								4	4		15,000
Negawnee,								2	1	1	11,000
Total,								7	5	2	36,000
MASON COUNTY.—Continued.											
Free Soil,								1		1	14,000
Little Sauble,								2	2		55,000
P Marquette,								1		1	25,000
Summit,											
Total,								4	2	2	94,000
MECOSTA COUNTY.—Continued.											
Green,								1	1		10,000
Hinton,											
Leonard,								1	1		15,000
Pearson,											
Total,								2	2		25,000
MIDLAND COUNTY.—Continued.											
Ingersoll,											
Jerome,											
Midland,								2		2	14,000
Total,								2		2	14,000

MARQUETTE COUNTY.—Continued.

Saw Mills.		Aggregate of all kinds of Manufactures, Mills included.				Estimated value of Real and Personal Estate.	
Annual product.		Capital invested in real and personal estate in the business.	Hands employ'd		Value of annual products.	By Assessors.	By assistant Marshals.
Feet of Lumber Sawed.	Value of.		Males.	Females.			
700,000	$9,450	$85,000	50		$9,450		....
1,848,533	19,927	105,100	142		253,624		...
600,000	6,000	736,000	209		565,000	.	.
3,148,533	17,377	926,100	401		828,074	861,670	$2,000,000

MASON COUNTY.—Continued.

Feet of Lumber Sawed.	Value of.	Capital invested in real and personal estate in the business.	Males.	Females.	Value of annual products.	By Assessors.	By assistant Marshals.
2,000,000	10,000	14,500	19	3	10,800		..
10,000,000	50,000	58,100	73	24	55,850	..	...
6,000,000	30,000	26,100	28	4	33,200		....
....							..
18,000,000	90,000	98,700	120	31	99,850	266,978	....

MECOSTA COUNTY.—Continued.

Feet of Lumber Sawed.	Value of.	Capital invested in real and personal estate in the business.	Males.	Females.	Value of annual products.	By Assessors.	By assistant Marshals.
*100,000	8,000	10,000	2		8,000	....	...
....		..			...		.....
*40,000	5,000	15,000	4		5,000	....	.....
.....						.	....
140,000	13,000	25,000	6		13,000	376,447	...

MIDLAND COUNTY.—Continued.

Feet of Lumber Sawed.	Value of.	Capital invested in real and personal estate in the business.	Males.	Females.	Value of annual products.	By Assessors.	By assistant Marshals.
....	....	......	.	.	...	509,948	$667,000
....	....	......		.	...	103,879	138,479
2,000,000	14,000	14,300	37		14,750	44,170	58,898
2,000,000	14,000	14,300	37	.	14,750	657,997	$844,377

* As returned, evidently a mistake.

MONROE COUNTY

TOWNSHIPS.	Dwelling Houses.		Number of Families.	Number of Inhabitants.				
	Whole number.	Number in Cities.		Whole number.	Colored.	Deaf and Dumb.	Blind.	Insane.
Ash,..	406		406	2,124		1		
Bedford,.	227		233	1,280	1			
Dundee,	375		374	1,940				
Erie,...	229		229	1,362			2	
Exeter,.	151		151	832				
Frenchtown,	324		324	1,777			1	1
Ida,..	121		122	673				
Lasalle,	239		242	1,327				
London,	174		174	849			1	
Milan,	211		211	1,045				
Monroe,	188		188	997				
City, 1st ward,	419	419	419	2,043	17	4		1
" 2d ward,	259	259	259	1 366	4			
" 3d ward,	80	80	80	486				
Raisinville,..	270		270	1,448	1		1	
Summerfield,	177		177	962		1		
Whiteford,..	229		231	1,137	2		1	
Total,	4,079	758	4,090	21,648	25	6	6	2

MONROE COUNTY.—Continued.

TOWNSHIPS.	Value of Real Estate owned.	Occupied Farms.			
		Whole number.	Acres improved.	Acres unimproved.	Cash value of.
Ash,. .	$410,350	216	7,426	19,505	$345,470
Bedford, ..	352,685	192	7,946	8,232	352,310
Dundee, . . .	479,930	220	8,686	10,796	402,050
Erie, ...	418,000	142	7,968	4,342	373,050
Exeter, ..	191,570	102	3,500	7,293	148,400
Frenchtown,	415,020	188	8,733	8,294	319,425
Ida,.	159,320	84	4,005	4 266	168,250
Lasalle, ...	395,635	171	8,184	6,393	380.215
London, ...	194,420	97	3,756	6,000	129,840
Milan,	266,860	131	4,886	5,940	232,130
Monroe, ...	245,310	125	7,202	2,426	257,603
City, 1st ward,	467,880		.....	. ..	.. . ..
" 2d ward,	443,250	.	. ...		.. ....
" 3d ward,	509,645	*23	1,985	570	96,900
Raisinville,	432,864	198	10,518	11,086	403,790
Summerfield,	284,600	103	4,344	5,776	199,750
Whiteford,	249,940	146	5,398	6,638	321,850
Total, ..	$5,917,297	2,138	94,537	107,557	$4,031,033

* This includes the whole city.

MONROE COUNTY.—Continued.

Value of Farming Implements and Machinery.	Live Stock, June 1st, 1860. Horses.	Asses and Mules.	Milch Cows.	Working Oxen.	Other Cattle.	Sheep.	Swine.	Value of Live Stock.
$17.410	617		572	143	925	1,732	1,413	$67,452
13,409	513	3	619	77	630	2,188	1,008	56,153
17,176	583	5	620	180	1,304	2,755	1,049	74,986
13,147	572	1	397	63	502	3,385	817	54,807
7,234	285	.	404	82	679	1,270	855	37,854
15,367	585	1	588	145	958	2,291	1,256	71,104
6,435	229		312	118	521	664	482	31,028
14,187	507		546	98	552	1,848	731	56,407
8,081	291		379	78	663	1,488	518	34,794
10,955	315	1	427	106	704	2,402	789	45,605
5,210	409		394	80	384	1.533	726	43,437
....							.	...
2,115	146	30	81	6	106	401	124	15,636
9,309	527		599	184	862	2,938	1,021	62,564
7,569	275		327	72	511	1,041	723	97.018
9.304	287		355	95	400	1,086	561	35,627
$156,914	6141	41	3611	1,522	9,701	27,022	12,073	$784,474

MONROE COUNTY.—Continued.

TOWNSHIPS.	Produce, during the Year						
	Wheat, bushels of.	Rye, bushels of.	Indian corn, bushels of.	Oats, bushels of.	Barley, bushels of.	Buckwheat, bushels of.	Potatoes, bushels of.
Ash, . .	21,808	619	37,045	10,855	411	3,483	17,169
Bedford,	9,668	957	38,913	5,975	709	3,712	27,577
Dundee,	14,422	750	65,253	9,756	690	4,852	22,462
Erie, .	16,550	1,234	50,165	11,240	7,030	2,821	19,091
Exeter,.	7,400	674	19,052	3,644		1,383	10,407
Frenchtown, :	15,903	942	43,863	9,857	1,705	2,591	20,204
Ida,	4,234	331	22,850	3,230	589	2,156	9,302
Lasalle,	18,005	723	37,225	11,[illegible]13	4,556	3,060	16,616
London,	1,661	707	16,343	4,041	80	1,742	10,137
Milan,	5,179	813	31,318	4,502	328	1,769	7,391
Monroe,	14,401	725	30,375	9,939	2,153	1,372	10,431
City, 1st ward,	.			.			.
" 2d ward,				.			. ...
" 3d ward,	2,563	300	7,790	3,710	470	101	2,950
Raisinville,	13,080	786	44,390	15,748	1,025	2,549	16,899
Summerfield,	7,476	362	23,867	4,486	209	2,393	16,969
Whiteford,	8,138	45	28,670	3,910	693	3 826	21,514
Total,	149488	9,468	497119	112006	20648	37810	229 19

MONROE COUNTY.—Continued.

ENDING JUNE 1st, 1860.

Wool, pounds of.	Value of Orchard products.	Butter, pounds of.	Cheese, pounds of.	Hay, tons of.	Clover seed, bushels.	Maple Sugar, pounds.	Value of home made manufactures.
3,012	2 461	48,727	565	2,890	311	928	$116
4,750	3 361	51,140	10,625	2,740	285	.	442
7,026	3,480	48,043	11,995	3,601	51	6,565	696
10,801	2,770	36 010	275	1,956	147	.	63
2,714	1,801	30,510	2,460	1,522		900	51
4,714	2,747	50,365	150	3,178	21	549	22
1,863	570	30,640	1,200	1,928	34		25
4,554	3,193	41,870	8,141	2,078	88		75
2,988	2,986	27,998	11,965	3,107		3,088	100
6,209	1,919	32,470	22,270	1,988	51	2,006	222
3,784	1,093	17,706	7,8[illegible]0	1,491	53	. ..	.. ...
......	.....		.... .	.	.	.. ..	. . .
.....	..	.	. .			....	. ...
1,145	440	4,565	.	532	.	.....	..
7,941	860	29,865	730	3,390	26	.	.. ..
2 221	2,132	31 370	5,144	1,488	67	240	122
2,793	1,229	29,500	700	1 699	10	.	.....
66,517	31,048	510,769	84,030	23394	1144	14,276	$1,934

MONROE COUNTY.—Continued.

TOWNSHIPS.	Flouring Mills.							Saw Mills.			
	Number of.	Runs of Stone.	Power used. Water.	Power used. Steam.	Capital invested in real and personal estate in the business.	Annual product. Bbls. flour made.	Annual product. Value of.	Number of.	Power used. Water.	Power used. Steam.	Capital invested in real and personal estate in the business.
Ash,								1		1	$5,000
Bedford,								1	1		500
Dundee,	1		1		$8,000	1,600	$8,000	3	1	2	9,000
Erie,								2	1	1	5,500
Exeter,											
Frenchtown,								2	1	1	4,500
Ida,											
Lasalle,								1		1	2,500
London,											
Milan,	1		1		500		1,000				
Monroe,											
City, 1st ward,											
" 2d ward,											
" 3d ward,	2	4	2		19,000	9,300	48,200	3	2	1	7,900
Raisinville,								2	2		4,300
Summerfield,	1		1		8,000	5,000	25,000	1	1		7,000
Whiteford,								1		1	4,000
Total,	5	4	5		35,500	15900	82,200	17	9	8	50,200

MONROE COUNTY.—Continued.

Saw Mills.		Aggregate of all kinds of Manufactures, Mills included.				Estimated value of Real and Personal Estate.	
Annual product.			Hands employ'd				
Feet of Lumber Sawed.	Value of.	Capital invested in real and personal estate in the business.	Males.	Females.	Value of annual product.	By Assessors.	By assistant Marshals.
1,500.000	$15000	$5,000	5		15,000	......	....
100,000	1,500	1,000	4		3,000	..	.... .
1,300,000	8,700	18,500	16		20,100	. . .	. . ...
450,000	3,600	5,500	5		3,600		. ...
.....	...	...			. .	.. ..	. ..
300,000	2,000	4,500	4		2,000	....	. ...
....	.	1,100	4		1,420	.....	.. ....
400,000	3,200	3,000	7		5,000	.	... .
.. ...	. .	. .				. ....	....
... .	. .	500	1		1,000	. ..	.. ....
. .. .	.	....				*	*
.. .. .	......	.		.	. ..	......	....
.. . .	....	... .			.	. ..	....
782,138	7,588	72,606	144	40	148,728	*	*
625,000	5,765	8,500	9	7	9,765	*	*
900,000	7.000	20,500	20		39,400	. ..	. .....
300,000	2,400	4,000	4		2,400	....	....
6,707,138	$56743	$144706	223	47	$251413	4059171	†4519737

† The footings of the two last columns are of towns marked thus *.

MONTCALM COUNTY.

TOWNSHIPS.	Dwelling Houses.		Number of Families.	Number of Inhabitants.				
	Whole number.	Number in Cities.		Whole number.	Colored.	Deaf and Dumb.	Blind.	Insane.
Bloomer,	140	...	125	630	1			
Bushnell,	147	...	131	645		1		
Cato,	39	...	34	192	..			
Crystal,	48	..	45	221				
Eureka,	139	....	120	591		2	1	
Evergreen,	21		20	89				
Fairplain,	108		99	492	7			
Ferris,	45	..	42	184				
Greenville village,	113		92	399				
Montcalm,	91	..	79	367				1
Sidney,	32		35	174		1		
Total,	923	...	822	3,984	8	4	1	1

MONTCALM COUNTY.—Continued.

TOWNSHIPS.	Value of Real Estate owned.	Occupied Farms.			
		Whole number.	Acres improved.	Acres unimproved.	Cash value of.
Bloomer,	$111,820	43	1,519	2,556	$58,980
Bushnell,	120,520	49	2,240	3,498	61,550
Cato,	18,830	9	241	956	7,300
Crystal,	35,480	12	434	684	13,400
Eureka,	207,300	77	5,398	4,914	183,200
Evergreen,	12,125	4	66	193	2,400
Fairplain,	121,000	38	2,192	2,174	75,200
Ferris,	22,375	18	486	1,897	14,600
Greenville vil.,	134,640	.	......	...	...
Montcalm,	88,900	41	1,521	2,657	56,300
Sidney,	14,950	7	150	694	5,800
Total,	$887,940	298	14,247	20,223	$478,730

MONTCALM COUNTY.—Continued.

Value of Farming Implements and Machinery.	Live Stock, June 1st, 1860.							
	Horses.	Asses and Mules.	Milch Cows.	Working Oxen.	Other Cattle.	Sheep.	Swine.	Value of Live Stock.
$1,497	36		99	54	125	301	218	$10,680
1,807	41		105	80	118	296	167	9,930
249	.	.	20	14	20	.....	18	1,150
446	7		26	20	27	7	60	2,205
5,482	111		197	108	256	1,216	314	24,182
133	2		6	6		...	10	590
2,429	78		96	38	119	499	138	11,705
396	.	2	36	34	30	7	71	2,885
...	.			..	.	.....	....	....
1,201	30	.	85	53	55	97	152	7,204
398	4		18	8	14	3	27	1,373
$14,038	309	2	688	415	764	2,426	1,175	$71,904

MONTCALM COUNTY.—Continued.

TOWNSHIPS.	Produce, during the Year						
	Wheat, bushels of.	Rye, bushels of.	Indian corn, bushels of.	Oats, bushels of.	Barley, bushels of.	Buckwheat, bushels of.	Potatoes, bushels of.
Bloomer, ...	2,574	2	1,728	1,624	42	129	766
Bushnell, ...	6,522	230	1,700	2,706	22	102	1,166
Cato, ...	259	20	300		13		433
Crystal, ...	792	39	542	240		29	607
Eureka, ...	12,349	1,346	6,550	5,745		189	4,672
Evergreen, .	340		450	50		30	185
Fairplain, ..	6,518	305	3,620	3,890	128	102	1,956
Ferris, ..	897	98	729	431	8	85	1,098
Greenville vil.							
Montcalm, .	5,589	148	4,240	1,663	1	59	2,089
Sidney ..	304	119	480	30		50	418
Total, ..	36,144	2,313	20,339	16,379	214	775	13,390

MONTCALM COUNTY.—Continued.

[illegible]nding June 1st, 1860.							
Wool, pounds of.	Value of Orchard products.	Butter, pounds of.	Cheese, pounds of.	Hay, tons of.	Clover seed, bushels.	Maple Sugar, pounds.	Value of home made manufactures.
666	.	6,295	1,07[illegible]	31[illegible]	1	22,78[illegible]	$18[illegible]
623	$2[illegible]	8,825	1,02[illegible]	27[illegible]	1	9,86[illegible]	34[illegible]
.....	.	1,650	2[illegible]	1[illegible]	.	5,75[illegible]	
20	...	1,700	270	33	2	3,660	.
3,124	56[illegible]	16,58[illegible]	1,62[illegible]	664	17	860	185
...	...	55[illegible]	...	10		1[illegible]	3
1,216	3[illegible]	6,92[illegible]	82[illegible]	345	6	2,77[illegible]	219
.....	..	2,14[illegible]	..	66		2,45[illegible]	....
.....			.....		.	.	..
21[illegible]	25[illegible]	6,47[illegible]	7[illegible]	161	1	1,495	48
9	...	1,37[illegible]	2[illegible]	37		1,490	325
5,875	$878	55,515	4,92[illegible]	1,915	28	51,130	$8[illegible]2

MONTCALM COUNTY.—Continued.

TOWNSHIPS.	Flouring Mills.							Saw Mills.			
			Power used.			Annual product.			Power used.		
	Number of.	Runs of Stone.	Water.	Steam.	Capital invested in real and personal estate in the business.	Bbls. flour made.	Value of.	Number of.	Water.	Steam.	Capital invested in real and personal estate in the business.
Bloomer,. .					. ..	.	..	.			.
Bushnell, . .					.		. ...				.. .
Cato,.					..		.	1	1	.	$2,500
Crystal,.. .				.	. ...		. .				.
Eureka, .					..		.				... ..
Evergreen,.					. .		....	1	1		7,000
Fairplain,.	1	.	1		$3,500	.	$3,000	1	1		10,000
Ferris, ...	.				. .. .	.	...				.... .
Greenville vil.	1	.	1		5,000	.	12,500	2	2		13,500
Montcalm, . .					....	..	.. . .	3	3		21,000
Sidney,......		.			.		.....				.. ...
Total,.	2		2		8,500	. .	15,500	8	8		54,000

MONTCALM COUNTY.—CONTINUED.

SAW MILLS.		AGGREGATE OF ALL KINDS OF MANUFACTURES, MILLS INCLUDED.				ESTIMATED VALUE OF REAL AND PERSONAL ESTATE.	
Annual product.			Hands employ'd				
Feet of Lumber Sawed.	Value of.	Capital invested in real and personal estate in the business.	Males.	Females.	Value of annual products.	By Assessors.	By assistant Marshals.
.....	..				..	.. .	..
....	.	.				.....	.
1,800,000	$7,200	$2,500	15	2	$ 7,200	... .	.
.. .	. .				.	.	
. .. .	. . .					. .	.
400,000	2,800	7,000	6		2,800	.	
500,000	3,500	13,500	8	2	6,500	. . .	
...	.					. . .	
1,800,000	9,000	24,300	29	4	27,500	.	
1,300,000	6,500	21,000	17	4	6,500	. . .	.
....	.	.. ..			.	.	.
5,800,000	29,000	68,300	75	12	50,500	907,722	1,361,584

MUSKEGON COUNTY

TOWNSHIPS.	Dwelling Houses.		Number of Families.	Number of Inhabitants.				
	Whole number.	Number in Cities.		Whole number.	Colored.	Deaf and Dumb.	Blind.	Insane.
Cazenovia,.	110	... .	107	605				
Dalton,..	72	.	56	243	.			
Eggleston, ...	17	.. .	14	29	.			
Moreland, ...	28		24	105	.			.
Muskegon,	51		45	285	.	1		
" village,	283	. .	268	1,448	12			
Norton, ..	49	..	46	197				
Oceana, .	40	..	. 31	214				..
Ravenna, ..	86	....	79	393				
White River, .	80	. .	69	374	9			
. Total,... .	816	......	739	3,893	21	1		

NEWAYGO COUNTY

TOWNSHIPS.	Dwelling Houses: Whole number.	Dwelling Houses: Number in Cities.	Number of Families.	Inhabitants: Whole number.	Colored.	Deaf and Dumb.	Blind.	Insane.
Ashland, ..	74	....	57	304	.. .		1	.
Barton, ...	10	..... .	8	38	..			
Big Prairie,.	70	..	52	275	.			
Bridgeton, . ..	56	.	41	226	16			
Brooks, ...	131	.. ..	103	574	23	2		
Croton,.	170	....	102	535	2			
Dayton,.	78	..	61	281	..			
Ensley, ...	34	. .. .	30	124	.			..
Everett, . .	45	....	34	158	.	1		
Fremont, ...	69	..	48	252	9			.
Total, .	737	.....	536	2,767	50	3	1	.

MUSKEGON COUNTY.—Continued.

TOWNSHIPS.	Value of Real Estate owned.	Occupied Farms.			
		Whole number.	Acres improved.	Acres unimproved.	Cash value of.
Cazenovia, . . .	$138,930	95	2,518	11,363	$138,330
Dalton, .	30,750	8	164	89[illegible]	8,000
Eggleston, ...	9,400	2	27	453	1,900
Moreland, . .	12,080	9	120	520	4,500
Muskegon,	97,455		.	. . . . .	. . . . .
" village,	510,295		. . .	. . .	. . . .
Norton, .	22,280	5	168	712	9,500
Oceana, .	51,650	10	184	734	9,650
Ravenna,	71,395	46	1,202	3,381	54,800
White River,	92,340	19	326	1,826	16,900
Total, .	$1,036,585	194	4,709	19,887	$243,580

NEWAYGO COUNTY.—Continued.

TOWNSHIPS.	Value of Real Estate owned.	Whole number.	Acres improved.	Acres unimproved.	Cash value of.
Ashland, ...	$48,975	8	315	696	$13,200
Barton, ...	5,760	.	. .	. . . . .	. . . . . .
Big Prairie,	21,155	19	1,842	1,338	19,700
Bridgeton, .	27,055	1	152	48	400
Brooks, .	76,595	1	75	85	2,000
Croton, ...	89,800	34	2,050	2,295	1,240
Dayton, ...	34,065	17	494	1,446	12,650
Ensley, . . .	22,366	11	368	1,129	17,400
Everett, . . .	15,925	6	385	1,215	9,500
Fremont, ...	46,770	10	589	1,835	23,100
Total, . . .	$388,460	107	6,269	10,087	$126,400

MUSKEGON COUNTY.—Continued.

Value of Farming Implements and Machinery.	Live Stock, June 1st, 1860. Horses.	Asses and Mules.	Milch Cows.	Working Oxen.	Other Cattle.	Sheep.	Swine.	Value of Live Stock.
$3,584	50		180	117	180	117	402	$14,289
522	7		21	12	27	.	36	1,798
150	2		6	2	2	...	1	350
264	2		11	13	15		6	1,026
....						. .	..	
. .					.	....	.	..
355	6		8	8	14	..	13	1,215
593	7		9	12	9	...	31	1,505
1,893	19		80	50	76	21	224	6,397
445	6		29	24	24	2	65	2,371
$7,806	99		344	238	347	140	778	$28,951

NEWAYGO COUNTY.—Continued.

Value of Farming Implements and Machinery.	Horses.	Asses and Mules.	Milch Cows.	Working Oxen.	Other Cattle.	Sheep.	Swine.	Value of Live Stock.
$1,100	5		16	13	20	36	16	$1,520
. .						.	.. ...	.
1,804	22		39	22	27	74	63	4,040
60	2		4	.	12	.	.	410
100	2	.		2	5	.....	...	400
1,230	46		59	32	51	50	134	4,294
640			35	27	25	.	66	2,531
505	5		14	18	18	3	31	1,295
392	4	.	16	10	10	39	59	1,115
502	3		21	22	25	1	199	3,623
$6,333	89		204	146	193	203	568	$19,228

MUSKEGON COUNTY.—CONTINUED.

TOWNSHIPS.	PRODUCE, DURING THE YEAR						
	Wheat, bushels of.	Rye, bushels of.	Indian corn, bushels of.	Oats, bushels of.	Barley, bushels of.	Buckwheat, bushels of.	Potatoes, bushels of.
Cazenovia,.	3,557	780	4,090	944	43	195	2,579
Dalton, ...	30	103	58	261		13	391
Eggleston,		60	6	.	.		33
Moreland,	183		375	170	14	8	365
Muskegon, .	.		..		.		....
" vil.	..			.			.....
Norton,	82	75	105	115	6	10	282
Gceana,	60	90	70	...			300
Ravenna, .	1,149	36	1,847	815		5	1,379
White River,	162	294	591	189	5		547
Total, .	5,223	1,444	7,142	2,494	68	231	5,876

NEWAYGO COUNTY.—CONTINUED.

TOWNSHIPS.	Wheat, bushels of.	Rye, bushels of.	Indian corn, bushels of.	Oats, bushels of.	Barley, bushels of.	Buckwheat, bushels of.	Potatoes, bushels of.
Ashland,. ..	653	55	785	350			445
Barton, . .	.		..	..		.	......
Big Prairie,..	1,018	4,437	2,025	250			1,034
Bridgeton,			..	50			75
Brooks, .	360		100	200			300
Croton, ...	1,460	2,572	1,765	325	.	40	1,513
Dayton, ...	352	24	1,015	86		4	525
Ensley,.	1,820	48	396	400		64	685
Everett, .	490	850	190	100		.	470
Fremont,	1,066	220	915	520	18		670
Total,..	7,226	8,206	7,191	2,281	18	108	5,717

MUSKEGON COUNTY.—Continued.

Wool, pounds of.	Value of Orchard products.	Butter, pounds of.	Cheese, pounds of.	Hay, tons of.	Clover seed, bushels.	Maple Sugar, pounds.	Value of home made manufactures.
		ENDING JUNE 1ST, 1860.					
..	..	18,115	1,585	459		35,07[illegible]	$10
.	. .	1,400		23		800	
..	.	200	. . .	30	. .	.	.
.. .	....	1,125		55		1,790	.
.....		.	. ...			. .	
......		.	..			.	.
... .	10	300	. .	122		100	
..	..	1,225		47		560	...
40	. .	3,980	150	223		7,445	70
. ..	.	1,700		15		1,990	.
40	10	28,045	1,735	974		47,760	$80

NEWAYGO COUNTY.—Continued.

Wool, pounds of.	Value of Orchard products.	Butter, pounds of.	Cheese, pounds of.	Hay, tons of.	Clover seed, bushels.	Maple Sugar, pounds.	Value of home made manufactures.
...	....	1,330	...	53		1,200	
...		. .	. .			.	
227	. .	3,735	. . .	49		2,664	. .
..	. . .	500	.	40		600	.
.. .	....		......	. 25	.	....	..
... ..	.	705	... .	168		550	
.....	.. ..	3,670	. .	53	.	9,920	
.... .		780	.	37		175	...
80	. :	950	..	31		.	..
...	.	1,865	. ...	47		3,050	. . .
357	.. ..	13,535	....	503		18,159	. .

MUSKEGON COUNTY—Continued.

TOWNSHIPS.	Flouring Mills. Number of.	Runs of Stone.	Power used. Water.	Steam.	Capital invested in real and personal estate in the business.	Annual product. Bbls. flour made.	Value of.	Saw Mills. Number of.	Power used. Water.	Steam.	Capital invested in real and personal estate in the business.
Cazenovia,								1	1		$6,600
Dalton,								3	2	1	21,500
Eggleston,											
Moreland,											
Muskegon,								4		4	153000
" vil.,								10		10	408750
Norton,								2	1	1	23,500
Oceana,								3	1	2	38,500
Ravenna,								2	2		3,800
White River,								3	2	1	50,000
Total,								28	9	19	705650

NEWAYGO COUNTY—Continued.

TOWNSHIPS.	Flouring Mills. Number of.	Runs of Stone.	Power used. Water.	Steam.	Capital invested in real and personal estate in the business.	Annual product. Bbls. flour made.	Value of.	Saw Mills. Number of.	Power used. Water.	Steam.	Capital invested in real and personal estate in the business.
Ashland,											
Barton,											
Big Prairie,											
Bridgeton,								2		2	$9,500
Brooks,	1		1		$4,000	600	$12060	2	1	1	23,500
Croton,	1		1		5,000	200	9,060	2	2		10,500
Dayton,											
Ensley,											
Everett,											
Fremont,											
Total,	2		2		$9,000	800	$21120	6	3		$43500

MUSKEGON COUNTY.—Continued.

Saw Mills.		Aggregate of all kinds of Manufactures, Mills included.				Estimated value of Real and Personal Estate.	
Annual product.			Hands employ'd				
Feet of Lumber Sawed.	Value of.	Capital invested in real and personal estate in the business.	Males.	Females.	Value of annual product.	By Assessors.	By assistant Marshals.
200 000	$1,200	$6,600	2		$1,200	$72,952	$218,826
2,100,000	19,500	21,500	17		19,500	.	.
...	..	...			.	..	.
...	.	...					....
9,000,000	56.835	153.000	100		56,835	404,665	809,328
49,100,000	310693	424,200	327		356,993	...	...
1,900.000	9,900	25,700	48		17,020	56,947	113,894
4,100,000	20,500	38,500	40		20.500		....
500,000	3,400	4,400	5		7,500	82,425	164,850
8,240.000	42,040	62.000	114		57,040	69.620	131,240
75,140,000	464068	735,900	653		536,588	$686609	$1438138

NEWAYGO COUNTY.—Continued.

Feet of Lumber Sawed.	Value of.	Capital invested in real and personal estate in the business.	Males.	Females.	Value of annual product.	By Assessors.	By assistant Marshals.
.	..				.	....	.
....	.	..			...	....	...
.....	.				...		....
1,200,000	$10800	$9,500	21		$10,800	..	.....
8,500,000	54,500	32.300	63		75,310	...	....
*1,000,000	10,050	15,500	13		19,110	....	...
....		.			..	..	...
....	.	...			...	.	
...		.			..	..	..
......						.	.
$10,700,000	$75350	$57,300	97		$105220	$964312	$964,312

* Only one returned.

OAKLAND COUNTY

TOWNSHIPS.	Dwelling Houses.		Number of Families.	Number of Inhabitants.				
	Whole number.	Number in Cities.		Whole number.	Colored.	Deaf and Dumb.	Blind.	Insane.
Addison,	204		197	1,068				
Avon,	338	.....	331	1,769	4		..	
Bloomfield,	355	.....	355	1,926	11	2	..	5
Brandon,	237	.....	237	1,314			..	
Clarkston village,	76	....	74	376				
Commerce,	272	.	273	1,424	5	2	1	1
Farmington,	362	.	362	1,914	32			
Groveland,	253		250	1,271			1	
Highland,	212	..	208	1,139	1			
Holly,	196	..	198	1,062	4	1		
Holly village,	114	.	115	542	1			
Independence,	238	.....	241	1,268		2	1	
Lyon,	301		294	1,629	8	1		2
Milford,	317		300	1,664		1	3	
Novi,	283	.. .	275	1,466	3			2
Oakland,	207		200	1,071				1
Orion,	181	.	181	1,000				
Orion village,	63	....	63	292				
Oxford,	244	. .	244	1,402	4			
Pontiac,	266	.	266	1,560	18			
Pontiac village,	472	.	472	2,576	135			
Rose,	228	.	223	1,129				
Royal Oak,	266	...	249	1,224	32			
Southfield,	296	.	296	1,496	16			
Springfield,	270		269	1,426			1	
Troy,	346		332	1,700	12	2	5	2
Waterford,	241	.	241	1,050				
West Bloomfield,	205	.. .	205	1,120	1	1		1
White Lake,	225	.	222	1,142		1	1	
Total,	7,268	.. .	7,173	38,020	287	13	13	14

OAKLAND COUNTY.—Continued.

TOWNSHIPS.	Value of Real Estate owned.	Occupied Farms.			
		Whole number.	Acres improved.	Acres unimproved.	Cash value of.
Addison,	$412,725	139	10,8[illegible]8	6,298	$350,715
Avon,	858,838	266	15,374	8,043	666,770
Bloomfield,	928,997	138	11,078	6,639	612,725
Brandon,	539,560	182	11,955	8,870	512,160
Clarkston vil.,	191,500	.	. .	. .	. .
Commerce,	618,485	169	13,558	7,024	528,700
Farmington,	1,030,360	226	15,973	10 031	981,171
Groveland,	407,075	178	10,992	9,971	414 150
Highland,	358,540	166	12,337	6 087	366,600
Holly,	399,260	135	9,443	9,096	391,520
Holly vil.,	135,470		...	. .	...
Independence,	561,210	150	12,571	10,096	544,800
Lyon,	711,100	171	13,407	8,226	601,830
Milford,	602,110	156	12,793	6,649	427,980
Novi,	797,549	187	14,004	8,338	726,600
Oakland,	632,330	152	14,199	6,984	574,400
Orion,	530,990	145	13,809	7,326	520,370
Orion vil.,	75,800		...	. ..	. .
Oxford,	641,900	162	14,400	7,877	593,580
Pontiac,	870,850	200	13,216	7,709	737,660
Pontiac vil.,	903,125		. ..	..	..
Rose,	416,450	153	9,541	7,177	398,300
Royal Oak,	432,870	163	6,984	7,144	400,054
Southfield,	710,005	170	10,597	7,800	620,575
Springfield,	513,445	159	11,598	8,767	470,800
Troy,	814,940	283	15,310	7,917	783,410
Waterford,	676,170	121	10,616	7,922	554,400
West Bloomfield,	599,791	142	12,421	8,908	580,290
White Lake,	355 925	139	9,745	6,758	307,650
Total,	16,727,370	4,252	306,789	197,657	13,667,210

OAKLAND COUNTY.—Continued.

Value of Farming Implements and Machinery	Live Stock, June 1st, 1860.							
	Horses.	Asses and Mules.	Milch Cows.	Working Oxen.	Other Cattle.	Sheep.	Swine.	Value of Live Stock.
$10,482	407		458	125	581	4,012	886	$68,192
17,091	839	14	703	77	842	7,571	1,190	115,394
19,208	509		572	78	614	5,178	719	69,128
14,485	395		532	180	602	4,527	931	74,240
23,428	512	2	500	82	736	5,104	933	82,627
35,565	811	3	834	113	791	10,309	941	136,727
17,047	392		494	209	577	4,273	756	68,639
16,634	400		443	118	547	3,363	660	61,741
16,645	293		394	211	524	4,884	550	64,526
20,784	424		548	180	683	3,558	839	82,024
20,516	571	4	571	118	920	7,960	1,020	91,052
20,545	470		550	109	708	5,760	693	80,703
25,529	618		640	90	831	8,451	1,09[illegible]	87,901
14,400	607		633	48	857	4,793	1,237	87,900
14,252	480	14	484	144	762	4,217	800	68,949
17,860	498		575	184	769	7,012	1,318	81,936
19,545	654		687	86	943	5,922	1,059	89,897
15,471	308		452	171	474	4,521	638	64,949
7,234	508		680	38	535	2,657	995	64,435
23,229	544		680	80	594	6,857	1,160	81,337
20,205	365		482	219	614	3,677	800	70,962
18,634	847	1	1,022	66	962	7,216	1 322	128,997
25,035	402		427	96	539	4,349	758	75,459
21,230	468		477	98	647	6,979	758	68,236
11,479	364	3	425	114	596	3 342	605	54,301
$466,539	12686	42	14263	3034	17248	136492	22665	2,020,252

OAKLAND COUNTY.—Continued.

TOWNSHIPS.	Produce, during the Year						
	Wheat, bushels of	Rye, bushels of.	Indian corn, bushels of.	Oats, bushels of.	Barley, bushels of.	Buckwheat, bushels of.	Potatoes, bushels of.
Addison,	21,955	3,334	20,120	12,177	2,499	2,850	6,906
Avon,	17,083	3,456	61,090	34,398	5,423	5,388	23,911
Bloomfield,	15,703	1,730	38,181	31,731	2,585	3,281	24,196
Brandon,	31,365	4,466	25,612	10,294	1,648	3,229	10,186
Clarkston vil.,	..		..				......
Commerce,	21,245	8,206	41,410	7,898	542	3,434	34,378
Farmington,	18,409	8,117	61,700	34,163	692	2,948	41,328
Groveland,	28,790	2,800	29,500	7,688	1,105	2,030	12,886
Highland,	33,619	8,639	35,925	9,460	507	1,642	16,837
Holly,	24,463	2,652	16,693	8,577	1,301	1,181	8,260
Holly vil.,	.		..	...			.. .
Independence,	34,051	1,283	27,570	11,242	2,069	2,965	13,297
Lyon,	25,361	4,623	49,339	20,373	1,450	2,028	20,099
Milford,	24,920	4,762	30,810	11,662	443	1,846	26,937
Novi,	21,362	3,524	51,103	29,339	2,492	2,966	24,606
Oakland,	21,760	4,034	38,253	21,605	7,064	3,632	12,144
Orion,	22,017	3,451	35,340	15,463	2,726	2,783	15,407
Orion vil.,		.	. .				. ...
Oxford,	31,425	4,486	30,142	15,173	3,304	2,561	12,020
Pontiac,	15,284	2,218	29,102	21,139	4,137	3,880	25,723
Pontiac vil.,			.	.			...
Rose,	28.494	5,876	14.590	6,819	884	1.605	12,347
Royal Oak,	1,935	684	16.192	16,600	706	3.050	19,617
Southfield,	6.530	1,272	37,235	38,844	385	3,171	52,352
Springfield,	31,234	2,488	25,985	12,956	856	1,497	12,812
Troy,	7,891	591	45,765	55,500	2,071	4,532	29,904
Waterford,	22,406	2,397	37,820	12,151	832	2.069	21,232
W Bloomfield,	18.642	5,463	37,621	22,371	1,068	2,782	26,110
White Lake,	25,160	3,140	23,768	8,311	422	826	14,441
Total,	551104	93692	890866	475934	47211	68176	517936

OAKLAND COUNTY — CONTINUED.

ENDING JUNE 1ST, 1860.

Wool, pounds of.	Value of Orchard products.	Butter, pounds of.	Cheese, pounds of.	Hay, tons of.	Clover seed, bushels.	Maple Sugar, pounds.	Value of home made manufactures.
12,855	$1,412	57,205	610	1,59[illegible]	228	670	$441
26,117	5,860	82,550	4,442	2,203	354	110	565
16 931	8,104	49,979	5,500	2,896	460	420	225
13,156	1,230	50,810	.	2,302	226		
15,358	2,223	38,870	1,660	2,513	292		
31,619	10,794	69,215	56,370	[illegible]	92	7,170	446
13,743	3,332	51,145	2,26[illegible]	2,414	301	535	806
9,287	705	35,060	2,11[illegible]	1,853	105		.
15,734	1,933	41,700	910	2,312	98	..	338
12,919	1,497	55,213	3,211	2,079	357	662	803
22,572	4,511	45,896	4,638	2,749	379	5,637	.
17,954	2,467	40,645	4,585	2,780	140	. ...	50
27,835	7,619	48,890	7,230	2,710	223	11,391	623
14,709	3,315	71,752	1,330	2,059	336	500	642
11,333	1,127	44,640	1,360	2,417	397	.	...
17,189	1,408	53,990	980	2,174	145		75
17,645	4,580	60,970	2,750	3,139	220	. .	
13,217	1,354	47,400	2,404	2,444	379	..	404
8,654	4,173	77,025	3,733	1,806		295	500
21,093	7,816	66,960	5,270	2,004	19	2,045	165
12,880	1,995	49,205	2,259	1,783	158		659
25,783	9,017	125,745	10,825	2,830	78	1,266	467
13,574	3,158	50,600	2,051	2,053	135	. .	255
23,988	6,768	44,970	2,630	2,612	257	780	70
10,651	497	33,306	2,510	1,737	104	..	. .
426,796	96,895	1,393,741	131,633	58735	5483	31,581	$7,535

OAKLAND COUNTY—Continued.

TOWNSHIPS.	Flouring Mills.							Saw Mills.			
			Power used.			Annual product.			Power used.		
	Number of.	Runs of Stone.	Water.	Steam.	Capital invested in real and personal estate in the business.	Bbls. flour made.	Value of.	Number of.	Water.	Steam.	Capital invested in real and personal estate in the business.
Addison,	1		1		$6,000	2,000	13,195				
Avon,	4		4		11,700	2,120	34,460				
Bloomfield,	1		1		5,000	300	4,000				
Brandon,											
Clarkston vil.,	1				10,000	2,000	12,000	1			1,500
Commerce,	1	2	1		8,000	400	9,000				
Farmington,	2		2		13,500	1,750	14,770				
Groveland,											
Highland,											
Holly,											
Holly vil.,	1				17,500	6,666	46,788				
Independence,											
Lyon,											
Milford,	2	6	2		11,000	1,118	8,090				
Novi,											
Oakland,	1		1		2,400	1,260	10,630				
Orion,											
Orion vil.,											
Oxford,											
Pontiac,											
Pontiac vil.,	3		3	1	52,000	29500	147500				
Rose,											
Royal Oak,											
Southfield,								1	1		1,500
Springfield,	1		1	1	10,000	4,500	27,100				
Troy,											
Waterford,	2		2		17,000	7,200	43,323	1	1		1,500
W Bloomfi'ld,											
White Lake,											
Total,	20	8	18	2	164100	58814	370850	3	2		$4,500

OAKLAND COUNTY.—CONTINUED.

SAW MILLS. Annual product.		AGGREGATE OF ALL KINDS OF MANUFACTURES, MILLS INCLUDED.				ESTIMATED VALUE OF REAL AND PERSONAL ESTATE.	
Feet of Lumber Sawed.	Value of.	Capital invested in real and personal estate in the business.	Hands employ'd Males.	Hands employ'd Females.	Value of annual products.	By Assessors.	By assistant Marshals.
		$8,000	4		$17,145		
		37,300	64		75 169		
		16,300	8		15,162		
125,000	1,000	23,700	36	1	39,467		
		15,960	14		16,740		
		24,811	23		32,754		
		850	5		1,798		
		26,178	31		68,846		
		500	2		583		
		33,200	29	8	30,715		
		7,200	10		9,015		
		2,400	1		10,630		
		148,700	138	67	334,500		
150,000	1,200	2,500	3		1,350		
		19,150	21		39,412		
60,000	480	19,325	12		46,786		
335,000	2,680	386,074	401	76	740,070	9953892	13942448

OCEANA COUNTY

TOWNSHIPS.	Dwelling Houses.		Number of Families.	Number of Inhabitants.				
	Whole number.	Number in Cities.		Whole number.	Colored.	Deaf and Dumb.	Blind.	Insane.
Benona,	81	.	79	275	...			
Clay Bank,	88	.	84	276	9	1		1
Elbridge,	71	..	70	237	.			
Greenwood,	24	...	26	83				
Indian Reserve,	132	.	140	463			2	
Otto,	31		31	119	1			
Pentwater,	68		64	244	.			.
Weare,	26	.	25	105				
Total,	521	..	519	1,802	10	1	2	1

ONTONAGON COUNTY

TOWNSHIPS.	Whole number.	Number in Cities.	Number of Families.	Whole number.	Colored.	Deaf and Dumb.	Blind.	Insane.
Algonquin,	16	..	16	77	..			
Greenland,	59		59	336				
Ontonagon,	145	.....	145	1,192	27			
Pewabic,	81	.....	81	109				.
Rockland,	283	..	283	2,861	2		1	.
Total,	684	....	684	4,575	29		1	.

OSCEOLA COUNTY

TOWNSHIPS.	Whole number.	Number in Cities.	Number of Families.	Whole number.	Colored.	Deaf and Dumb.	Blind.	Insane.
Green,	12		9	27				..

OCEANA COUNTY.—Continued.

TOWNSHIPS.	Value of Real Estate owned.	Occupied Farms.			
		Whole number.	Acres improved.	Acres unimproved.	Cash value of.
Benona,	$38,290	16	247	1,496	$8,920
Clay Bank,.	48,920	46	1,245	4,076	42,010
Eldridge,	26,850	19	337	2,033	13,040
Greenwood,	10,500		...	...	..
Indian Reserve,.	27,110		..	..	... .
Otto,	3 350		....	...	.
Pentwater,	35,760		.	.	..
Weare,. .	6,525	2	62	323	3,000
Total, .	$197,305	83	1,891	7,928	$66,970

ONTONAGON COUNTY.—Continued.

TOWNSHIPS.	Value of Real Estate owned.	Whole number.	Acres improved.	Acres unimproved.	Cash value of.
Algonquin,. .	$10,750	6	163	3,223	$8,250
Greenland,	11,600	12	336	2,186	18,000
Ontonagon, .	258,600	29	767	1,951	33,100
Pewabic,	16,300	10	421	5 954	32,700
Rockland, ..	178,050	15	1,158	7,137	71,900
Total, . . .	$475,300	72	2,845	20,451	$163,950

OSCEOLA COUNTY.—Continued.

TOWNSHIPS.	Value of Real Estate owned.	Whole number.	Acres improved.	Acres unimproved.	Cash value of.
Green,	$10,680	3	220	815	$5,200

OCEANA COUNTY.—Continued.

Value of Farming Implements and Machinery.	Live Stock, June 1st, 1860.							
	Horses.	Asses and Mules.	Milch Cows.	Working Oxen.	Other Cattle.	Sheep.	Swine.	Value of Live Stock.
$399	3		23	19	18		39	$1,555
2,131	27		64	54	80	11	96	7,770
455	6		33	20	33		58	2,110
......								
5			2	2	1		4	145
$2,990	36		122	95	132	11	191	$11,580

ONTONAGON COUNTY.—Continued.

Value of Farming Implements and Machinery.	Horses.	Asses and Mules.	Milch Cows.	Working Oxen.	Other Cattle.	Sheep.	Swine.	Value of Live Stock.
$300	4		2	3	2		2	$1,020
525	3		7	4	1			1,070
1,315	35		31	12	9	1	29	5,515
1,100	7		14	10	10		12	2,310
4,250	48	4	13	36	3		89	10,325
$7,490	97	4	67	65	25	1	132	$20,240

OSCEOLA COUNTY.—Continued.

Value of Farming Implements and Machinery.	Horses.	Asses and Mules.	Milch Cows.	Working Oxen.	Other Cattle.	Sheep.	Swine.	Value of Live Stock.
	9		8	8	9		27	$1,370

OCEANA COUNTY.—CONTINUED.

TOWNSHIPS.	PRODUCE, DURING THE YEAR						
	Wheat, bushels of.	Rye, bushels of.	Indian corn, bushels of.	Oats, bushels of.	Barley, bushels of.	Buckwheat, bushels of.	Potatoes, bushels of.
Benona,	65	10	1,525	87	10		1,620
Clay Bank,	1,043	438	5,575	30	11	545	4,918
Elbridge,	305	30	1,853	100			1,545
Greenwood,							
Ind'n Reserve,							
Otto,							
Pentwater,							
Weare,	190	25	420	80			170
Total,	1,603	503	9,373	297	21	545	8,253

ONTONAGON COUNTY.—CONTINUED.

TOWNSHIPS.	Wheat, bushels of.	Rye, bushels of.	Indian corn, bushels of.	Oats, bushels of.	Barley, bushels of.	Buckwheat, bushels of.	Potatoes, bushels of.
Algonquin,							530
Greenland,				90			2,050
Ontonagon,				380	5		4,360
Pewabic,				100			1,150
Rockland,				1,200			10,840
Total,				1,771	5		18,930

OSCEOLA COUNTY.—CONTINUED.

TOWNSHIPS.	Wheat, bushels of.	Rye, bushels of.	Indian corn, bushels of.	Oats, bushels of.	Barley, bushels of.	Buckwheat, bushels of.	Potatoes, bushels of.
Green,	150			500			225

OCEANA COUNTY.—Continued.

ENDING JUNE 1ST, 1860.							
Wool, pounds of.	Value of Orchard products.	Butter, pounds of.	Cheese, pounds of.	Hay, tons of.	Clover seed, bushels.	Maple Sugar, pounds.	Value of home made manufactures.
....	363	1,396	...	19	.	1,825	..
...	633	5,705	100	56	.	8,621	.
..	110	1,900	200	12		5,750	....
...	..					...	...
....	...	..		.		..	..
....	...	..			...	..	..
..	.	.	.			......	
....	20	75		3		125	...
	1,126	9,076	300	90		16,320	......

ONTONAGON COUNTY.—Continued.

Wool, pounds of.	Value of Orchard products.	Butter, pounds of.	Cheese, pounds of.	Hay, tons of.	Clover seed, bushels.	Maple Sugar, pounds.	Value of home made manufactures.
.....	.....	.	.	77		..	..
...	.			131	.		..
....	....	900		374		.....	...
.....	....	300	.....	143		...	.....
.....	...	.	..	343	..	200	......
..	..	1,200	...	1,068		200	.

OSCEOLA COUNTY.—Continued.

Wool, pounds of.	Value of Orchard products.	Butter, pounds of.	Cheese, pounds of.	Hay, tons of.	Clover seed, bushels.	Maple Sugar, pounds.	Value of home made manufactures.
.	..			36		1,500	....

OCEANA COUNTY.—Continued.

TOWNSHIPS.	Flouring Mills.							Saw Mills.			
	Number of.	Runs of Stone.	Power used. Water.	Power used. Steam.	Capital invested in real and personal estate in the business.	Annual product. Bbls. flour made.	Annual product. Value of.	Number of.	Power used. Water.	Power used. Steam.	Capital invested in real and personal estate in the business.
Benona, ...					....	.	. .				....
Clay Bank,					...			2	2		$50000
Elbridge,					...		. .				. .
Greenwood,					.		..				.....
Ind'n Reserve,					.	.	.. .				. ..
Otto, ...					.		.. .				.....
Pentwater,							.	2		2	31,000
Weare, .					.	.					.. ..
Total,					.		. .	4	2	2	$81000

ONTONAGON COUNTY.—Continued.

TOWNSHIPS.	Number of.	Runs of Stone.	Water.	Steam.	Capital.	Bbls. flour made.	Value of.	Number of.	Water.	Steam.	Capital.
Algonquin,					.		. .				. .
Greenland,					..	.	...				....
Ontonagon, .					..	..	.	1		.	$3,000
Pewabic,							....				. ...
Rockland,					..		...	3	1	2	$9,000
Total,. .					.. .	.		4	1	2	$12000

OSCEOLA COUNTY.—Continued.

TOWNSHIPS.	Number of.	Runs of Stone.	Water.	Steam.	Capital.	Bbls. flour made.	Value of.	Number of.	Water.	Steam.	Capital.
Green, . ..					.....	.	.... .	1	1		$2,000

OCEANA COUNTY.—Continued.

Saw Mills. Annual product. Feet of Lumber Sawed.	Saw Mills. Annual product. Value of.	Aggregate of all kinds of Manufactures, Mills included. Capital invested in real and personal estate in the business.	Hands employ'd. Males.	Hands employ'd. Females.	Value of annual product.	Estimated value of Real and Personal Estate. By Assessors.	Estimated value of Real and Personal Estate. By assistant Marshals.
......	..	$2,200	18	6	$6,650	.	.
1,800,000	$8,000	54,000	51	8	12,000	.	..
.....	....	..			.....	..	...
......	...	...			....	..	.
....	...				...		.
....	.				..		..
5,000,000	25,000	31,000	70	8	25,000	...	......
....	....	...					
6,800,000	$38000	$78,200	139	22	$43,650	$505916	.

ONTONAGON COUNTY.—Continued.

Feet of Lumber Sawed.	Value of.	Capital invested.	Males.	Females.	Value of annual product.	By Assessors.	By assistant Marshals.
....		$87,500	41		$11,480	$82,000	$112,000
.....		900,000	65		27,780	101,100	125,000
600,000	$5,400	20,100	23		46,750	311,535	500,000
....	.	573,000	51		14,400	207,730	250,000
1,250,000	15,000	596,600	1239		865,690	549,197	3,500,000
1,850,000	$20400	2177200	1419		$966100	1251563	$4487000

OSCEOLA COUNTY.—Continued.

Feet of Lumber Sawed.	Value of.	Capital invested.	Males.	Females.	Value of annual product.	By Assessors.	By assistant Marshals.
100,000	$800	$2,000	3		$800	.	....

OTTAWA COUNTY

TOWNSHIPS.	Dwelling Houses.		Number of Families.	Number of Inhabitants.				
	Whole number.	Number in Cities.		Whole number.	Colored.	Deaf and Dumb.	Blind.	Insane.
Allendale,	52		52	245				
Blendon,	74		70	381				
Chester,	147		147	721				
Crockery,	118		102	396				
Georgetown,	195		185	973	1			
Holland,	417		419	1,991				
Jamestown,	113		108	519				
Olive,	72		69	317				
Ottawa,	297		289	1,359	23		1	
Polkton,	250		239	1,222		1		
Robinson,	24		25	128				
Spring Lake,	180		155	743	10			1
Tallmadge,	215		212	1,145		2		
Wright,	288		288	1,520				
Zeeland,	321		308	1,467				
Total,	2,763		2,668	13,127	24	3	1	1

PRESQUE ISLE COUNTY

Total,	9		5	26				

OTTAWA COUNTY.—Continued.

Townships.	Value of Real Estate owned.	Occupied Farms. Whole number.	Acres improved.	Acres unimproved.	Cash value of.
Allendale, ...	$74,267	27	989	2,666	$54,400
Blendon, ...	50,224	21	502	1,187	24,400
Chester, ...	189,140	108	3,664	6,144	153,350
Crockery,.	137,020	40	1,632	5,033	89,730
Georgetown, ..	215,595	77	2,405	5,780	117,300
Holland, ..	314,029	134	3,203	4,366	130,210
Jamestown, .	105,355	67	1,336	3,639	72,235
Olive,..	37,360	24	602	1,600	21,900
Ottawa, ...	427,760	15	260	758	9,310
Polkton, ...	292,720	114	3,838	6,407	188,300
Robinson, ...	25,120	6	260	923	11,650
Spring Lake,. ..	127,000	2	90	354	3,000
Tallmadge, . .	354,900	116	4,786	7,572	259,400
Wright, ...	420,245	200	7,927	8,728	378,265
Zeeland, ...	291,640	223	6,028	7,869	246,690
Total,. .	$3,062,375	1,174	37,522	63,026	$1,760,145

PRESQUE ISLE COUNTY.—Continued.

Total, ...	..	..	....	..	.....

OTTAWA COUNTY.—Continued.

Value of Farming Implements and Machinery.	Live Stock, June 1st, 1860.							
	Horses.	Asses and Mules.	Milch Cows.	Working Oxen.	Other Cattle.	Sheep.	Swine.	Value of Live Stock.
$980	23		64	53	145	66	197	$6,622
508	3		41	29	36	2	65	2,509
4,000	139		228	112	397	420	621	21,871
2,110	63		112	46	139	58	208	11,145
4,870	85		192	106	236	100	379	15,685
7,245	88		297	163	388	.....	956	22,632
1,649	35		125	75	138	152	277	9,854
620	16		49	36	73	.....	127	4,250
343	8	2	35	20	18	....	64	2,822
5,110	115	1	300	133	576	407	549	25,070
255	16		19	18	25	30	40	2,305
150	5		6	...	6	....	8	650
6,304	173	4	320	99	506	673	612	31,266
10,805	282		455	186	737	1,354	1,062	45,764
8,537	129		677	245	593	52	1,042	38,941
$53,486	1180	7	2920	1,321	4,011	3,314	6,207	$241,386

PRESQUE ISLE COUNTY.—Continued.

......	.	.	...	. .		. .	...	....

OTTAWA COUNTY.—Continued.

TOWNSHIPS.	Produce, during the Year						
	Wheat, bushels of.	Rye, bushels of.	Indian corn, bushels of.	Oats, bushels of.	Barley, bushels of.	Buckwheat, bushels of.	Potatoes, bushels of.
Allendale,	824	10	3,838	1,008	82	100	1,614
Blendon, .	496	158	925	323	4	23	1,135
Chester,. .	6,177	584	9,255	4,888	135	480	5,595
Crockery, .	1,423	375	2,300	500	95	106	3,765
Georgetown,. .	3,131	396	5,575	2,424	106	252	3,617
Holland, . .	7,095	2,809	8,772	2,733	65	370	4,685
Jamestown, .	1,694	281	6,945	1,570	2	156	2,547
Olive, ...	1,542	379	1,535	751	40	82	1,031
Ottawa,. .	34	270	635	52	5	15	1,615
Polkton, .	3,400	394	7,906	3,786	424	97	4,657
Robinson, . ..	50	40	325			28	480
Spring Lake,	...	.	110	50		60	200
Tallmadge,	7,757	1,941	10,456	7,650	419	147	5,738
Wright,......	13,422	3,214	19,902	13,842	839	478	6,772
Zeeland, .	14,153	4,479	15,319	8,772	672	565	6,858
Total,.. .	61,198	15330	92,798	47,349	2,888	2,959	50,309

PRESQUE ISLE COUNTY.—Continued.

Total,. .				.		..	.....

OTTAWA COUNTY.—Continued.

ENDING JUNE 1ST, 1860.							
Wool, pounds of.	Value of Orchard products.	Butter, pounds of.	Cheese, pounds of.	Hay, tons of.	Clover seed, bushels.	Maple Sugar, pounds.	Value of home made manufactures.
203	$40	4,895	200	379	5	2,190	.
....	..	4,050	.	180		1,850	..
1,028	425	18,043	1,080	787	10	38,780	$236
142	315	8,005	900	760	15	6,970	65
220	343	14,727	810	947		18,494	
..	286	22,930	. .	723	8	908	593
365	92	11,685	460	362	2	15,110	20
		2,890		125		695	..
.....	4	2,000		81		30	
704	188	22,140	1,028	737	20	20,385	90
60	.....	650	200	187		150	.. ..
.....	20	400	.	7		....	.. ...
1,739	1,496	27,065	2,890	1,396	29	25,825	490
3,206	782	35,060	2,180	1,545	3	54,579	593
184	170	53,333	2,080	1,925	3	2,876	......
7,851	$4,151	227,873	11,828	10141	95	188842	$2,087

PRESQUE ISLE COUNTY.—Continued.

..	.					..	.

OTTAWA COUNTY.—Continued.

TOWNSHIPS.	Flouring Mills.							Saw Mills.			
	Number of.	Runs of Stone.	Power used.		Capital invested in real and personal estate in the business.	Annual product.		Number of.	Power used.		Capital invested in real and personal estate in the business.
			Water.	Steam.		Bbls. flour made.	Value of.		Water.	Steam.	
Allendale,					...	.	. .	1		1	10,000
Blendon, ..					. ...	.	...	1		1	8,000
Chester,						.	.	1	1		1,000
Crockery, ..					.. .	.	....	*4	2	2	47,000
Georgetown,					...	.	..	3	1	2	65,000
Holland, ..	1			1	10,000	8,000	40,000	3	1	2	19,100
Jamestown, .					....		....	1	1		1,400
Olive, ...					.. .		....				...
Ottawa, . .			.		.		.....	2		2	21,500
Polkton, .					..	.	.	*4		4	51,500
Robinson,.							. .				. ...
Spring Lake,					.		..	†6		6	99,500
Tallmadge,	*2		1		11,000	3,000	14,000	6	3	3	37,200
Wright, .	1		1		3,000		8,500	1	..	1	3,000
Zeeland,.					..						... ..
Total,.	4		2	1	24,000	11000	62,500	33	9	24	334200

PRESQUE ISLE COUNTY.—Continued.

Total,	.	.			. .		.			.	..

* One at rest. † Two at rest.

OTTAWA COUNTY.—Continued.

Saw Mills.		Aggregate of all kinds of Manufactures, Mills included.				Estimated value of Real and Personal Estate.	
Annual product.			Hands employ'd				
Feet of Lumber Sawed.	Value of.	Capital invested in real and personal estate in the business.	Males.	Females.	Value of annual products.	By Assessors.	By assistant Marshals.
800,000	$4,000	$10,000	12		$4,000	$69,151	$92,200
1,300,000	7,800	8,000	12		7,800	59,385	200 000
200,000	1,500	1,000	3		1,500	83,710	111,613
5,000,000	30,000	47,000	34		30,000	89,846	119,794
7,050,000	56,700	85,000	87		66,700	136,597	300,000
3,200,000	19,200	36,800	46		79,400	185,343	247,124
200,000	1,600	1,400	2		1,600	117,000	290,000
....	.				.	48,562	64,749
6,200,000	37,200	48,500	46		70,200	317,181	400,180
2,900,000	22,840	41,425	56		44,240	175,707	234,276
......	.	.			..	79,057	105,409
18,000,000	108000	134,300	158		196,200	111,330	148,440
4,450,000	23,300	49,000	26		39,550	213,859	285,136
200,000	1,200	8,000	10		13,930	144,538	194,538
....	...	.			...	170,000	320,000
49,500,000	313340	470,425	492		555,120	2001259	3,113,459
PRESQUE ISLE COUNTY.—Continued.							
....	...	$50	1		$100	......	....

SAGINAW COUNTY

TOWNSHIPS.	Dwelling Houses.		Number of Families.	Number of Inhabitants.				
	Whole number.	Number in Cities.		Whole number.	Colored.	Deaf and Dumb.	Blind.	Insane.
Birch Run,	124		123	703				
Blumfield,	119		119	557				
Brady,	68		62	279				
Brant,	20		20	88				
Bridgeport,	95		95	491	1			
Buena Vista,	46		48	232				
Chesaning,	116		107	539				
E.Saginaw, 3 wards	598	598	572	3,005	21	3	1	
Frankinmuth,	220		220	1,120				1
Fremont,	13		12	62				
Kochville,	146		146	658				
Maple Grove,	47		46	201				
Saginaw,	147		147	880				
City, 3 wards,	339		339	1,699	7		1	
Spaulding,	34		34	216				
St. Charles,	147		147	605		1	1	
Taymouth,	59		59	269				
Thomaston,	97		97	480				
Tittabawassee,	107		106	514				
Zilwaukie,	35		34	160				
Total,	2,577	937	2,510	12,758	29	4	3	1

SAGINAW COUNTY.—Continued.

TOWNSHIPS.	Value of Real Estate owned.	Occupied Farms.			
		Whole number.	Acres improved.	Acres unimproved.	Cash value of.
Birch Run,	$78,125	22	636	1,674	$25,500
Blumfield,	45,693	77	1,508	5,096	35,230
Brady,	19,150	3	104	555	2,600
Brant,	5,700	1	100	635	2,200
Bridgeport,	102,300	22	1,065	1,946	46,700
Buena Vista,	58,100	22	722	1,173	26,900
Chesaning,	73,340	11	707	3,864	24,600
E. Saginaw, 3 w.,	935,965				..
Fankinmuth,	203,760	134	3,861	5,563	143,100
Fremont,	3,350	1	20	200	700
Kochville,	42,295	84	1,265	4,231	30,264
Maple Grove,	15,960	3	70	420	2,700
Saginaw,	163,280	55	2,689	3,947	120,500
City, 3 wards,	653 350		... ...	..	......
Spaulding,	106,600	12	668	443	34,500
St. Charles,	33,355	8	213	1,884	7,400
Taymouth,	28,610	11	605	1;100	16,500
Thomaston,	97,370	41	1,612	3·521	60,760
Tittabawassec,	117,710	57	2,079	3,616	85,500
Zilwaukie,	25 400		...	.. ..	....
Total,	$2,809,413	564	17,924	40,368	$665,654

SAGINAW COUNTY.—Continued.

Value of Farming Implements and Machinery.	Live Stock, June 1st, 1860. Horses.	Asses and Mules.	Milch Cows.	Working Oxen.	Other Cattle.	Sheep.	Swine.	Value of Live Stock.
$2,850	14		52	49	84	..	93	$3,700
3,826	74		186	104	250		329	10,268
255	3		11	16	13		18	795
200	2		3	2	4		2	400
3,670	58		79	30	131	154	105	6,170
3,050	27		70	37	106	3	107	5,050
1,510	21		33	18	65	142	47	3,875
10,414	121		357	208	366	80	610	19,260
75			4	2	10		5	250
4,933	41		222	135	347	24	321	10,723
100	2		10	4	10	13	11	600
9,330	117		206	56	311	572	320	23,775
1,675	33		42	14	62	2	74	3,775
205	2		19	16	42	15	26	1,650
1,550	39		36	26	63	28	72	2,875
5,070	73		128	60	199	224	234	14,005
6,500	88		147	70	217	174	308	16,830
$55,213	715		1605	847	2,480	1,431	2,682	$124,001

SAGINAW COUNTY.—Continued.

TOWNSHIPS.	Produce, during the Year						
	Wheat, bushels of.	Rye, bushels of.	Indian corn, bushels of.	Oats, bushels of.	Barley, bushels of.	Buckwheat, bushels of.	Potatoes, bushels of.
Birch Run,	437	385	2,026	795	10	10	1,621
Blumfield,	3,445	1,838	10,465	8,785	278	.	6,296
Brady, ...	51		220	80			125
Brant, .	.		50	175			60
Bridgeport,	1,482	705	2,870	2,230	130	.	1,912
Buena Vista,.	425	533	1,545	2,065	2	35	1,208
Chesaning,	995		2,860	200	40		980
E. Saginaw,				.			. . .
Frankinmuth,	5,268	2,810	3,749	11,231	243	33	5,012
Fremont,	. . .		50	.			50
Kochville,	3,255	2,805	6,275	1,867	179		7,790
Maple Grove,	40		350	200	.	.	250
Saginaw,	5,805	1,738	6,213	5,680	200	..	6,190
City, 3 wards,				.		.	..
Spaulding,.	875	461	1,650	1,020		49	871
St. Charles,.	....		385	25			660
Taymouth,.	690	260	3,110	1,645	80		1,627
Thomaston,.	4,778	746	8,865	2,897	20	.	4,112
Tittabawassee	4,192	971	6,561	3,138		27	3,542
Zilwaukie,	.		.....			.	. . .
Total,	31,739	13252	57,244	42,027	1,182	154	42,306

SAGINAW COUNTY.—Continued.

Ending June 1st, 1860.							
Wool, pounds of.	Value of Orchard products.	Butter, pounds of.	Cheese, pounds of.	Hay, tons of.	Clover seed, bushels.	Maple Sugar, pounds.	Value of home made manufactures.
......	.	3,350	.. ..	250	.	....	.... ..
......	....	17,700	....	687	..	..	......
......	....	800	.....	20		1,300	......
......	. .	.	.....	12	.	..	. . .
326	.....	6,550	.....	477	.	. ..	. . . .
......	.	4,900	.....	178	..	.. ..	.. ....
400	.. .	1,900	....	166	.	2,700	.. ...
......	. .	..	.....			...	.....
183	. .	26,035	400	11 27		.. .	. .
......	....	. .	.....	10	.	400	......
50	.....	15,005	.....	813		..	....
50	. .	600	. . .	29	3	1,200	... ..
1,707	...	12,395	500	889	5	1,500	. . .
......	....	...	.....	..	. .		. ..
......	....	3,090	800	260	.	.	. .....
40	.....	600	.....	66	..	...	...
60	.....	2,775	.....	177	..	...	......
480	..	8,400	.....	489	.	350	....
380	....	9,265	....	627	.	1,414	....
.....	.. .		. . .	..	.	..	......
3,682	.....	113,365	1,700	6,295	8	8,864	....

SAGINAW COUNTY.—Continued.

TOWNSHIPS.	Flouring Mills.							Saw Mills.			
	Number of.	Runs of Stone.	Power used.		Capital invested in real and personal estate in the business.	Annual product.		Number of.	Power used.		Capital invested in real and personal estate in the business.
			Water.	Steam.		Bbls. flour made.	Value of.		Water.	Steam.	
Birch Run,											
Blumfield,											
Brady,											
Brant,											
Bridgeport,											
Buena Vista,											
Chesaning,								3	3		$9,000
E. Saginaw,	2	6		2	$33000	11000	$91500	6		6	113000
Frankinmuth,											
Fremont,											
Kochville,											
Maple Grove,											
Saginaw,								4		4	175000
City, 3 wards	1			1	10,000	1,500	10,000	2		2	62,000
Spaulding,								3		3	68,000
St. Charles,								3		3	109000
Taymouth,											
Thomaston,											
Tittabawassee								1		1	3,000
Zilwaukie,								1		1	20,000
Total,	3	8		3	$43000	12500	101500	23	3	20	559000

SAGINAW COUNTY.—Continued.

Saw Mills. Annual product.		Aggregate of all kinds of Manufactures, Mills included.				Estimated value of Real and Personal Estate.	
Feet of Lumber Sawed.	Value of.	Capital invested in real and personal estate in the business.	Hands employ'd: Males.	Hands employ'd: Females.	Value of annual product.	By Assessors.	By assistant Marshals.
...	...					...	...
...	...					...	...
...	...	...					...
...	...	...			...		...
...		...			...		
...		...				...	
2,000,000	$14000	$9,000	11		$14,000	...	...
16,800,000	161500	202,500	201	2	317,820		...
...	...	...			...	...	...
...	...				...		...
...	...						...
...		...			...	...	...
13,500,000	111500	175,000	97		111,500	...	...
8,000 000	61 200	77,000	63		78,900		...
6,500 000	51,000	68,000	38		51,000		...
16,000,000	156100	109,000	68	3	156,100		...
...	...	...			...	...	...
...					...		...
300 000	2 800	3,000	4		2,800		...
3.000.000	18 000	20 000	30		18.000	...	...
66,100,000	576100	$663500	512	5	$750120	2006831	$3910246

SANILAC COUNTY.

TOWNSHIPS.	Dwelling Houses. Whole number.	Number in Cities.	Number of Families.	Number of Inhabitants. Whole number.	Colored.	Deaf and Dumb.	Blind.	Insane.
Austin, ...	77	. . ..	74	302				1
Bridgehampton, .	79	. ...	74	305	.			..
Buell, ...	39	. ...	35	176				.
Delaware,.......	103	.... .	95	437	.			..
Elk,......... ...	54	..	51	229				..
Forester, ...	66	. ...	60	375				.
Fremont,..	51	.....	46	223				.
Lexington, . . .	251	.....	244	1,378	..			.
Lexington village,	147	.....	143	690	..			1
Marion,....... .	49	.. .	45	197	.			..
Marlette, ...	50	. .	48	196	.			..
Maple Valley,. .	27	.....	27	132	.			..
Sanilac,...... .	252	...	237	1,205	.			.
Speaker,... ..	72	....,	68	326	.			..
Washington, .	44	....	41	173				.
Worth, ...	211	....	210	1,279				.
Total, ...	1,572	. .	1,498	7,623	..			2

SCHOOLCRAFT COUNTY

TOWNSHIPS.	Dwelling Houses. Whole number.	Number in Cities.	Number of Families.	Number of Inhabitants. Whole number.	Colored.	Deaf and Dumb.	Blind.	Insane.
Grand Island, ..	14	. .	9	43	..			...
Munsing & M'n L'd.	14	....	5	35	4		1	..
Total, ...	28	......	14	78	4	..	1	..

SANILAC COUNTY.—Continued.

TOWNSHIPS.	Value of Real Estate owned.	Occupied Farms.			
		Whole number.	Acres improved.	Acres unimproved.	Cash value of.
Austin, ..	$27,300	44	687	5,271	$18,450
Bridgehampton,	21,250	18	376	1,036	7,400
Buell, ...	10,000	5	218	227	3,100
Delaware, ...	29,700	14	332	1,718	7,050
Elk, ...	11,850	9	300	1,005	4,800
Forester, ...	45,030	2	60	540	1,900
Fremont, ...	14,225	3	150	270	2,200
Lexington, . .	140,730	98	4,620	5,814	118,100
" vil., .	149,450				
Marion, .	10,150	7	159	1,156	3,700
Marlette, ...	18,200	7	320	2,030	5,400
Maple Valley, .	7,400	6	178	757	3,300
Sanilac,	94,700	48	1,014	2,097	25,650
Speaker, ...	28,530	6	181	624	3,400
Washington,	32,600	14	501	2,500	20,500
Worth, . .	216,200	127	6,277	7,412	201,240
Total, ...	$857,315	408	15,378	32,457	$426,190

SCHOOLCRAFT COUNTY.—Continued.

Grand Island,	$21,800		. . . .	.	. .
Muns'g & M'n L'd,	6,400		. . .	. . . .	. . . .
Total, .	$28,200		. . . .	. .	.

SANILAC COUNTY.—CONTINUED.

Value of Farming Implements and Machinery.	Live Stock, June 1st, 1860. Horses.	Asses and Mules.	Milch Cows.	Working Oxen.	Other Cattle.	Sheep.	Swine.	Value of Live Stock.
$335	11		51	57	1	12	71	$1,780
110	5		23	22	14	..	20	1,105
30	2		13	6	10	...	9	470
217	9		26	22	29	[illegible]	43	1,430
98	9		20	14	10	....	14	1,150
40	2		8	2	20	....	10	300
85	.		11	6	17	73	15	390
4,065	185		249	81	276	582	353	14,975
....			.			...	....	...
53	4		11	8	7	...	25	540
125	5		21	11	16	..	11	935
70	7		10	10	14	...	18	595
954	38		87	46	45	94	104	4,705
67	2		16	12	15	..	4	790
260	18		37	24	1	37	30	2,100
8,110	271		339	100	508	839	515	22,480
$14,619	568		922	421	1,006	1,640	1,242	$53,745

SCHOOLCRAFT COUNTY.—CONTINUED.

.	.		.			...	.....	
...	.			.		..	. ..	....
. ..	...		..	....	.	...	.....	.. .

SANILAC COUNTY.—Continued.

TOWNSHIPS.	Produce, during the Year						
	Wheat, bushels of.	Rye, bushels of.	Indian corn, bushels of.	Oats, bushels of.	Barley, bushels of.	Buckwheat, bushels of.	Potatoes, bushels of.
Austin, . .	1,477		430	973	.	10	2,622
Bridgehampt'n	570	.	60	592	.	.	1,505
Buell, ..	125	..	..	56		40	220
Delaware,	305	.	177	645		20	635
Elk, ...	115	.	.....	1,055		50	1,220
Forester, .	...	...	25	75		..	200
Fremont, ...	140	.	....	540		45	450
Lexington,	7,998	35	2,900	13,697	50	499	7,786
" vil..	.	.	..	. .			.....
Marion, ..	268	:	..	50	.		840
Marlette,	375	.	40	421		20	690
Maple Valley,	110		155	405		18	265
Sanilac, ...	1,404	225	1 430	1,28		87	3,017
Speaker,	240	.	180	290			230
Washington,	736		280	1,160	: .	15	730
Worth, . .	10.851	50	3 570	24.950	.	309	9,959
Total, . .	24,714	310	9,247	46,184	50	1,113	30,369

SCHOOLCRAFT COUNTY.—Continued.

TOWNSHIPS.	Wheat	Rye	Indian corn	Oats	Barley	Buckwheat	Potatoes
Grand Island..	.	.	.	....	...	.	.....
Muns'g & M. L		.	..	. .		.	.....
Total,....	......	....	......	......	.....	.	....

SANILAC COUNTY.—Continued.

ENDING JUNE 1ST, 1860.							
Wool, pounds of.	Value of Orchard products.	Butter, pounds of.	Cheese, pounds of.	Hay, tons of.	Clover seed, bushels.	Maple Sugar, pounds.	Value of home made manufactures.
......	...	300	...	83		50	....
......	...		....	30		45	...
.....	..	.	......	20	.	400	..
10	.	..	....	36		195	..
.....	.	150	..	74		....	..
...	.		.	15		..	.
65	..		...	20	..	250	.
1,657	$25	7,605	230	509		.	....
....	..				.		....
.....	.	.	.	18	.		..
......	..	...		26		1,100	....
.....		..	.	18		750	.....
340	...	500	..	163		....	....
....	...	.	...	28	..	..	....
94	.	300	.	40		800	....
2,692	10	10,710	200	836		200	....
4,858	$35	19,565	430	1,928		4,195	....

SCHOOLCRAFT COUNTY.—Continued.

.....	....	...	....	.		......	.....
......	...	..	...	.		...	.....
......	.....	....	.....	..	..	.....	....

SANILAC COUNTY—Continued.

Townships.	Flouring Mills.							Saw Mills.			
	Number of.	Runs of Stone.	Power used.		Capital invested in real and personal estate in the business.	Annual product		Number of.	Power used.		Capital invested in real and personal estate in the business.
			Water	Steam.		Bbls. flour made.	Value of.		Water.	Steam.	
Austin,											
Br'dg'hampt'n											
Buell,											
Delaware,											
Elk,											
Forester,								1		1	25,000
Eremont,											
Lexington,	1		1		2,000	300	3,000	2		2	20,000
" vil.,											
Marion,								1		1	7,000
Marlette,											
Maple Valley											
Sanilac,								1		1	10,000
Speaker,											
Washington,								1	1		3,000
Worth,	1		1		5,000	2,400	12,000	3	2	1	10,500
Total,	2		2		$7,000	2,700	15,000	9	3	6	75,500

SCHOOLCRAFT COUNTY—Continued.

Townships.	Number of.	Runs of Stone.	Water	Steam.	Capital	Bbls. flour made.	Value of.	Number of.	Water.	Steam.	Capital
Grand Island Mun'g & M. L											
Total,											

SANILAC COUNTY.—Continued.

Saw Mills.		Aggregate of all kinds of manufactures, Mills included.				Estimated value of Real and Personal Estate.	
Annual product.			Hands employ'd				
Feet of Lumber Sawed.	Value of.	Capital invested in real and personal estate in the business.	Males.	Females.	Value of annual products.	By Assessors.	By assistant Marshals.
4,000,000	35,000	$25,000	40		$35,000		
4,000,000	35,000	26,800	41		50,000		
2,000,000	18,000	7,000	10		18,000		
3,000,000	25,000	10,000	15		25.000		
300,000	3,000	3.000	2		3,000		
2,400,000	23.200	15.500	19		35 200		
18,700,000	139200	$87,300	127		166,200	1456939	1,456,939

SCHOOLCRAFT COUNTY.—Continued.

Feet of Lumber Sawed.	Value of.	Capital invested	Males.	Females.	Value of annual products.	By Assessors.	By assistant Marshals.
.....	.....	.....			.....	250,579	$500,000

SHIAWASSEE COUNTY 1 2

TOWNSHIPS.	Dwelling Houses.		Number of Families.	Number of Inhabitants.				
	Whole number.	Number in Cities.		Whole number.	Colored.	Deaf and Dumb.	Blind.	Insane.
Antrim,	140	...	138	640				
Bennington,	185	.....	174	895				
Burns,	239	...	215	1,067				
Caledonia,	138	....	128	1,203				
Corunna village,	158	....	138	864				
Fairfield,	71	.....	70	340				
Hazelton,	77	.....	71	350				
Middlebury,	126	.	120	616	8			1
New Haven,	101	....	96	448				
Owosso,	120	....	112	573				
City, 1st ward,	105	105	98	523	2			
" 2d ward,	61	61	58	207	2			1
" 3d ward,	33	33	28	172				
" 4th ward,	46	46	41	227				
Perry,	140	.....	130	670				
Rush,	72	.....	63	346				
Sciota,	111	.....	99	499			1	
Shiawassee,	260	.....	227	1,146				1
Venice,	134	.....	115	575				
Vernon,	224	.....	207	1,100			1	
Woodbull,	109	...	103	387		1		
Total,	2,656	245	2,432	12,888	12	1	2	3

SHIAWASSEE COUNTY.—Continued.

TOWNSHIPS.	Value of Real Estate owned.	Occupied Farms.			
		Whole number.	Acres Improved.	Acres unimproved.	Cash value of.
Antrim,	$132,000	46	2 320	4,201	97,170
Bennington,	290,880	72	5,478	7,496	240,000
Burns,	311,186	85	5,899	5,790	209,855
Caledonia,	185,780	55	2,748	4,250	136,320
Corunna village,	284,975	.		..	.
Fairfield,	45,940	30	755	1,840	34,650
Hazelton,	57,550	64	1,100	3,992	57,950
Middlebury,	141,755	41	2,150	2.485	108,150
New Haven,	96 660	76	1,574	4,857	74,850
Owosso,	119,300	32	1,615	2,543	95,500
City, 1st ward,	673,550		.....	.	.....
" 2d ward,	81,550		....	.....	.
" 3d ward,	19 700	.		.	.
" 4th ward,	49,700		.	.	.
Perry,	209,135	61	4,117	4.609	151,720
Rush,	58,985	40	1 049	1,325	46,375
Sciota,	162 785	59	2,946	4,222	118,809
Shiawassee,	345 771	81	4 398	6,636	247,400
Venice,	91 980	25	1,388	1,373	58,260
Vernon,	270,790	66	2 837	4 674	140,325
Woodhull,	144,720	59	3 333	6 525	140,500
Total,	$3,774,702	892	43,727	66,818	$1,957,834

SHIAWASSEE COUNTY.—CONTINUED.

Value of Farming Implements and Machinery.	Live Stock, June 1st, 1860.							
	Horses.	Asses and Mules.	Milch Cows.	Working Oxen.	Other Cattle.	Sheep.	Swine.	Value of Live Stock.
$4,704	97		152	96	243	1,280	310	$19,022
12,167	210		284	140	387	2,88[illegible]	712	39,908
11,129	189		304	136	493	3,493	602	39,221
5,180	135	1	221	66	210	515	291	20,270
......			.	.	.	.	.....	.
1,008	17		71	52	90	69	94	5,340
1,386	32		117	74	115	89	180	8,488
2,905	59		111	59	139	318	191	11,891
2,645	52		160	80	165	121	233	11,690
3,780	84		114	32	212	409	184	13,526
....						.	....	. .
....						. .		. . .
. . ..			.	..		. . .	...	. .
..				. . .				. .
8,723	144		243	133	438	2,164	491	32,236
1,980	33		93	46	130	108	111	6,491
4,907	9[illegible]		167	109	264	919	328	20,784
8,656	23[illegible]		302	119	886	3,299	509	27,615
2,453	9[illegible]		74	24	146	351	154	10,492
5,490	139		281	94	406	1,697	402	29,069
7,847	171		214	127	308	1,862	364	30,680
$84,968	1793	1	2908	1,387	4,132	19,379	5,156	$326,724

SHIAWASSEE COUNTY.—Continued.

TOWNSHIPS.	Produce, during the Year						
	Wheat, bushels of.	Rye, bushels of.	Indian corn, bushels of.	Oats, bushels of.	Barley, bushels of.	Buckwheat, bushels of.	Potatoes, bushels of.
Antrim,	6,640	340	4,100	1,543	80	170	2,741
Bennington, .	16,241	2,054	9,491	4 628	280	247	6,424
Burns, . .	11,542	737	11,230	6,355	300	250	9,154
Caledonia, .	3,941	180	6,135	2,634	669	293	4,223
Corunna vil.,.	...		.	.	.		...
Fairfield,	958	68	1,518	317		70	877
Hazelton,. .	620	48	3,290	700	4	93	1,707
Middlebury,	5,934	450	3.955	890	268	3[illegible]	1,423
New Haven,	734	100	3,54[illegible]	816		91	1,772
Owosso, .	2,471	123	3,260	2,443	339	117	2,085
City, 1st ward.	.. .		.. ..	....		.	......
" 2d ward.	.	..	.....	.			.....
" 3d ward.			....	. .	..		. ...
" 4th ward.	.		..	. .		.	.. ..
Perry, ...	10,154		7,256	3,816	13[illegible]	112	3,750
Rush, ...	938	40	2,023	956		27	1,014
Sciota, ...	8,327	578	3,780	2 923	101	188	3,230
Shiawassee,	12 926	988	12,753	5,943	179	331	5,141
Venice, ...	2,518	9	4,150	2,890	341	290	1,650
Vernon, ...	5,561	50	8,130	4,091	793	331	3,328
Woodhull, .	11,596	8	8,845	9,120	33	187	5,680
Total,	101101	5,773	93,467	43,071	3,829	2,830	54,199

SHIAWASSEE COUNTY.—Continued.

Ending June 1st, 1860.							
Wool, pounds of.	Value of Orchard products.	Butter, pounds of.	Cheese, pounds of.	Hay, tons of.	Clover seed, bushels.	Maple Sugar, pounds.	Value of home made manufactures.
3,214	511	12 314	726	720		527	$159
7,807	1,8[illegible]	25 893	1,33[illegible]	1.574		10,425	524
8,154	765	24 344	1,[illegible]	1,424	11	790	108
1,942	382	16,178	1,730	850	12	10,767	244
....	...	.	.	.		.	...
202	. .	6,450	300	265		7,685	31
217	...	9,280	.. .	273	3	11,597	76
433	10	9.270	765	41.	5	4,480	15
757	52	13,858	640	524	. .	9,46.	12
1,051	.	12,510	750	489	.	4,320	215
.....	...	.	.....	.	.	. ..	......
......	.		. ...	.	.	...	. ...
......		.	.. .		..	....	. ....
.....	. ..		... .		. .	.. ..	. . ....
5,674	1,054	19.899	620	1,341	9	5.78[illegible]	222
228	....	7,700	.. .	253	4	4,141	30
1,799	295	16,500	1,175	854	13	3.695	339
6,608	2,442	22,964	5,180	1,604	26	7,810	425
1,058	57	7,990	778	309	8	3 2 [illegible]	383
3,238	480	26.364	2,686	53	.	11,980	424
4.388	1,030	19.497	840	1,173	13	15	121
46,770	8,976	251,011	18,582	12579	104	96,723	$3,328

SHIAWASSEE COUNTY.—Continued.

TOWNSHIPS.	Flouring Mills.							Saw Mills.			
	Number of.	Runs of Stone.	Power used.		Capital invested in real and personal estate in the business.	Annual product.		Number of.	Power used.		Capital invested in real and personal estate in the business.
			Water.	Steam.		Bbls. flour made.	Value of.		Water.	Steam.	
Antrim,							..	1	2		$5,000
Bennington,					.		.	1		1	3,000
Burns,	1	2	1		$10000	9,412	$50025	1	1		3,000
Caledonia,	1	2	1		8,000	.		1	1		1,500
Corunna vil.,					...		....				.....
Fairfield,					. ..		.				.....
Hazelton,					.	.	..				.. ..
Middlebury,					. . .		. .	1		1	5,000
Hew Haven,					. .	.	. .	1	1		2,000
Owosso,					... ..		..				. ...
City, 1st ward,					.....	. .	....				...
" 2d ward					..	.	.....				.....
" 3d ward,					.		.. ..				....
" 4th ward,	*1	3	1		47,000	10372	65,803	2		2	6,500
Perry, ...					....	. .	.				......
Rush, ...					..		.. .				......
Sciota,. .					. .		..				......
Shiawassee,	2	3	2		33,500	†6000	†38000	2	2		6,000
Venice, .					.	.	.				. .
Vernon,			.		.			1		1	1,500
Woodhull,											...
Total,	5	10	5		$98500	25784	153828	11	6	5	$33500

* Whole city. † Of one.

SHIAWASSEE COUNTY.—Continued.

Saw Mills.		Aggregate of all kinds of Manufactures, Mills included.				Estimated value of Real and Personal Estate.	
Annual product.			Hands employ'd				
Feet of Lumber Sawed.	Value of.	Capital invested in real and personal estate in the business.	Males.	Females.	Value of annual product.	By Assessors.	By assistant Marshals.
200,000	$1,400	$5,000	2		$1,400		...
400,000	4,000	3,000	3		4,000	.	...
...	2,400	17,000	12		57,625		...
...	...	21,400	29	4	†29,832	...	...
...	...				...	...	...
...	...	...	...		...	...	...
...	...	...			...	...	...
500,000	*40000	5,000	10	4	40,000	...	...
100,000	* 8,000	2,000	4	3	8,000	...	...
...	...	...			...	...	...
...	...	...			...	...	...
...	...	...			...	...	...
...	...	...			...	...	...
1,200,000	8,800	84,100	52	2	110,523	...	...
...	...	...			...	...	...
...	...	...			...	...	...
...	...	...			...	...	...
‡350,000	3,600	39,500	8		41,600	...	...
...	...	...			...	...	...
250,000	2,500	1,500	3		2,500	...	...
...	...	...			...		...
2,900,000	$34700	$178500	123	13	$295480	2346756	$4325000

* As returned, evidently a mistake. † Exclusive of mills. ‡ Whole city.

ST CLAIR COUNTY.

TOWNSHIPS.	Dwelling Houses.		Number of Families.	Number of Inhabitants.				
	Whole number.	Number in Cities.		Whole number.	Colored.	Deaf and Dumb.	Blind.	Insane.
Berlin, ...	202	..	19[illegible]	1,032	4			1
Brockway,..... ..	148	....	134	749				..
Burchville,.... ..	315	..	307	1,80[illegible]	.	4		..
Casco, . ,.......	24[illegible]	....	232	1,085	..			.
China, ...	247	.. .	259	1,340				..
Clay,...........	232	. .	199	1,085				.
Clyde, ...	222	..	202	1,129	.	2		2
Columbus, ...	185	. ..	18[illegible]	1,03[illegible]	1			.
Cottrelville,. ..	29[illegible]	...	28[illegible]	1,531	.			.
East China, .	57	...	57	31[illegible]				1
Emmet, ...	13[illegible]	....	12[illegible]	647	.			1
Greenwood,.... .	114	...	105	538			1	.
Ira, .	20	...	200	1,130	.			.
Kenokee, . ..	14[illegible]	...	14[illegible]	778		[illegible]		..
Kimball, .	16	....	149	838		2		
Lynn, ...	5[illegible]	..	4	225	..			.
Mussey,. . . .	104	..	80	441			1	.
Port Huron, ...	271		264	1,494	[illegible]	3		1
City, 1st ward,..	210	210	207	1,160	.	[illegible]		..
" 2d ward, ..	198	198	19[illegible]	99[illegible]	[illegible]			.
" 3d ward,	248	248	23	1,200	14	1		.
" 4th ward, .	209	209	190	1,021	.	1		..
Riley, ...	200	....	18[illegible]	938				..
St. Clair, ...	297	...	29[illegible]	1,688				...
City, 1st ward,	142	142	140	904	[illegible]			1
" 2d ward,	170	170	164	760	..	1		..
Wales, ...	167	.	160	903	..	1	.	1
Total,.. .	5,170	1,177	4,950	26,814	30	19	2	8

ST. CLAIR COUNTY.—CONTINUED.

TOWNSHIPS.	Value of Real Estate owned.	Occupied Farms.			
		Whole number.	Acres improved.	Acres unimproved.	Cash value of.
Berlin,	$288,650	133	6,541	8,684	$270,150
Brockway,	183,088	48	3,107	4,957	112,700
Burchville,	317,353	87	4,408	5,608	187,378
Casco,	117,280	31	1,204	1,088	45,500
China,	280,245	62	2,483	2,932	130,400
Clay,	194,935	50	1,513	4,338	73,900
Clyde,	285,004	52	3,639	7,068	166,114
Columbus,	216,100	53	2,698	3,798	134,450
Cottrelville,	254,455	54	2,666	5,117	171,400
East China,	118,100	29	2,095	1,970	164,000
Emmet,	98,120	16	677	1,741	27,100
Greenwood,	84,850	16	626	1,662	24,300
Ira,	111,365	51	1,432	2,876	61,450
Kenokee,	121,250	18	911	1,366	32,600
Kimball,	173,480	16	1,264	3,164	66,100
Lynn,	35,050	14	479	1,155	17,000
Mussey,	76,090	10	400	760	13,200
Port Huron,	257,155	26	1,620	2,288	116,000
City, 1st ward,	410,950	.	.	....	.
" 2d ward,	882,400	.	..	....	....
" 3d ward,	347,860		......	.....	.
" 4th ward,	394,395	.	......	.. .	....
Riley,	255,060	82	4,189	5,334	179,600
St. Clair,	444,690	68	2,887	4,560	192,700
City, 1st ward,	319,700			.....	...
" 2d ward,	296,970	10	630	1,209	54,900
Wales,	155,426	29	1,433	1,865	70,200
Total,	$6,720,021	955	46,902	73,540	$2,311,142

ST CLAIR COUNTY.—Continued.

Value of Farming Implements and Machinery.	Live Stock, June 1st, 1860.							
	Horses.	Asses and Mules.	Milch Cows.	Working Oxen.	Other Cattle.	Sheep.	Swine.	Value of Live Stock.
$14,34[illegible]	326		370	86	624	1,816	513	$47,707
5.938	113		132	68	132	286	164	17,493
6,332	207		246	72	290	548	275	24,381
2,025	61		91	22	1,188	280	102	6,980
5,372	172		214	36	260	79[illegible]	241	17,020
2,475	182		223	34	231	542	200	15,279
5,935	150		157	52	205	1,110	172	20,913
5,392	172		214	51	232	1,023	250	22,685
7,036	149		201	24	171	1,322	200	16,171
5,485	130	9	127	4	139	817	142	15,015
1,420	25		44	20	35	16	50	4,372
1,912	23		47	18	59	3	47	4,857
2,991	116		162	45	203	297	196	11,141
1,240	39		46	16	46	35	77	4,340
2,710	54	1	60	47	108	66	93	9,068
1,032	19		32	14	39	45	28	3,139
995	11		25	14	31	15	25	2,546
3,248	77		86	20	89	194	72	10,158
…	…			…	…	…	…	…
…				…		…	…	…
…				…		…	…	…
…			…			…	…	…
8,705	159		227	76	277	649	269	26,124
6,865	174		220	74	226	697	212	24,010
…	…		…	…		…	…	…
1,900	35		36	10	55	100	17	5,170
3.264	94		85	24	97	55	108	10,656
$96,620	2488	11	3045	827	4,737	10,709	3,452	$319,225

ST. CLAIR COUNTY.—Continued.

TOWNSHIPS.	Produce, during the Year						
	Wheat, bushels of.	Rye, bushels of.	Indian corn, bushels of.	Oats, bushels of.	Barley, bushels of.	Buckwheat, bushels of.	Potatoes, bushels of.
Berlin, ...	5,719	641	21,332	21,705	304	840	13,335
Brockway,..	1,934	29[illegible]	2,648	3,547	130	710	4,337
Burchville, ..	7,760	70	5,074	9,730		394	8,543
Casco, ...	1,288	730	5,240	3,101	. .	701	4,575
China, ...	3,598	1,844	9,010	5,984		2,984	9,000
Clay, ...	1,460	.	7,901	2 630	50	1,986	8,170
Clyde, ...	4,890	576	3 324	9.657	46	[illegible]21	10,131
Columbus,.	1,933	520	9,725	9,197	90	1,552	10.815
Cottrelville,.	1,338	50	11,275	9.138	781	1,59[illegible]	7,693
East China,.	1,670	13	4,950	6,048	140	797	6,879
Emmet,. .	39[illegible]	182	287	660	.	3[illegible]	1,165
Greenwood,.	605	30	267	774	15	9[illegible]	1,088
Ira, . .	1,548	428	6,460	4,889	197	1,097	9.055
Kenokee,...	918	163	734	1,060		169	2,405
Kimball, ..	768	295	2,925	3,099	20	225	3,205
Lynn, . ..	178	100	710	405		50	1,080
Mussey, . .	94		405	290	.	53	950
Port Huron,	1,003	220	3,140	4,726	5	507	8,106
City, 1st ward,			.	...		.	..
" 2d ward			.				.....
" 3d ward	...			.	.		..
" 4th ward,			.	.			.
Riley, ...	3,552	86	8,185	15,033	80	850	5,809
St. Clair, .	1,539	267	5,652	9,[illegible]90	120	1,230	10,100
City, 1st ward,		.					.....
" 2d ward.	95		1,540	2.190	48	[illegible]210	2,345
Wales,	950	452	4,835	1 966	25	36[illegible]	6 020
Total,.. .	43,243	7,862	115647	125523	2,051	17048	134806

ST CLAIR COUNTY.—CONTINUED.

ENDING JUNE 1ST, 1860.

Wool, pounds of.	Value of Orchard products.	Butter, pounds of.	Cheese, pounds of.	Hay, tons of.	Clover seed, bushels.	Maple Sugar, pounds.	Value of home made manufactures.
5,101	558	59 788	4,084	1,080	14	15,278	$1,523
733	....	16,550	861	547		2,292	61
1,889	.	17,555	230	773	9	11,718	547
701	.	7,350	250	385			
2,556	..	18.400	300	944		.	...
1,118	1,300	11,280	1,890	1,166			...
3,385		14.979	375	821	.	3,735	446
2,751	. .	17 650	800	981		....	..
3,412	...	13,415	260	629			.. ...
2,640		11,550	11,000	915	..		. .
123	. .	4,500		120	.	1,220	389
12		4 900		120		1,025	45
705	.	11 915	450	599			.. .. .
142	.	4,130	700	217		1,270	12
233	.	6 275	100	539		300	.
58	.	3,750	..	17		120	..
33	. .	2 900		91		2,000	....
632	.	6,800	100	491		.	.
... ..	....			.		..	..
....	.		.	.		.	
.....	.	.	.	.		.. .	.. .. .
...	.		.			..	....
2 060	40	35,190	2,845	448		17,435	222
1,924	....	19,715	710	1,570		.	..
.....		.	. ..	.	.	. .	. ...
390	..	3 050	.	308			..
185	.	7.375	350	274		2.105	42
80,788	1,898	299,573	25,315	15195	23	58,498	8,423

ST. CLAIR COUNTY.—Continued.

Townships.	Flouring Mills.							Saw Mills.			
	Number of.	Runs of Stone.	Power used.		Capital invested in real and personal estate in the business.	Annual product.		Number of.	Power used.		Capital invested in real and personal estate in the business.
			Water.	Steam.		Bbls. flour made.	Value of.		Water.	Steam.	
Berlin,								1	1		$6,500
Brockway,	1		1		$5,000	800	$5,935	1	1		3,720
Burchville,								1	1		4,000
Casco,	*										
China,	*										
Clay,	*										
Clyde,	1			1	3,000	3,000	20,062	2	1	1	16,800
Columbus,	*										
Cottrelville,	*										
East China,	*										
Emmet,											
Greenwood,											
Ira,	*										
Kenokee,											
Kimball,	1		1		4,000	400	5,550	1	1		2,000
Lynn,											
Mussey,								2		1	†126000
Port Huron,								2	1	1	8,000
City, 1st w'rd,											
" 2d w'rd,											
" 3d w'rd,											
" 4th w'rd,	1			1	10,000	5,500	74,000	7		7	155,000
Riley,	1		1		5,000	1,200	13,000	2	2		5,000
St. Clair,	*										
City, 1st w'rd,											
" 2d w'rd,	*										
Wales,											
**								9	1	8	194,000
Total,	5		3	2	27,000	10900	118547	28	9	18	$521020

** Aggregate of the townships marked thus *.
† As returned, evidently a mistake.

ST. CLAIR COUNTY—CONTINUED.

Saw Mills.		Aggregate of all kinds of Manufactures, Mills included.				Estimated value of Real and Personal Estate.	
Annual product.			Hands employ'd				
Feet of Lumber Sawed.	Value of.	Capital invested in real and personal estate in the business.	Males.	Females.	Value of annual products.	By Assessors.	By assistant Marshals.
500,000	*40000	$6 506	5		$40,000	1533777	†1533777
250,000	*20000	8,720	3		25,935	...	...
300,000	3,000	4,000	4		3,000	188,450	407,861
...	...	...			...		...
...	...	...				...	...
...	...				...		
1,100,000	9,784	21,000	17		31,946	125,543	285,054
...	...	...				...	...
...	...	...					...
...	...	...			...	...	...
...	...	...			...	...	...
...	...	...			...	...	...
...	...	...			...	...	
...	...	...			...	61,540	151,225
300,000	2,100	6,000	9		7,650	130,797	218,968
...	...	...			...		...
1,100,000	17,750	126,000	14		17,750	...	...
2,650,000	26,500	8,000	29		26,500	205,858	342,945
...		...			...	...	...
...	...	...			...	...	...
...	...				...	...	...
23,000,000	264540	179,500	210		353,981	670,390	3,310,159
600,000	*39000	12,000	8		55,000	...	...
...	...	...			...	...	...
...	...	...			...	...	...
...	...	...			...	...	...
...	...	...			...	10,007	198,995
24,900,000	238100	229,050	258		326,740	5797192	4,733,985
54,700,000	660774	600,770	557		$888502	6813554	11182969

* As returned, evidently a mistake.
†The two last columns includes Brockway, Emmet, Greenwood, Lynn, Mussey and Riley

ST. JOSEPH COUNTY.

TOWNSHIPS.	Dwelling Houses.		Number of Families.	Number of Inhabitants.				
	Whole number.	Number in Cities.		Whole number.	Colored.	Deaf and Dumb.	Blind.	Insane.
Burr Oak,	208	.	209	1,107	2			.
Burr Oak village,	142	....	142	666	3			.
Centerville village.	99	...	99	47[illegible]	..			..
Colon, . :. .	167	...	167	958				
Colon village,	71	....	71	311	1			
Constantine, ..	97[illegible]	.. ..	99[illegible]	1,889	3		1	
Fabius, ...	16[illegible]	....	164	876				.
Fawn River,. ..	112	.	112	570	11			
Florence, ...	616	. ..	62[illegible]	981				.
Flowerfield, .	210	...	21[illegible]	1,097	.		1	.
Leonidas, . .	250	..	249	1,259	..			1
Lockport, ...	174	.....	174	960				..
Lockport village,	65	.. ..	65	312	.			
Mendon, ...	225	...	221	1,141		1		.
Mendon village,	86	......	86	409	3			.
Mottville, .	150	.....	143	735				
Nottawa, ...	204	...	204	1,185	1			.
Park, ...	196	...	19[illegible]	1,009	.			1
Parkville village,	23	......	23	112				..
Sherman,.	170	.....	17[illegible]	865	2			..
Sturgis,.	97	...	97	53[illegible]				..
Sturgis village,	218	...	218	1,020	5			.
Three Rivers vil.,	281	. ...	281	960	7			..
White Pigeon,	444	...	449	1,680	7			.
Total,.... .	5,347	......	5,362	21,111	45	1	2	2

ST JOSEPH COUNTY.—Continued.

TOWNSHIPS.	Value of Real Estate owned.	Occupied Farms.			
		Whole number.	Acres improved.	Acres unimproved.	Cash value of.
Burr Oak,	$476,930	163	10,479	7,285	$458,610
" vil.,	134,705				
Centerville vil.,	195,585				
Colon,	455,715	145	8,803	7,483	437,860
" village,	100,250				
Constantine,	769,393	171	11,018	9,564	529,123
Fabius,	261,605	131	6,936	7,213	268,118
Fawn River,	255,910	80	5,500	3,517	263,065
Florence,	556 610	147	11,618	17,838	553,595
Flowerfield,	319,755	149	7,195	6,451	211,725
Leonidas,	450,795	162	9,062	9,235	401,565
Lockport,	494,819	157	14,384	7,247	604,055
" vil.,	71,495				
Mendon,	537,875	159	11,141	5,374	305,200
" vil.,	166,780				
Mottville,	379,675	108	7,892	3,764	374,655
Nottawa,	647,450	160	12,873	8,731	576,165
Park,	672,235	162	11,695	7,116	626,855
Parkville village.	41.500				
Sherman,	280,585	134	6,960	5,880	309,335
Sturgis,	388,620	96	7,934	3,974	458,560
" village,	274,800				
Three Rivers vil.,	493,334				
White Pigeon,	488,372	109	7,702	5 312	375,959
Total,	$8,914,793	2,233	151,192	115,983	$6,754,445

ST. JOSEPH COUNTY.—Continued.

Value of Farming Implements and Machinery.	Live Stock, June 1st, 1860.							
	Horses.	Asses and Mules.	Milch Cows.	Working Oxen.	Other Cattle.	Sheep.	Swine.	Value of Live Stock.
$11,208	389		442	85	581	1,394	1,958	$64,455
10,165	275		414	124	583	3,267	1,503	63,651
25,216	425	2	445	74	581	2,203	1,232	67,571
12,610	216	1	322	90	391	1,438	1,046	40,826
5,605	212	5	219	44	235	1,041	1,092	32,782
23,179	459	2	455	36	608	1,792	1,080	58,892
17,650	224		353	163	383	1,382	883	45,719
10,475	337		376	135	566	2,467	1,697	57,186
29,798	371	2	433	49	572	2,257	1,221	62,935
11,533	380		447	80	494	2,210	1,359	66,040
10,672	290	2	288	7	385	815	800	37,973
16,555	486	7	502	110	900	3,402	2,279	101,359
30,267	420		476	34	487	2,435	2,484	68,576
7,280	268	2	291	114	291	1,099	1,347	42,485
9,635	289		283	34	394	785	867	44,770
13,823	297		249	35	410	730	656	43,926
$245,671	5336	23	5995	1,212	7,867	28,717	21,499	$899,156

ST. JOSEPH COUNTY.—Continued.

TOWNSHIPS.	Produce, during the Year						
	Wheat, bushels of.	Rye, bushels of.	Indian corn, bushels of.	Oats, bushels of.	Barley, bushels of.	Buckwheat, bushels of.	Potatoes, bushels of.
Burr Oak,	29,562	1,087	52,510	6,995	65	948	26,042
" vil.,	..	.	.	.	.		....
Centerville vil.	...	.		.			...
Colon, . . .	37,697	65	51,250	5,933	20	1,047	13,101
" vil.,			..	..	.		.
Constantine,	45,628	900	70,100	5,892	1,691	557	14,478
Fabius, . . .	24,485	324	32,870	4,704	375	490	9,430
Fawn River,	21,70[illegible]	139	36,070	1,040	20	288	10,325
Florence,.	46,370	959	84,267	4,087	109	1,382	33,722
Flowerfield,	80,646	50	36,060	5,522	460	684	8,015
Leonidas,	30,930	335	57,315	5,332	500	470	8,168
Lockport,	46,631	884	99,655	2,827	150	1,065	18,141
" vil.,			.	.			...
Mendon,	34,390	446	51,315	4,921	110	418	8,107
" vil.,	..	.	..	.			..
Mottville, .	31,421	233	47,990	4,210	85	187	5,966
Nottawa,	54,255	327	82,685	7,541	80	897	15,000
Park, ...	46,829	659	71,390	3,836	404	1,032	10,267
Parkville vil.,				..			....
Sherman,. .	20,005	720	30,765	2,538		269	21,670
Sturgis,. .	35,518	390	51,210	1,790	10	.	22,924
" vil.,	.		.	...	.	.	....
Three Riv vil.			..				....
White Pigeon,	29,877	575	47,651	2,565	92	867	39,190
Total,	613953	8,093	909103	69,733	4,171	10591	264546

ST. JOSEPH COUNTY.—Continued.

Ending June 1st, 1860.							
Wool, pounds of.	Value of Orchard products.	Butter, pounds of.	Cheese, pounds of.	Hay, tons of.	Clover seed, bushels.	Maple Sugar, pounds.	Value of home made manufactures.
4,651	$2,590	5,918	1,081	1,254	7	..	$143
.... .	.	..	.. .	.	.	. ..	. ..
......			..			.....	......
10,655	2,96[illegible]	34 79[illegible]	5,57[illegible]	2,04[illegible]	62[illegible]	. ..	835
......	.		..		.	....	....
8,859	4,10[illegible]	39 60[illegible]	3 73[illegible]	1,87[illegible]	29[illegible]	10	677
3,651	2,49[illegible]	32,10[illegible]	28[illegible]	1,25[illegible]	19[illegible]	38[illegible]	173
8,311	925	16,935	2,10[illegible]	90[illegible]	184	.. ..	224
6,125	2 856	37,70[illegible]	1,48[illegible]	1,87[illegible]	23[illegible]	.. .	468
3,88[illegible]	1 88[illegible]	34 797	7,24[illegible]	1 424	4[illegible]	904	111
6,391	2 43[illegible]	32,420	3,76[illegible]	1 44[illegible]	25[illegible]	5,71[illegible]	452
7,326	1,90[illegible]	44,873	1,94[illegible]	1,87[illegible]	19[illegible]	.. ..	535
.....	....	.	....			...	......
8,711	2,09[illegible]	36,030	5,31[illegible]	2,13[illegible]	26[illegible]	68[illegible]	792
......	.. .	. ..	...	.		...	....
3,351	1 69[illegible]	20 009	. ..	879	28[illegible]	100	41
12,894	3,396	39,99[illegible]	2,85[illegible]	2 23[illegible]	32[illegible]	....	778
9,251	3,32[illegible]	38,81[illegible]	1,70[illegible]	1,864	47[illegible]	.....	405
.... .	.	..	....	.	..	....	... .
2,95[illegible]	1,57[illegible]	25 62[illegible]	20[illegible]	48[illegible]		....	135
2,26[illegible]	1,41[illegible]	22,95[illegible]	15[illegible]	84[illegible]	3[illegible]	....	269
......	...	. ..	. ....		.	.....	.. ....
......	.	.	...	.	..	...	.. ....
3 239	2 081	22,961	1,505	1,36[illegible]	211	.....	238
97,52[illegible]	37,738	515,213	38,937	23753	3700	7,79[illegible]	$6,2[illegible]6

ST. JOSEPH COUNTY.—Continued.

Townships.	Flouring Mills.							Saw Mills.			
	Number of.	Runs of Stone.	Power used.		Capital invested in real and personal estate in the business.	Annual product.		Number of.	Power used.		Capital invested in real and personal estate in the business.
			Water.	Steam.		Bbls. flour made.	Value of.		Water.	Steam.	
Burr Oak,	1		1		$6,000	..	109700				.....
" vil.,	.		.		. ..	.	...			.	....
Centerville v.,	1	.	1		10,000	.	171916	1	1		$500
Colon,				.	.....		...				.....
" village,	1		1		1,000		25,874	1	1		2,500
Constantine,	3		3		25,000	5,916	37,977	5	5		10,500
Fabius,. ..	.	.			. ...		. .	3	2	1	6,500
Fawn River,	1		1		10,000	1,800	29,140	1	1		500
Florence,	.			.	.....		.....			.	....
Flowerfield,..	1	.	1		15,000	7,777	62,885	3	3		4,500
Leonidas, ...	1		1		5,000	666	4,807	6	4	2	17,000
Lockport, ..	3		2		50,000	1,880	109324	2	2	.	8,000
" vil.,	.	.			. ...	...	. .			..	......
Mendon,	.			.	.....	...	... .	1	1		9,000
" vil.,	.		..		.... .	. ..	......				......
Mottville,. .				.	... .	..	.....	.			.....
Nottawa, .	.		.		....	.	....				. ....
Park, . .	1		1		5,000	2,666	20,030	1	1		2,000
Parkville vil.	.		.	.	. ....	.	. ...				.....
Sherman,.. .	.			.	. ...	.	......				......
Sturgis, ..	.		.		.....	.	......			..	.....
" vil.,	1		.	1	6,000	4,000	21,450			.	......
Three R. vil.,	.		.		.....	.	...			.	.....
White Pigeon,	1		1	..	10,000	6,000	41,000	1	1	.	2,600
Total, ...	15	..	13	1	143000	30705	634103	25	22	3	63,600

ST. JOSEPH COUNTY.—Continued.

Saw Mills.		Aggregate of all kinds of Manufactures, Mills included.				Estimated value of Real and Personal Estate.	
Annual product.			Hands employ'd				
Feet of Lumber Sawed.	Value of.	Capital invested in real and personal estate in the business.	Males.	Females.	Value of annual product.	By Assessors.	By assistant Marshals.
....	.	$11,850	25		133,734	372,846	$466,057
....		....			. .	....	. . ..
250,000	2,000	18,200	24		189,156	.....	...
....	.. .	.. .			....	302,511	377,511
90,000	950	11,700	22		38,998	......	... .
1,625,000	14,400	87,360	80	10	129,976	......	....
740,000	7,400	7,000	15		12,320	......	.. ....
50,000	500	18,700	9		35,727	152,350	190,437
....	....	1,400	14		5,250	.....	....
590,000	5,275	26,300	17		91,802	. ...	.. ....
2,400,000	15,705	22,250	23		23,387	269,378	350,000
500,000	5,000	140,750	128	2	135,446	......	. ...
......	...	....	.		... .	......	.. ...
800,000	8,800	12,550	10		12,600	324,900	406,125
....	......	. ..	.	.	.... .	. ..	....
....	.. ..	1,700	4		2,280	...	....
....	.....	. ....	.		...	.....	....
60,000	540	13,000	8		28,070	.....	....
....	......	.....			..	....	.. ....
......	....	......			. ....	191,460	239,325
......	....	..			... ..	383,940	479,925
....	.....	26,665	55	12	71,942	.. ..	. ...
..... .	....	..			. .. .	.....	....
300 000	30,000	61,400	62		138,300	...	...
7,405,000	90,560	460,815	496	24	1048983	1997485	2,509,380

TUSCOLA COUNTY.

TOWNSHIPS.	Dwelling Houses.		Number of Families.	Number of Inhabitants.				
	Whole number.	Number in Cities.		Whole number.	Colored.	Deaf and Dumb.	Blind.	Insane.
Akron, ...	41	..	41	18[illegible]				.
Alma, ...	4[illegible]	.	4[illegible]	26[illegible]			1	.
Arbela, ...	124	...	124	527			1	..
Columbia, ...	24	....	2[illegible]	94	.			..
Dayton, ...	2[illegible]	. ..	2[illegible]	129				..
Denmark, ...	60	....	60	309	.			.
Elkland, ...	1[illegible]	....	13	5[illegible]	.			..
Ellington, ...	1[illegible]	....	11	92	.			.
Fair Grove, ...	91	....	91	367	.	1		.
Fremont, .. .	2[illegible]	.. .	21	96	.			1
Geneva, ...	10	...	10	45	.			.
Gilford, ...	21	. .	21	114				.
Indian Fields,	3[illegible]	. ..	26	12[illegible]				.
Junietta, ...	134	..	134	64				.
Koylton, . .	17	.	16	60				..
Millington, .. .	64	...	64	285				.
Tuscola, ...	12[illegible]	. ..	121	954			1	.
Vassar, ...	5[illegible]	.	52	22[illegible]	.			.
Watertown, .	4[illegible]	.	4[illegible]	20[illegible]	.			.
Waterloo, . ..	[illegible]	. .	[illegible]	3[illegible]				.
Wells, ...	11	.. .	10	7	.			.
Total, ...	977	. ..	967	4,885	.	1	3	1

TUSCOLA COUNTY.—Continued.

TOWNSHIPS.	Value of Real Estate owned.	Occupied Farms. Whole number.	Acres improved.	Acres unimproved.	Cash value of.
Akron, . ..	$25,682	26	558	2.477	$20,590
Alma, ...	50,265	40	1,054	4,846	45.790
Arbela, ...	2,510	97	1,423	6,860	81,890
Columbia, ...	26,291	18	494	1 867	17,951
Dayton, ...	23,010	18	514	1,866	19,180
Denmark, ...	100	76	1,461	4,588	57,660
Elkland, ...	18,580	9	228	1,770	15,200
Ellington, ...	24,482	15	480	2,696	20,552
Fair Grove, ...	230	87	1,398	6 414	64,770
Fremont, ...	13,350	15	340	1,406	11,750
Geneva, ...	11,900	6	185	695	6,860
Gilford, ...	...	22	345	1,515	13,175
Indian Fields, ..	62,815	22	790	2,374	33,515
Junietta, ...	15,880	135	3,045	12,376	176.988
Koylton, ...	4,880	7	112	923	3,390
Millington, ...	... ..	55	922	9,766	70,080
Tuscola, ...	38,670	156	3,627	19,907	221,295
Vassar, ...	27,100	34	715	11,897	89,695
Watertown, ...	42,570	33	833	2,604	30,470
Waterloo, ...	7,630	6	180	850	7,290
Wells, ...	10,590	5	133	912	6,920
Total, ...	$406,535	882	18,837	98,609	$1,015,011

TUSCOLA COUNTY.—CONTINUED.

Value of Farming Implements and Machinery.	Live Stock, June 1st, 1860. Horses.	Asses and Mules.	Milch Cows.	Working Oxen.	Other Cattle.	Sheep.	Swine.	Value of Live Stock.
$755	9		60	37	55	......	37	$4,328
1,333	15		71	64	83	26	142	6,804
1,353	42		141	107	154	10	253	13,995
867	1		42	34	40	4	37	3,001
499	1		25	25	9	[illegible]	20	2,129
1,433	35		121	84	171	5	243	11,975
244	2		12	12	11	......	9	1,151
627	7		19	24	24	......	41	2,196
660	15		114	96	127	..	196	9,610
387	1		19	16	27	....	39	1,637
165	3		19	16	12	...	9	1,330
220	5		30	24	27	14	54	2,383
1,161	27		38	28	30	40	61	4,559
3,505	82		192	140	242	182	449	21,955
165	2		9	12	4	....	11	855
766	14		80	70	69	18	207	7,634
2,363	126	2	243	143	263	408	498	28,443
565	19		26	26	20	14	61	4,130
682	5		46	45	35	32	72	4,026
252			9	12	5	.....	20	919
193			7	4	...	......	2	345
$18,195	411	2	1323	1,019	1,408	753	2,461	$133,405

TUSCOLA COUNTY.—Continued.

TOWNSHIPS.	Produce, during the Year						
	Wheat, bushels of.	Rye, bushels of.	Indian corn, bushels of.	Oats, bushels of.	Barley, bushels of.	Buckwheat, bushels of.	Potatoes, bushels of.
Akron, ...	620	173	1,379	127		240	1,465
Alma, ...	2,164	53	2,210	1,522	10	16	2,684
Arbela, ...	730	652	3,139	1,040	.	246	2,418
Columbia, .	529	129	663	365	..	69	769
Dayton, ...	707	.	1,635	395	15	40	1,340
Denmark, ..	2,124	862	2,891	2,551	35	29	1,881
Elkland, ...	158	..	415	170	30	9	557
Ellington,...	957	.	720	455	.	95	967
Fair Grove, .	1,396	48	1,363	1,082	34	101	1,325
Fremont, ...	670	.	885	278	15	17	392
Geneva, ...	368		290	160		11	207
Gilford, ...	155	8	420	150	27	86	434
Indian Fields,	1,011	47	990	1,072	57	38	633
Junietta, ..	7,625	152	7,250	4,579	..	372	3,579
Koylton, ...	121	.	395	. .	..	. .	395
Millington, .	913	235	2,978	756	..	30	2,360
Tuscola, ...	4,308	844	7,941	6,001	14	180	4,441
Vassar, ...	380	120	89[illegible]	620	90	..	1,062
Watertown, .	859	80	1,808	444	80	110	1,425
Waterloo, .	445		54	385	15	11	195
Wells, ...	120		520	150	...	10	660
Total, . .	26,43[illegible]	3,482	39,332	22,308	428	1,710	29,190

TUSCOLA COUNTY—Continued.

Ending June 1st, 1860.							
Wool, pounds of.	Value of Orchard products.	Butter, pounds of.	Cheese, pounds of.	Hay, tons of.	Clover seed, bushels.	Maple Sugar pounds.	Value of home made manufactures.
....	...	5,80(		9:		2 04(	..
.....	...	6,07:	..	12:		6,55:	. .
32	....	14 73(	20(	32	.	3 87	. ...
......	... .	2 8 (	50(	71		1,35:	...
......	.. ..	1,55(	..	25	.	2 614	..
... ..	. .	9 44:	. 10(	26(	2	5 76	. ...
......	.	1 12:	....	1:		1 16	. ...
... .	...	1,90(		6(	.	4 95:	. ..
.. ..	.. .	5,94(	..	8:		6 46(	. ..
.... .	.. .	1,80(		2:		2,45:	. ..
.....	. ..	1 30(	30(	2:	1	5(	. .
2:	....	1,82(	4(	4	.	2,12.	.
6l	....	3,35(		10l		1,08:	...
51:	....	14,77	50(	33:		10,13:	.
......	....	60(		4		1 15:	.
4:	. ..	7,95:		16:		4 78(	.
1,369	.	4 35(	2,45(	70		11 244	$100
3(	. .	2 62(	...	11:		81(	.
...	.	4 20(	...	9		6 19(	.
....	..	70(	..	14		1 40(	.
.....	.	65(		4	1	70	.
1,97:	.. ..	93,453	4,09(	2,79(	3	19,92(	$100

TUSCOLA COUNTY.—Continued.

TOWNSHIPS.	Flouring Mills.							Saw Mills.			
	Number of.	Runs of Stone.	Power used. Water.	Power used. Steam.	Capital invested in real and personal estate in the business.	Annual product. Bbls. flour made.	Annual product. Value of.	Number of.	Power used. Water.	Power used. Steam.	Capital invested in real and personal estate in the business.
Akron,											
Alma,											
Arbela,								2		2	$7,000
Columbia,											
Dayton,											
Denmark,											
Elkland,											
Ellington,											
Fair Grove,											
Fremont,											
Geneva,											
Gilford,											
Indian Fields,	1		1		$2,500		$2,500	1	1		2,500
Junietta,	1			1	2,500		8,000	1		1	2,500
Koylton,											
Millington,								1	1		2,000
Tuscola,	1		1		1,000		4,700	1	1		8,000
Vassar,	1		1		7,000		13,250	2	1	1	10,000
Watertown,											
Waterloo,											
Wells,											
Total,	4		3	1	13,000		28,450	8	4	4	32,000

TUSCOLA COUNTY.—Continued.

Saw Mills. Annual product.		Aggregate of all kinds of Manufactures, Mills included.				Estimated Value of Real and Personal Estate.	
Feet of Lumber Sawed.	Value of.	Capital invested in real and personal estate in the business.	Hands employ'd Males.	Hands employ'd Females.	Value of annual products.	By Assessors.	By assistant Marshals.
1,600,000	12,800	$7,000	12		$12,800		
500,000	4,000	5,000	5		6,500		
800,000	6,400	5,200	10	1	16,400		
500,000	4,000	2,000	3		4,000		
500,000	4,000	12,200	18		19,700		
1,800,000	17,400	22,450	27		37,650		
5,700,000	48,600	$53,850	75	1	$97,050	1172346	

VAN BUREN COUNTY.

TOWNSHIPS.	Dwelling Houses.		Number of Families.	Number of Inhabitants.				
	Whole number.	Number in Cities.		Whole number.	Colored.	Deaf and Dumb.	Blind.	Insane.
Almena, . ..	130	. ..	140	749	24	3		.
Antwerp, ...	194	.....	200	1,023	6		1	
Arlington,..	171	...	171	854	22			..
Bangor,.	119	. ..	119	672				..
Bloomingdale, .	131	.. .	129	629	..			.
Breedsville village	48	.....	48	252	..			.
Columbia,.	67	...	67	320	.		1	.
Decatur, ...	135	.....	134	654	..		1	..
" village, .	118	.....	123	564	5			..
Deerfield, .. .	38	....	38	207	...		.	..
Geneva, ...	45	....	45	240				.
Hamilton,..	153	......	153	785	11	.		.
Hartford, ...	130	... ..	130	1,073	3			1
Keeler, ...	177	.....	177	97[illegible]		1		1
La Fayette, ...	175	.....	174	890	20	1		..
Lawrence, ...	188	.....	190	1,008	23	.	1	.
" village,	79	...	77	339	..			
Lawton village,	95	.....	92	420	.			1
Paw Paw village,	219	.....	217	1,098	1[illegible]		3	..
Pine Grove, ...	100	. ..	101	490	1			..
Porter, ...	181	...	182	960	5		1	.
South Haven,	18	....	18	9[illegible]	..			..
" " village	71	. .	61	308	.			.
Waverly,.	124	...	120	614	13		.	..
Total,... ..	2,912	...	2,918	15,230	140	6	8	3

VAN BUREN COUNTY—Continued.

TOWNSHIPS.	Value of Real Estate owned.	Occupied Farms.			
		Whole number.	Acres improved.	Acres unimproved.	Cash value of.
Almena, ...	$278,990	63	4,622	4,056	$198,020
Antwerp, ...	466,800	96	7,542	5,249	341,080
Arlington, ..	227,430	129	3,787	6,392	203,600
Bangor, ...	143,610	79	2,219	6,262	113,000
Bloomingdale, ..	151,300	58	1,899	4,320	106,900
Breedsville vil.,.	57,025		. .	. .	. . . .
Columbia, ...	72,100	55	1,810	2,967	89,800
Decatur,.	195,490	64	2,842	4,292	158,200
" village,.	154,650	.	.....	...	. . . .
Deerfield, ...	20,840	19	320	1,237	12,800
Geneva, . .	39,750	17	412	1,437	21,400
Hamilton, ...	314,490	107	5,825	6,916	284,850
Hartford, ...	262,865	80	4,070	5 466	185,850
Keeler,..	370,555	126	8 146	7,285	337,815
La Fayette,....	387,775	130	7,174	6,579	388,750
Lawrence,. ..	249,125	169	5,356	9,349	286,630
" village,	95,440	. .	. ...	......	... .
Lawton village,	94,710	....	.... .	.... .	....
Paw Paw village,	519,575	...	. ..	. ..	.. ..
Pine Grove,..	115,170	29	735	1,837	31,800
Porter, ...	316,225	109	5,364	6,025	273,900
South Haven, ..	21,600	19	387	879	36,900
" " village.	77,065		......	..	. ..
Waverly, . ..	130,100	46	1,996	2,578	73,650
Total,.... .	$4,762,680	1,395	64,506	83,124	$3,144,945

VAN BUREN COUNTY.—Continued.

Value of Farming Implements and Machinery.	Live Stock, June 1st, 1860.							
	Horses.	Asses and Mules.	Milch Cows.	Working Oxen.	Other Cattle.	Sheep.	Swine.	Value of Live Stock.
6,551	158		174	75	228	612	400	$26,336
12,218	243		266	82	261	929	515	40,452
6,944	110	2	244	166	416	290	585	25,446
4,511	74		185	101	221	132	469	17,450
3,556	62		134	70	104	128	276	14,628
....	....	....	....	....	....	....	....	....
3,420	57		115	58	114	161	235	11,560
5,779	122	3	148	70	165	255	369	21,713
....	....	....	....	....	....	....	....	....
421	1		31	30	17	10	89	2,275
735	7		30	26	20	....	57	2,350
9,952	168		225	164	286	623	483	33,257
9,367	122		233	126	293	865	375	24,251
11,015	245		322	197	366	1,448	597	45,071
12,923	289		326	123	378	906	697	46,965
10,079	198		351	220	377	482	846	21,965
....	....	....	....	....	....	....	....	....
....	....	....	....	....	....	....	....	....
....	....	....	....	....	....	....	....	....
1,370	19		51	35	55	33	150	5,512
9,315	233		243	94	288	493	582	35,902
1,265	5		24	30	21	....	59	2,445
....	....	....	....	....	....	....	....	....
3,040	65		131	48	138	154	198	13,132
$112,461	2178	5	3233	1,715	3,748	7,521	6,982	$400,710

VAN BUREN COUNTY.—Continued.

TOWNSHIPS.	Produce, during the Year.						
	Wheat, bushels of.	Rye, bushels of.	Indian corn, bushels of.	Oats, bushels of.	Barley, bushels of.	Buckwheat, bushels of.	Potatoes, bushels of.
Almena,	9,53-	16	19 900	2,140	23	688	6,282
Antwerp, .	20 530	180	37,825	1 9[illegible]	199	45	10,603
Arlington, .	9,52	18-	21,81	3,531	219	278	5,726
Bangor, .	4,034	70	14,730	2 010	78	69.	3 997
Bloomingdale.	5,281	110	9,630	1,734		250	3,491
Breedsville vil			....	...	.	.	. ...
Columbia,	1 75[illegible]	34.	6,550	1,01	10	12	3 306
Decatur, .	9,299	285	14,61	3,647	....	249	3,447
" village.	...	. .	..	.. ..	..	...	......
Deerfield, .	301	.	2 20.	. ..	..	412	835
Geneva,	437	30	1,820	155	15	...	915
Hamilton,	16,40[illegible]	654	42,520	6 29.	68	437	8,828
Hartford, ...	11,329	80	16,140	4,56[illegible]	5	77	4,118
Keeler, ...	31,907	280	42,510	8,610	...	118	11,044
La Fayette,	23 540	42[illegible]	37,585	5 700	.	449	9,458
Lawrence, .	13,690	5[illegible]	28,015	5,101	25	487	8,431
" village	. .		..	... .	..	..	.....
Lawton "	...	.	... .	...	...	..	......
Paw Paw "	.. .	.	. .	....	..		.....
Pine Grove,	1 59[illegible]	40	4 79[illegible]	281	..	153	3 400
Porter.	19,2[illegible]	60[illegible]	28,035	6,925	88	961	7,003
South Haven,	167	20	2,930	179	.	24	1,635
" " vil.	.. .	.	....	...	..	..	.. ..
Waverly,	4 53	[illegible]	10 170	1 92[illegible]	30	335	2,760
Total, ..	18315[illegible]	3,517	341,785	55,779	1,518	5,788	95,278

VAN BUREN COUNTY.—CONTINUED.

ENDING JUNE 1ST, 1860.							
Wool, pounds of.	Value of Orchard products.	Butter, pounds of.	Cheese, pounds of.	Hay, tons of.	Clover seed, bushels.	Maple Sugar, pounds.	Value of home made manufactures.
1,607	1,755	14,375	850	1,013	12	700	$300
3,187	2,370	22,849	1,050	1,382	183	. ..	79
560	1,616	20,965	1,250	469	.	17,655	. .....
336	490	23,900	1,879	549		17,286	20
200	420	11,480	610	379	7	8,358	. . .
.....	.		.....			.	. ....
320	650	11,675	1,550	449	.	4,798	100
800	1,950	14,425	200	726	17	480	55
....					.	. .	... ..
.. .	....	2,900	. ..	26	.	1,370	. .
.. ..	.	3,858	. ..	96	.	2,120	. ....
2,984	1,640	21,900	450	926	71		... .
1,898	1,470	22,550	1,220	709		8,623	... ...
4,614	3,093	30,640	2,385	1,570	96	485	40
3,183	2,655	30,235	1,000	1,724	77	2,700	175
1,413	3,239	32,720	365	955	2	15,075	53
... . .		.	.....	.		..	. . ..
... .		.. . .	. .	.		...	... ..
......	. .	... .	..	. .		..	.. ...
55	25	5,080	..	65		580	.. ...
1,516	3,252	25,100	500	795	74	2,855	177
103	..	2,225	. ..	37	..	900	.. ...
......	. ..	.	......		.	......	....
361	252	10,450	6,610	391	..	11,118	....
22,237	24,887	307,327	19,849	12506	539	95,103	999

VAN BUREN COUNTY—Continued.

TOWNSHIPS.	Flouring Mills.							Saw Mills.			
	Number of.	Runs of Stone.	Power used.		Capital invested in real and personal est. in the business.	Annual product.		Number of.	Power used.		Capital invested in real and personal estate in the business.
			Water.	Steam.		Bbls. flour made.	Value of.		Water.	Steam.	
Almena,								1	1		$12000
Antwerp,											
Arlington,											
Bangor,	1		1		$2,500	750	$4,500	1	1		2,500
Bloomingdale,								1		1	17,550
Breedsville v.,											
Columbia,								3	1	2	11,500
Decatur,								1		1	3,000
" village											
Deerfield,											
Geneva,											
Hamilton,	1		1		4,500	4,000	24,000	2	2		6,500
Hartford,								2	2		18,000
Keeler,								3	3		8,500
La Fayette,	1	5	1		75 000	8,500	42,500	2	1	1	10,000
Lawrence,	1		1		6,000	5,000	30,000	2	2		6,500
" village,											
Lawton "											
Paw Paw "											
Pine Grove,								2		2	29,000
Porter,											
South Haven,								2		2	36,000
" " vil.											
Waverly,											
Total,	4	5	4		$88000	18250	101000	22	13	9	161050

VAN BUREN COUNTY.—Continued.

Saw Mills.		Aggregate of all kinds of Manufactures, Mills included.				Estimated value of Real and Personal Estate.	
Annual product.			Hands employ'd				
Feet of Lumber Sawed.	Value of.	Capital invested in real and personal estate in the business.	Males.	Females.	Value of annual product.	By Assessors.	By assistant Marshals.
1,000,000	$17000	$12,000	11		$17,000		
300,000	1,800	5,000	4		6,500		
500,000	7,000	17,550	8		7,000		
2,300,000	16,100	13,500	22		17,600		
600,000	5,400	34,000	41		65,700		
1,200,000	12,000	11,000	7		36,000		
1,200,000	9,600	18,000	5		9,600		
1,100,000	11,000	8,500	6		11,000		
600,000	6,900	100,500	34		76,375		
900,000	8,000	12,500	9		38,000		
3,500,000	36,500	29,000	35		36,500		
2,500,000	15,000	36,000	30		15,000		
15,700,000	146300	297,550	212		$336075	2598780	$3248475

WASHTENAW COUNTY

TOWNSHIPS.	Dwelling Houses.		Number of Families.	Number of Inhabitants.				
	Whole number.	Number in Cities.		Whole number.	Colored.	Deaf and Dumb.	Blind.	Insane.
Ann Arbor,	396		421	2,055	35	1	1	
City, 1st ward,	248	248	263	1,352	5	1	1	
" 2d "	193	193	209	1,134	7			
" 3d "	147	147	141	871	15			
" 4th "	206	206	222	1,090	27			
Augusta,	222		220	1,139	5		2	
Bridgewater,	239		238	1,291				
Dexter,	151		150	857			1	1
Freedom,	251		248	1,336				
Lima,	190		190	992		1		
Lodi,	242		240	1,319	6		1	1
Lyndon,	141		141	823				
Manchester,	345		338	1,712	1		1	
Northfield,	260		260	1,373	1	1		
Pittsfield,	210		207	1,331	26		5	7
Saline,	383		379	1,967	16			
Salem,	250		250	1,360	38		1	
Scio,	345		345	1,820				
Sharon,	187		184	1,000	1			
Superior,	247		247	1,346	50			1
Sylvan,	294		292	1,587				
Webster,	214		214	1,106				1
York,	299		297	1,573	31	1		1
Ypsilanti,	255		248	1,357	39	1	3	1
City, 1st ward,	114	114	110	594	60		1	
" 2d "	123	123	126	675	12			
" 3d "	167	167	165	885	78		2	
" 4th "	131	131	137	712	20		1	
" 5th "	202	202	198	1,090	49		1	
Total,	6,652	1,531	6,680	35,747	522	6	21	13

WASHTENAW COUNTY.—Continued.

TOWNSHIPS.	Value of Real Estate owned.	Occupied Farms. Whole number.	Acres improved.	Acres unimproved.	Cash value of.
Ann Arbor,	$825,290	142	10,490	5,527	$579,090
City, 1st ward,	848,200	....	....	....	....
" 2d "	555,100	....	....	....	....
" 3d "	311,400	....	....	....	....
" 4th "	589,850	....	....	....	....
Augusta,	420,990	138	6,202	7,499	309,900
Bridgewater,	610,315	185	13,249	8,011	640,370
Dexter,	439,700	112	9,520	7,677	425,700
Freedom,	506,300	219	12,674	7,578	495,495
Lima,	650,200	147	11,650	9,429	631,050
Lodi,	626,310	126	10,075	5,074	480,900
Lyndon,	336,250	115	9,868	8,819	346,950
Manchester,	627,270	177	11,554	8,996	511,400
Northfield,	587,150	190	11,625	9,530	556,540
Pittsfield,	909,095	165	15,750	6,275	916,580
Saline,	821,990	194	14,831	7,527	673,860
Salem,	683,427	203	13,296	8,089	676,390
Scio,	903,750	139	12,276	7,831	685,700
Sharon,	659,650	151	14,544	7,828	644,500
Superior,	704,175	167	13,379	6,600	696,890
Sylvan,	616,650	147	10,439	9,580	495,900
Webster,	491,000	139	11,128	6,815	477,380
York,	666,610	205	12,945	7,164	630,700
Ypsilanti,	908,663	179	15,194	6,334	987,825
City, 1st ward,	254,400	....	....	....	....
" 2d "	449,414	....	....	....	....
" 3d "	364,900	....	....	....	....
" 4th "	245,900	....	....	....	....
" 5th "	330,150	....	....	....	....
Total,	16,944,099	3,230	240,681	152,183	11,863,150

WASHTENAW COUNTY—Continued.

Value of Farming Implements and Machinery.	Live Stock, June 1st, 1860.							
	Horses.	Asses and Mules.	Milch Cows.	Working Oxen.	Other Cattle.	Sheep.	Swine.	Value of Live Stock.
$23,235	390		462	171	720	7,637	746	$78,744
.....								
.....								
.....								
.....								
14,070	424		550	87	685	3,099	638	62,760
28,013	568		656	216	919	9,701	1,080	127,835
17,825	256		373	160	511	7,476	718	77,150
21,895	461		656	260	907	6,010	1,279	76,970
24,815	427		581	161	777	8,917	735	106,733
17,090	355	4	437	153	5[illegible]	7,664	721	80,990
15,120	257		363	180	548	5,577	862	44,411
16,317	392		481	166	557	8,665	703	86,690
25,000	589		572	224	910	9,432	1,300	85,335
31,197	552		655	12[illegible]	761	12,299	1,296	129,548
22,833	617		737	200	897	9,809	983	121,409
21,215	669		689	139	9[illegible]9	7,850	1,288	110,547
25,495	448		500	160	78[illegible]	9,049	972	103,340
22,422	450		432	126	59[illegible]	11,99[illegible]	1,047	112,865
20,870	615		655	89	894	7,560	1,515	95,374
19,450	375		490	210	691	6,275	741	92,255
19,490	394		502	246	93[illegible]	8,994	1,037	77,405
26,135	654		744	107	90[illegible]	8,410	1,036	114,165
25,295	641		810	89	82[illegible]	9,004	1,235	114,621
.....								
.....								
.....								
....	*150		200				100	17,900
$437,782	9634	4	11545	3272	15320	165424	20,032	1,917,047

*This includes the whole city.

WASHTENAW COUNTY.—Continued.

TOWNSHIPS.	Produce, during the Year						
	Wheat, bushels of.	Rye, bushels of.	Indian corn, bushels of.	Oats, bushels of.	Barley, bushels of.	Buckwheat, bushels of.	Potatoes, bushels of.
Ann Arbor,	26,411	2,094	34,285	11,916	2,719	1,683	13,018
City, 1st ward,	...		.....	....	.		......
" 2d ward,	.	.	...	.		...	......
" 3d ward,	..	..	..	......	...		......
" 4th ward	.....		.....	....	..	..	......
Augusta,	11,670	537	25,742	6 432	91	1,964	10,675
Bridgewater,	35,875	1,126	45,612	11,261	326	2,157	17,109
Dexter,	27,159	256	23,721	4,664	661	1,190	13,420
Freedom,	41,520	1,899	30,397	9,390	958	2,224	13,639
Lima,	40,253	405	28,870	17,901	3,471	1,896	15,397
Lodi,	27,989	450	26,570	11,890	1,072	1,645	8,019
Lyndon,	26,989	75	22,137	4,149	291	1,922	17,431
Manchester,	34,260	791	31,360	9,740	304	2,214	12,024
Northfield,	27,534	1,343	34,267	21,415	1,189	3,700	17,990
Pittsfield,	51,088	520	53,610	26,698	2,374	2,717	14,454
Saline,	38,515	1,057	51,150	16,853	1,125	2,760	17,929
Salem,	20,746	3,433	52,974	31,913	1,571	3,110	19,317
Scio,	42,810	1,599	35,715	17,350	1,708	1,211	15,573
Sharon,	57,197	185	47,613	14,545	529	1,249	12,148
Superior,	23,771	2,463	52,101	30,462	1,015	2,735	21,387
Sylvan,	32,309	1,090	28,075	8,408	901	2,585	17,350
Webster,	30,776	294	34,640	11,713	4,289	2,170	14,346
York,	34,140	1,076	56,650	12,688	570	2,566	18,554
Ypsilanti,	32,756	1,066	75,940	24,104	765	2,766	28,338
City, 1st ward,	.....	..	......	.	.	...	......
" 2d "	....	..	.....	..	.	..	.....
" 3d "	.....	...	....		....	...	......
" 4th "	...	.		....	.	.	..
" 5th "	.						
Total,	663768	21759	791429	303349	25929	44152	318713

WASHTENAW COUNTY.—Continued.

ENDING JUNE 1ST, 1860.

Wool, pounds of.	Value of Orchard products.	Butter, pounds of.	Cheese, pounds of.	Hay, tons of.	Clover seed, bushels.	Maple Sugar, pounds.	Value of home made manufactures.
24,795	$6,226	42,905	925	2,937	278	...	$346
......	...	..	...			...	.
......	....	.	...		.	.	.
.....	...	.	..			.	.
...	.....		.. .		.	.	..
10,862	4,884	47,567	7,665	2,182	121	500	358
31,630	7,658	61,494	6,105	4 175	657	430	832
21 941	4,577	37,075	1,830	3 037	285	...	.. . .
18,985	6.244	34,850	11,850	3,573	1258	200	. ...
30,782	7,402	51,887	27 295	4 246	825	....	.. .
26,200	6,036	38,305	2,235	2.535	309	2,080	375
18,622	4,012	38,620	1,200	2,709	450	.	50
29,617	6,476	42.110	2,330	3.353	161	. ...	729
26,555	5,835	39,329	1,620	3,784	796	..	.
45,413	8,557	53,335	4 0[illegible]0	3,776	955	....	20
37 955	7,882	67,715	9,555	3,819	391	925	640
23,260	10,077	36,325	3,354	3 073	19[illegible]	5,160	.....
27,943	5,418	54,609	1,350	3,504	768	..	.. .
36,254	8,155	39,371	7,96[illegible]	3,290	412	..	80
27.598	7,345	52,525	1,330	3.279	3[illegible]	3,100	.. ...
23,740	5,294	45,850	3,92[illegible]	3.336	294	....	.. ...
27,008	5,442	30,820	3,250	3 572	318	..	.. . ..
31,116	9,904	68,075	14,695	3 062	573	1,749	1,122
30,956	8,105	59,649	2,000	3,501	539	.. .	136
....	....	. .	....	.		. .	. ....
......	.....	. .	....	.		. ...	.. ....
......	.....	. ...	.... .			...	.....
. . .	...	. .	.....			. .	.....
		8,000	.	.		..	
551,232	135529	950,316	114,482	68741	9619	14,144	$4,688

WASHTENAW COUNTY.—Continued.

Townships.	Flouring Mills.							Saw Mills.			
			Power used.			Annual product.			Power used.		
	Number of.	Runs of Stone.	Water.	Steam.	Capital invested in real and personal estate in the business.	Bbls. flour made.	Value of.	Number of.	Water.	Steam.	Capital invested in real and personal estate in the business.
Ann Arbor,	2	10	2		50,000	28,000	189300	2	2		$4,500
City, 1st w'd,											
" 2d "											
" 3d "											
" 4th "	1	3	1		8,000	4,500	27,000	1		1	2,200
Augusta,								4	2	2	8,700
Bridgewater,	1	3	1		3,500	3,780	23,600	3	3		6,000
Dexter,	2	5	2		16,000	8,350	42,250				
Freedom,								1		1	2,200
Lima,											
Lodi,								1		1	2,000
Lyndon,											
Manchester,	3	8	3		36,000	20,946	131880	3	3		6,300
Northfield,											
Pittsfield,											
Saline,	2	6	2	1	22,000	14,000	76,000	3	1	2	6,500
Salem,								2		2	7,600
Scio,	3	8	3		49,000	34,555	183200	2	2		3,900
Sharon,	1	1	1		5,000	2,500	12,790	2	2		4,800
Superior,								2	1	1	3,500
Sylvan,	2	3	1	1	19,000	14,580	82,400	2	2		3,900
Webster,											
York,	1	3	1		4,000	4,000	16,800	2	2		2,500
Ypsilanti,	1	4	1		10,000		23,000	2	1	1	8,000
City, 1st w'd,											
" 2d "											
" 3d "											
" 4th "											
" 5th "	2	10	2		38,000	26,000	175000	1	1		10,000
Total,	21	64	20	2	260500	161211	983220	33	22	11	82,600

WASHTENAW COUNTY.—Continued.

Saw Mills. Annual product. Feet of Lumber Sawed.	Saw Mills. Annual product. Value of.	Aggregate of all kinds of manufactures, Mills included. Capital invested in real and personal estate in the business.	Hands employ'd. Males.	Hands employ'd. Females.	Value of annual products.	Estimated value of Real and Personal Estate. By Assessors.	Estimated value of Real and Personal Estate. By assistant Marshals.
240,000	$2,700	$92000	50	24	$260560	…	…
…	…	…			…	…	…
…	…						…
…	…	…					…
150,000	2,600	252250	328	73	452,399	…	…
1,310,000	11,900	9,600	10		14,500		…
550,000	5,400	10,000	6		29,700		…
…	…	16,000	4		42,250		…
190,000	17,100	4,100	11		22,368		
…	…	…				…	…
200,000	2,000	2,925	7		6,300	…	…
…	…	1,500	8		3,300	…	…
510,000	4,740	68,950	62	3	164,830	…	…
…	…	…			…	…	
…	…	…					…
780,000	6,180	48,025	52	3	120,025	…	…
*400,000	6,200	9,600	11		8,700		…
260,000	2,400	92,800	53	4	222,525	…	…
460,000	4,060	9,800	3		16,850	…	…
*400,000	5,500	3,500	3		5,500	…	…
305,700	3,057	28,100	24		99,937		
…	…	…			…		…
480,000	4,560	8,400	11		27,230	…	…
1,000,000	10,000	21,100	15		38,500	…	…
…	…				…	…	…
…	…				…		…
…	…	…			…	…	…
…		…			…	…	…
1,300,000	2,000	234000	246	57	464,894		…
8,535,700	109397	910650	904	164	2000458	8900000	17800000

*Of one.

WAYNE COUNTY.

TOWNSHIPS.	Dwelling Houses. Whole number.	Dwelling Houses. Number in Cities.	Number of Families.	Number of Inhabitants. Whole number.	Colored.	Deaf and Dumb.	Blind.	Insane.
Brownstown,	310	..	280	1,380	23		1	1
Canton,	299	..	278	1,554	33	1	.	1
Dearborn,	314	.....	288	1,546	12	.		3
" village,	68	.. .	68	320	12			
Detroit City, 1st w.	605	605	648	3,780	59		1	
" " 2d w.	204	204	212	1,428	15	.	.	.
" " 3d w.	532	532	570	3,701	301			.
" " 4th w.	871	871	1,041	5,064	376	4		3
" " 5th w	1,040	1,040	1 016	5,519	48	1	2	
" " 6th w.	1,336	1 336	1,429	7,008	163	4	1	6
" " 7th w.	1,222	1,222	1,341	6,560	251	2	2	..
" " 8th w.	1,045	1,045	1,112	5,573	9	1	2	.
" " 9th w.	680	680	699	3,520	68	.	1	.
" " 10th w.	708	708	740	3,234	31		3	3
Ecorse,	478	. . .	481	2,399				.
Greenfield,	462		441	2,185	12	3	2	1
Grosse Point,	371	. . .	361	2,086	5	.	1	.
Hamtramck,	328	.. ..	320	1,638	18		.	
Huron,	185	. .	173	833	.	2	1	1
Livonia,	328	..	329	1,665	14	1	3	1
Monguagon,	266	.. .	267	1,335	6			1
Nankin,	388		367	2,108	24	1	3	22
Northville village,	118	....	114	621	2	..	1	1
Plymouth,	302	...	294	1,557	2			1
" village,	186	.	174	821	8		..	.
Redford,	381	....	364	1,861	3			..
Romulus,	231	....	215	1,106	15	.	1	1
Springwells,	286	.....	290	1,518	34			14
Sumpter,	173	.. ..	160	736			..	..
Taylor,	122	..	117	567		.		..
Van Buren,	387	......	372	1,757	25		.	1
Wayne village,	68	.. .	64	304		.	.	.
Total,	14,294	8,243	14,623	75,284	1570	20	25	61

WAYNE COUNTY.—Continued.

Townships.	Value of Real Estate owned.	Occupied Farms.			
		Whole number.	Acres improved.	Acres unimproved.	Cash value of.
Brownstown,	$408,805	129	5,734	10,183	$348,700
Canton,	1,009,683	203	11,732	9,044	743,765
Dearborn,	697,810	130	8,230	8,745	622,300
" village,	106,000	48	791	1,513	56,550
Det. City, 1st w.	3 862,050		...		
" " 2d w.,	4,829,650	.	.....	...	
" " 3d w.,	1,500,600	.	...	.	...
" " 4th w.,	1,489,845		..	.	..
" " 5th w.,	2,908,075	3	290	100	570,000
" " 6th w.,	3 385,750	.	..	..	..
" " 7th w.	2,115,562	...	.	..	..
" " 8th w.,	1,360,645		.	.....	
" " 9th w.,	1,756,536	15	767	550	209,500
" " 10th w,	987,575	.		..	.
Ecorse,	444,045	80	3,093	4,729	204,965
Greenfield,	956,200	210	9,156	5,441	764,420
Grosse Point,	773,725	177	6,438	9,618	703,475
Hamtramck,	832 250	67	3,056	1,551	374,435
Huron,	241,780	101	4,073	5,710	204,700
Livonia,	798,412	202	9,362	5,976	536,440
Monguagon,	741,915	60	4,110	4,898	411,605
Nankin,	631,480	130	8,365	6,243	484,800
Northville vil.,	230,650		....	.	...
Plymouth,	1,250,855	221	16,681	6,851	1,015,405
" village,	406,135		..	.	..
Redford,	915,825	214	11,505	7,859	779,790
Romulus,	249,575	39	2,015	2,054	97,800
Springwells,	514,960	69	2,658	1,312	234,625
Sumpter,	151,925	79	2,746	4,379	123,150
Taylor,	118,035	79	2,570	3,600	115,620
Van Buren,	683,560	217	10,346	8,985	578,685
Wayne village,	78,950		.	...	...
Total,	$36,433,863	2,473	123,718	109,341	$9,180,730

WAYNE COUNTY.—Continued.

Value of Farming Implements and Machinery.	Live Stock, June 1st, 1860.							
	Horses.	Asses and Mules.	Milch Cows.	Working Oxen.	Other Cattle.	Sheep.	Swine.	Value of Live Stock.
$24,600	579		421	81	523	920	1,122	$61,366
29,167	759		783	138	1,543	6,647	3,087	140,171
16,225	647	...	729	58	691	1,344	1,021	54,880
875	75		82	12	72	100	64	7,996
.....								....
.....								
..								
..								
325	11		34		16	.	12	1,900
..								
.....								
......								
1,415	26		28		610	.	26	3,200
......								
8,171	281		254	48	247	330	454	24,963
17,999	622		889	102	599	867	1,057	72,830
13,328	628		438	20	483	324	892	42,644
6,306	220	.	268	6	186	72	346	24,204
11,928	302		319	80	407	643	678	37,422
15,054	466	.	577	56	491	3,036	781	72,010
9,276	382		274	24	479	1,645	577	41,864
13,550	438		550	81	574	2,601	573	58,038
..								
44,384	639		890	118	1,536	8,336	2,348	159,059
..								
27,251	720		849	78	643	2,466	1,284	99,962
3,403	123		189	21	213	411	174	15,946
5,810	195		265	10	126	114	319	18,229
11,800	162		255	70	337	525	369	28,421
4,115	210		256	20	422	255	399	23,164
45,974	556		689	139	715	3,226	1,024	86,826
..						..	..	...
$311,856	8041		9039	1,162	10913	33,862	16,607	1,075,095

WAYNE COUNTY.—Continued.

TOWNSHIPS.				Produce, during the Year			
	Wheat, bushels of.	Rye, bushels of.	Indian corn, bushels of.	Oats, bushels of.	Barley, bushels of.	Buckwheat, bushels of.	Potatoes, bushels of.
Brownstown,	6,883	587	20,075	8,870	286	2,583	12,488
Canton,	8,965	1,664	58,920	33,578	1,029	4,700	36,390
Dearborn,	1,728	4,020	33,589	18,208	160	2,859	36,685
" village,	88	104	2,580	691	87	225	2,650
Det. city, 1st w.,	....		.	. . .			.....
" " 2d w.,	.		..	.			...
" " 3d w.,	.. ..			. ..	..		...
" " 4th w.,			..		.	.	..
" " 5th w.,	.		1,100	. .		.	250
" " 6th w.,			.			.	....
" " 7th w.,			.. .		.		. : .
" " 8th w.,			....		.		. ...
" " 9th w.,	..	.	1,530	215	..	100	1,229
" " 10th w.,	..	.	.....	..	.		...
Ecorse,	1,281	239	12,518	6,284	163	1,273	10,071
Greenfield,	323	923	24,508	15,658	1,233	1,474	39,712
Grosse Point,	2,092	3,600	30,850	25,622	2,624	3,352	28,214
Hamtramck,	69	518	10,170	6,536	109	700	11,308
Huron,	2,644	397	20,355	4,429	72	1,703	9,648
Livonia,	2,453	1,990	36,078	15,579		2,948	51.432
Monguagon,	2,808	368	15,990	10,375	2,400	709	6,953
Nankin,	1,298	826	31,890	14,221	110	3,041	43,545
Northville vil.,				..		.	.....
Plymouth,	21,361	2,214	83,300	33,055	2,449	4,050	65,842
" village,	.		.				.....
Redford,	2,074	3,225	44.751	30,050	561	3 749	62,395
Romulus,	169	225	6,610	3,255		1,728	7,455
Springwells,	105	558	7,725	5,293	607	391	13 435
Sumpter,	1,154	517	16,103	3,952		1,880	8,978
Taylor,	497	50	6,738	2,442	..	1,245	10,027
Van Buren,	2,782	606	69,675	19,576	374	4,384	27,015
Wayne vil.,	.....			. .		.	.....
Total,	68,774	22631	535055	525889	12274	43094	485752

WAYNE COUNTY.—Continued.

ENDING JUNE 1ST, 1860.							
Wool, pounds of.	Value of Orchard products.	Butter, pounds of.	Cheese, pounds of.	Hay, tons of.	Clover seed, bushels.	Maple Sugar, pounds.	Value of home made manufactures.
2,373	4,300	52,950	695	2,332	267	30	$111
16,662	8,454	75,010	19,770	3,016	2	2,980	115
4,120	4,138	40,132	1,075	2,348	1	635	633
.	95	3,482	200	308		100	.
.. ..	...		.			.	. ...
.. .	.		...				
... ..			.. ..		.	...	. ...
.. .			. .			.	
. ..	.	400	. ..	70		.	. .
.. ..			.			.	. . .
. .	. ..					.	. ..
. ..	.		.			. .	
...	575	1,000		155		.	....
. ...			.		..	.	...
876	.	11,995	. .. .	1,125		..	.
3,429	844	55,695	880	3,018		130	111
687	2,844	22,015	150	2,209		...	4
.....	307	16,321	30	1,118		...	. .
1,122	2,584	37,450	1,280	1,564	184	115	98
9,775	8,675	40,335	21,146	1,788	85	897	760
5,426	1,632	18,260	224	2,260	.	.	10
7,586	6,900	44,855	10,821	2,325	20	1,450	575
..					.	. ...	.
28,361	20,640	81,417	47,242	3,902	238	6,680	287
. .						. ..	... .
7,252	6,887	72,494	11,625	2,619	..	1,025	211
977	1,433	14,425	250	717	10	60	512
539	257	17,750	276	1,257		.	....
1,299	2,606	28,000	.	1,195	35	90	90
616	730	20,895	825	1,133	40	.....	109
8,930	9,418	6,170	3,123	2,283	405	70	75
...	.	.	. ..	...	.	... .	. ...
100,030	83,319	717,331	119,622	36742	1287	14,262	$3,701

WAYNE COUNTY.—Continued.

Townships.	Flouring Mills.							Saw Mills.			
	Number of.	Runs of Stone.	Power used.		Capital invested in real and personal estate in the business.	Annual product.		Number of.	Power used.		Capital invested in real and personal estate in the business.
			Water.	Steam.		Bbls. flour made.	Value of.		Water.	Steam.	
Brownstown,	1		1		$10000	3,000	$14000	1		1	$10000
Canton,					....		..	4		4	5,600
Dearborn,	1	2	1		10,000	1,500	27,544	2	2		7,000
" village,					..	.	..				...
Dt. city, 1st w.,					.		...				.
" 2d w.,					....		...				....
" 3d w.,					...		....				....
" 4th w.,					..		...				...
" 5th w.,	1			1	6,000	8,000	55,000				......
" 6th w.,	1			1	14,000	6,600	46,150				......
" 7th w.,					.....		...				...
" 8th w.,							...				....
" 9th w.,					..	.	...	3		3	135000
" 10th w.,					..		..	4		4	540000
Ecorse,						.	.	2		2	41,000
Greenfield,					..	...	...	4	1	3	9,200
Grosse Point,					....		.	1		1	5,000
Hamtramck,					....		..	3		3	21,000
Huron,					....		..	2		2	5,500
Livonia,					...		..	1		1	2,000
Monguagon,	1	2		1	5,000	5,500	27,500	1		1	60,000
Nankin,	1	4	1		6,000	.	3,935	3		3	28,000
Northville vil.							.				....
Plymouth,	5		5		29,800	11504	80,003	5	5		5,550
" village,					..		..				.....
Redford,	1		1		6,000	625	7,430	2	1	1	2,000
Romulus,					.....		....				....
Springwells,					.		...				......
Sumpter,					...		....	1		1	4,700
Taylor,					..	.	.	1		1	2,400
Van Buren,	2	.	1	1	18,500	4,500	21,000	3	2	1	18,000
Wayne vil.,					......	.	.				......
Total,	14	8	10	4	105300	41229	282562	43	11	32	901950

WAYNE COUNTY.—Continued.

Saw Mills.		Aggregate of all kinds of Manufactures, Mills included.				Estimated value of Real and Personal Estate.	
Annual product.			Hands employ'd				
Feet of Lumber Sawed.	Value of.	Capital invested in real and personal estate in the business.	Males.	Females.	Value of annual product.	By Assessors.	By assistant Marshals.
1,500,000	$10000	$27,500	26	3	$36,800	..	..
1,080,000	10,320	6,450	15		12,920		....
1,150,000	9,000	17,000	8		36,944	..	....
....	..				..		..
...	.	..			...		.....
....	.	....					.....
..	..	.					....
.....	.	253,850	255	2	335,105		....
	..	162,500	343	3	586,500		..
...	...	85,850	74	38	160,570	.	...
...	...	129,500	93		137,788		....
.....	...	39,000	26		46,000	...	.....
11000000	138250	192,400	162		357,150	..	....
22250000	276800	712,880	367		508,630	15766610	21022046
3,000,000	32,000	425,000	416		731,565	...	......
1,263,000	10,504	13,250	19		21,964	.....	....
700,000	5,600	20,594	72		17,142	......	.....
910,000	7,600	209,360	224		224,022	.	.....
2,075,000	14,500	8,000	9		19,000	.	...
600,000	5,000	4,400	19		10,960		...
4,000,000	40,000	87,100	130		106,424	...	..
1,750,000	15,500	40,700	36		30,923	..	...
	..	...			..	...	...
1,015,000	9,675	132,607	172	60	223,931	...	..
..	..	...	.		.		...
450,000	3,600	9,325	14		16,732	..	.....
....	...	.....			...		.....
...	....	240,600	253		1585070	...	.....
1,000,000	10,000	4,700	4		10,000	..	......
400,000	3,200	2,750	7		4,200	.....	......
2,600,000	26,000	51,400	45		64,100	..	....
......	...	.....	.		.....	4,600,473	6,133,964
56743000	627549	2876716	2789	106	5284040	20367083	27156010

Note.—The first line of figures in the last two columns includes the city; the 2d, the county.

RECAPITULATION

COUNTIES.	Dwelling Houses.		Number of Families.	Number of Inhabitants.				
	Whole number.	Number in Cities.		Whole number.	Colored.	Deaf and Dumb.	Blind.	Insane.
Allegan,	3,308	....	3,163	16,091	56	6	4	4
Alcona,	75	....	34	181	... .	....	....	....
Alpena,	108	....	49	291	....	....	....	....
Barry,	2,933	....	2,707	14,041	58	12	6	5
Bay,	654	....	635	3,169	6	2	2	2
Berrien,	4,471	544	4,406	22,274	404	8	6	9
Branch,	4,092	....	4,144	21,197	32	6	2	4
Calhoun,	6,028	1,553	5,623	29,398	372	5	13	12
Cass,	3,408	....	3,453	17,895	1,366	10	7	7
Cheboygan,	171	....	106	599	....	....	....	....
Chippewa,	354	....	354	1,544	8	....	....	....
Clinton,	2,946	....	2,669	13,923	13	3	4	8
Delta,	244	....	215	1,172	....	....	....	....
Eaton,	3,370	....	3,291	16,574	20	6	5	2
Emmet,	522	....	248	1,155	....	4	3	....
Genesee,	4,451	583	4,423	22,607	35	93	10	11
Grand Traverse,	375	....	260	1,288	....	....	....	....
Gratiot,	838	....	838	4,027	5	....	1	1
Hillsdale,	4,952	....	5,049	26,301	31	5	5	8
Houghton,	1,239	....	1,273	9,253	61	....	....	....
Huron,	645	....	641	3,167	1	....	1	....
Ingham,	3,454	607	3,458	17,456	32	4	5	3
Ionia,	3,499	....	3,385	16,665	1	27	11	3
Iosco,	113	....	47	175	....	....	....	....
Isabella,	328	....	304	1,445	....	....	....	....
Jackson,	5,060	782	5,033	26,664	167	9	9	4
Kalamazoo,	4,787	....	4,668	24,663	297	9	8	89
Kent,	6,894	1,816	6,310	30,743	114	11	1	8
Lapeer,	3,005	....	2,847	14,875	52	11	6	6
Leelenaw,	427	....	436	2,445	3	1	....	....
Lenawee,	7,313	1,188	7,476	38,497	219	15	8	27
Livingston,	3,182	....	3,174	16,629	30	2	9	6
Mackinaw,	415	....	356	1,939	6	1	1	....
Macomb,	4,448	....	4,498	23,112	51	15	12	6
Manistee,	247	.... ..	191	874	4	....	....	....
Manitou,	231	....	225	1,043	....	....	1	....
Marquette,	524	....	482	2,821	59	....	....	....
Mason,	241	....	208	831	....	....	....	....
Mecosta,	223	....	209	1,017	4	....	....	....
Midland,	173	....	173	782	1	....	....	....
Monroe,	4,079	758	4,090	21,648	25	6	6	2
Montcalm,	923	....	822	3,984	8	4	1	1
Muskegon,	816	....	739	3,893	21	1	....	....
Newaygo,	737	....	536	2,767	50	3	1	....
Oakland,	7,268	....	7,173	38,020	287	13	13	14
Oceana,	521	....	519	1,802	10	1	2	1
Ontonagon,	684	....	684	4,575	29	....	1	....
Osceola,	12	....	9	27	....	....	....	....
Ottawa,	2,763	....	2,668	13,127	24	8	1	1
Presque Isle,	9	....	5	26	....	....	....	....
Saginaw,	2,577	937	2,510	12,758	29	4	8	1
Sanilac,	1,572	....	1,498	7,623	... .	....	....	2
Schoolcraft,	28	....	14	78	4	....	1	....
Shiawassee,	2,656	245	2,432	12,888	12	1	2	3
St. Clair,	5,170	1,177	4,950	26,814	30	19	2	8
St. Joseph,	5,347	... .	5,362	21,111	45	1	2	2
Tuscola,	977	... .	967	4,885	... .	1	3	1
Van Buren,	2,912	....	2,918	15,230	146	6	8	3
Washtenaw,	6,652	1,531	6,680	35,747	522	6	21	13
Wayne,	14,294	8,248	14,623	75,284	1,670	20	25	61
Total,	149,655	19,964	146,290	751,110	16,310	354	233	338

RECAPITULATION.—Continued.

COUNTIES.	Value of Real Estate owned.	Occupied Farms.			
		Whole number.	Acres improved.	Acres unimproved.	Cash value of.
Allegan,	$4,624,156	1,828	60,804	108,226	$3,200,990
Alcona,	55,100	......	......	......	......
Alpena,	44,600	......	......	......	......
Barry,	3,690 590	1,470	74,179	91,412	2,876,965
Bay,	921,230	102	2,567	5 963	134,110
Berrien,	7,672 600	1,656	73,952	102 895	4,646,198
Branch,	6,754 089	2,162	107,853	106,912	5,076,834
Calhoun,	12,191,988	2,843	195,032	144 800	8,630,484
Cass,	7,070,992	1,789	114,413	109 294	5,773,850
Cheboygan,	30,755	80	573	2,860	12,977
Chippewa,	165 550	48	1,479	9,221	70,530
Clinton,	3,993 515	2,074	78,425	112,932	3,578,230
Delta,	315,323	16	457	1,722	12,170
Eaton,	4,546,192	1,606	71,913	92,969	3,175,019
Emmet,	68,052	55	668	6.339	21,285
Genesee,	8,451,720	1,781	99,093	87,859	4,666,460
Grand Traverse,	143,130	70	2,102	7,702	67,230
Gratiot,	569 560	333	7,858	33 427	338,230
Hillsdale,	8,827,687	3,162	163,276	140 705	7,293,970
Houghton,	757,450	25	1,541	16 271	115,740
Huron,	569,000	148	3,471	16,354	124,800
Ingham,	6,106,798	1,576	81,296	93,151	3,690,164
Ionia,	5,274,184	2,027	79,712	99,478	4,051,276
Iosco,	12,950	......	......	......	......
Isabella,	94,095	99	2,075	12.016	97,600
Jackson,	11,712 271	2,596	209,023	158,504	8,448,019
Kalamazoo,	12,574,943	1,940	137,663	129 276	8,152,813
Kent,	11,409,435	2,634	111.558	143,866	6,453,320
Lapeer,	4,765 560	1,544	83,383	88.941	3,405,481
Leelenaw,	239,138	54	1,373	8,372	66,813
Lenawee,	14,190,595	3,258	198,955	147,241	9,348,941
Livingston,	5,826,194	1,779	130,770	122,192	4,535,115
Mackinaw,	132,207	8	646	2.323	16,350
Macomb,	8,144,516	2,484	127,929	106,052	6,411,849
Manistee,	46,680	......	......	......	......
Manitou,	23,797	3	320	350	6,000
Marquette,	136.330	30	1,082	1,573	64,185
Mason,	29.950	43	1,214	28,600	165,250
Mecosta,	101,500	30	907	3,845	29,400
Midland,	146,450	71	1,660	26.244	92,800
Monroe,	5,917,297	2,128	94,687	107,557	4,031,033
Montcalm,	887,940	298	14.247	20,223	478,730
Muskegon,	1,036,585	194	4,709	19,887	243,580
Newaygo,	388,460	107	6,269	10,087	126,400
Oakland,	16,727,870	4,252	305,759	197.657	13,667,210
Oceana,	197,305	83	1,891	7,925	66,970
Ontonagon,	475,300	72	2,845	20,451	163,950
Osceola,	10,680	3	220	815	5,200
Ottawa,	3,062,375	1,174	37,522	63,026	1,760,145
Presque Isle,	......	......	......	......	......
Saginaw,	2,809 413	564	17,924	40,368	665,654
Sanilac,	857,315	408	15,373	32,457	426,190
Schoolcraft,	28,200	......	......	......	......
Shiawassee,	3,774,702	892	43,727	66 818	1,957,834
St. Clair,	6,720,021	955	46,902	73 540	2,311,142
St. Joseph,	8,914,793	2,233	151,192	115.983	6,754,445
Tuscola,	406 535	882	18.837	98,609	1,015.011
Van Buren,	4.762 680	1.395	64.506	83.125	3,144,945
Washtenaw,	16.944.099	3.230	240.681	152.183	11,863,150
Wayne,	36 433 863	2.473	123.718	109 341	9,180,730
Total,	$262,785,750	62,722	3,421,120	3,589,442	$162,713,267

RECAPITULATION.—CONTINUED.

Value of Farming Implements and Machinery.	Live Stock, June 1st, 1860. Horses.	Asses and Mules.	Milch Cows.	Working Oxen.	Other Cattle.	Sheep.	Swine.	Value of Live Stock.
$143,097	1,946	16	4,242	2,320	4,809	9,889	9,706	$490,984
...	...	...	...	...	...	...	...	...
...	...	...	...	...	...	...	...	...
113,124	2,174	3	3,502	2,212	5,132	22,585	8,172	463,248
8,060	101	..	204	100	250	45	207	22,533
125,457	3,591	13	4,328	1,697	5,729	8,702	14,473	567,264
138,064	4,862	3	6,076	1,877	8,445	36,507	19,985	786,828
334,993	6,561	9	8,353	3,041	10,195	96,309	18,312	1,248,976
154,275	4,638	7	4,928	1,255	6,792	23,058	17,815	712,687
538	35	..	36	25	52	14	104	5,106
4,985	56	2	95	45	67	18	45	9,294
125,969	2,016	2	4,858	2,546	7,488	17,527	9,626	509,571
1,025	40	...	44	60	55	11	142	5,300
125,315	2,669	....	4,822	1,832	7,937	26,923	9,541	538,019
953	91	....	2[illegible]	13	40	3	266	6,481
173,082	4,432	6	5,407	1,986	8,103	49,820	10,266	725,258
2,300	49	9	101	176	128	21	266	22,107
11,344	183	...	713	533	863	586	1,269	50,842
273,514	6,288	4	8,936	2,793	11,668	68,168	14,583	1,192,651
2,170	67	...	23	31	76	....	13	9,950
400	71	3	244	284	280	41	155	28,657
120,327	2,721	11	4,323	1,858	5,961	33,240	7,446	547,280
157,740	3,179	36	5,070	3,064	7,259	25,425	11,492	533,750
...	...	...	...	...	...	...	...	...
5,776	16	....	141	131	184	75	276	11,491
251,321	6,507	14	7,782	3,273	9,868	107,931	12,549	1,279,313
264,335	5,345	17	5,774	1,577	7,383	54,567	13,697	912,165
105,898	3,893	3	6,806	2,929	7,900	22,737	12,019	709,744
158,537	3,356	6	4,078	1,645	5,201	26,966	5,517	548,636
3,155	34	...	53	65	47	10	208	7,170
329,372	9,561	16	11,256	2,219	17,749	90,538	24,854	1,511,304
162,506	4,199	6	5,561	2,158	8,027	56,681	8,922	749,699
155	23	...	50	10	48	....	60	3,170
293,941	6,879	2	7,467	1,246	8,316	49,176	9,785	919,928
...	...	...	...	...	...	...	...	...
1,180	13	...	16	26	35	40	20	2,411
1,622	30	...	27	15	23	....	6	5,946
8,460	50	....	53	129	54	....	464	13,615
710	22	....	66	41	68	12	91	5,277
3,113	48	...	141	137	155	....	290	13,360
156,914	6,141	41	6,611	1,522	9,701	27,022	12,073	784,474
14,038	309	2	688	415	764	2,426	1,175	71,904
7,806	99	....	344	238	347	140	778	28,951
6,333	89	..	204	146	193	203	568	19,228
466,539	12,686	42	14,263	3,034	17,248	136,492	22,665	2,020,252
2,990	36	....	122	95	132	11	191	11,580
7,490	98	4	67	65	25	1	132	20,240
....	9	...	8	8	9	....	27	1,370
53,486	1,180	7	2,920	1,321	4,011	3,314	6,207	241,386
...	...	...	...	...	...	...	...	...
55,213	715	..	1,605	847	2,480	1,431	2,682	124,001
14,619	568	...	922	421	1,006	1,640	1,242	53,745
...	...	...	...	...	...	...	...	...
84,968	1,793	1	2,90[illegible]	1,387	4,132	19,379	5,156	326,724
96,620	2,488	11	3,045	827	4,737	10,709	3,452	319,225
245,671	5,336	23	5,99[illegible]	1,212	7,867	28,717	21,499	899,156
18,1[illegible]	411	2	1,32[illegible]	1,019	1,40[illegible]	753	2,462	133,405
112,461	2,17[illegible]	5	3,23[illegible]	1,71[illegible]	3,74[illegible]	7,521	6,982	400,710
437,782	9,634	4	11,[illegible]	3,272	15,320	165,424	20,032	1,917,047
311,856	8,041	..	9,0[illegible]	1,1[illegible]	10,913	33,862	16,607	1,075,095
$5,799,744	137,551	330	1[illegible]0,441	62,055	240,428	1,266,680	366,572	$23,618,458

RECAPITULATION.—CONTINUED.

COUNTIES.	PRODUCE, DURING THE YEAR						
	Wheat, bushels of	Rye, bushels of.	Indian corn, bushels of.	Oats, bushels of.	Barley, bushels of.	Buckwheat, bushels of.	Potatoes, bushels of.
Allegan,..	147,684	13,154	274,532	49,611	2,682	9,704	107,405
Alcona,........	......	......	......	......	......	......	......
Alpena,.......	......	......	......	......	......	......	......
Barry,....... ..	230,200	9,871	224,326	63,186	3,989	7,610	85,879
Bay,..........	4,690	1,670	4,655	3,989	25	834	6,404
Berrien,........	255,936	26,132	438,520	72,545	1,680	3,703	118,886
Branch,.........	288,176	11,219	545,132	76,645	5,691	17,709	211,282
Calhoun,........	692,804	12,197	612,109	187,216	18,455	8,194	217,656
Cass,..........	424,029	3,140	680,328	125,936	2,843	5,807	142,979
Cheboygan, ...	113	64	309	1,792	150	......	5,127
Chippewa,......	50	240	......	3,555	200	......	9,760
Clinton, ...	149,182	5,731	161,105	90,123	4,146	5,963	59,780
Delta,....... ..	65	......	210	2,370	155	......	6,180
Eaton,..........	79,598	7,479	166,312	84,208	8,938	7,384	62,702
Emmet,.........	100	15	1,996	1,643	......	36	7,060
Genesee,........	166,308	12,514	234,969	159,480	25,849	9,352	105,309
Grand Traverse,.	5,523	436	3,400	4,370	28	169	7,015
Gratiot,.........	14,472	822	17,671	9,202	388	922	8,122
Hillsdale,.......	378,416	22,438	813,994	107,075	6,623	41,270	264,047
Houghton,......	100	20	......	3,030	......	......	8,050
Huron,........	5,143	762	2,756	5,944	......	......	14,450
Ingham, ...	140,043	7,683	233,426	103,757	4,657	9,472	85,607
Ionia, ...	227,906	13,049	156,829	105,597	4,970	6,122	69,876
Iosco,...... ..	......	......	......	......	......	......	......
Isabella,........	2,165	736	1,777	937	28	135	1,974
Jackson,........	667,694	19,591	600,268	145,641	17,487	23,822	216,152
Kalamazoo,.....	585,235	6,368	548,691	147,529	15,944	4,868	128,053
Kent, ...	287,121	34,456	227,682	134,774	3,046	7,367	131,684
Lapeer,..... ..	169,668	18,630	177,468	110,880	11,061	12,430	111,955
Leelenaw,......	1,240	618	5,371	1,770	3	212	10,644
Lenawee,.......	424,302	13,119	1,225,371	204,271	18,147	48,330	296,682
Livingston,.....	273,545	39,534	268,473	105,371	10,067	17,885	161,222
Mackinaw,......	2	......	10	600	60	2	1,582
Macomb,........	74,923	24,914	329,238	319,993	12,438	36,399	265,318
Manistee,.......	......	......	......	......	......	......	......
Manitou,........	......	200	1,630	......	......	930	50
Marquette,......	......	30	......	2,897	......	......	9,845
Mason, ...	555	27	8,360	810	5	81	7,920
Mecosta,........	1,312	406	687	2,020	47	44	1,000
Midland,........	3,961	1,026	9,565	114	644	471	4,794
Monroe,........	140,408	9,468	497,119	112,006	20,648	37,810	229,119
Montcalm,......	36,144	2,313	20,339	16,379	214	775	13,390
Muskegon,.....	5,223	1,444	7,142	2,494	68	231	5,876
Newaygo, ...	7,226	8,206	7,191	2,281	18	103	5,717
Oakland, ...	551,104	93,692	870,866	475,934	47,211	68,176	517,936
Oceana, ...	1,603	503	9,373	297	21	545	8,253
Ontonagon,... .	......	......	......	1,771	5	......	18,930
Osceola,... ...	150	......	......	500	......	......	225
Ottawa, ...	61,198	15,330	92,798	47,349	2,888	2,959	50,309
Presque Isle,....	......	......	......	......	......	......	......
Saginaw,........	31,739	13,252	57,244	42,027	1,182	154	42,306
Sanilac, ...	24,714	310	9,247	46,184	50	1,113	30,369
Schoolcraft, ...	......	......	......	......	......	......	......
Shiawassee, ...	101,101	5,773	93,467	43,071	3,829	2,830	54,199
St. Clair,.... ...	43,243	7,862	115,647	125,523	2,051	17,048	134,806
St. Joseph,......	613,953	8,093	909,103	69,733	4,171	10,591	264,546
Tuscola, ...	26,435	3,482	39,332	22,308	428	1,710	28,190
Van Buren,...	183,159	3,517	341,785	55,779	1,518	5,788	95,278
Washtenaw,...	663,768	21,759	791,429	303,492	25,929	44,458	318,113
Wayne,..	68,774	22,631	535,055	255,889	12,274	43,094	485,752
Total,......	8,171,688	525,716	12,372,877	4,063,528	302,951	523,687	5,258,628

RECAPITULATION.—CONTINUED.

ENDING JUNE 1ST, 1860.							
Wool, pounds of.	Value of Orchard products.	Butter, pounds of.	Cheese, pounds of.	Hay, tons of.	Clover seed, bushels.	Maple Sugar, pounds.	Value of home made manufactures.
26,162	12,205	332,731	51,069	15,774	72	272,065	$3,311
....	....	....	....	....	....	....	....
....	....	....	....	....	....	....	....
60,501	10,610	310,138	24,494	17,919	273	241,550	2,610
....	....	9,615	1,640	2,416	....	895	....
26,689	75,265	322,483	30,379	13,812	648	55,410	6,530
101,373	33,186	389,392	49,801	21,996	1,996	110,480	1,088
299,905	61,771	834,289	67,324	42,361	6,247	4,725	7,134
63,781	70,724	335,367	27,041	16,177	1,545	70,891	2,595
....	....	1,950	....	113	....	9,200	....
....	....	3,110	....	565	....	2,750	....
50,855	7,003	459,271	32,463	16,352	223	339,273	1,244
....	....	640	....	293	....	2,250	....
90,134	14,853	428,350	74,519	16,085	285	460,645	7,658
....	150	187	....	48	....	43,538	50
143,643	13,886	489,868	53,385	21,297	612	163,197	1,986
....	....	9,290	....	54	15	16,440	....
1,878	....	51,775	1,175	1,756	....	93,150	....
220,301	64,230	903,517	110,319	33,054	2,067	122,014	8,945
....	....	....	....	625	....	300	....
....	....	1,550	....	850	....	....	....
89,803	20,895	400,055	37,788	19,485	492	190,514	16,744
66,908	12,599	408,248	44,879	19,893	1,051	315,323	7,906
....	....	....	....	....	....	....	....
143	....	2,043	200	186	2	23,806	....
352,304	85,579	662,559	58,279	51,707	3,124	400	6,588
187,160	39,920	496,158	68,237	24,442	2,263	141,490	2,890
69,102	23,214	608,422	47,070	32,281	234	282,378	13,193
87,968	10,572	439,313	42,770	15,134	661	175,397	6,863
30	....	2,415	....	155	....	22,628	....
279,193	88,534	982,855	131,233	48,241	2,927	40,566	2,155
167,028	18,389	440,874	36,065	33,037	2,890	14,378	3,635
....	30	650	....	206	....	1,600	....
177,640	25,544	652.509	62,411	18,645	413	51,608	6,660
....	....	....	....	....	....	....	....
50	....	750	....	28	....	500	....
....	....	....	....	243	....	400	....
....	620	2,765	....	65	....	4,024	....
35	....	3,050	....	165	....	12,060	....
....	....	8,830	....	293	....	10,650	....
66,517	31,048	510,769	84,030	23,394	1,144	14,276	1,934
5,875	878	55,515	4,923	1,913	28	51,136	832
40	10	28,045	1,735	974	....	47,760	80
357	....	13,535	....	503	....	18,159	....
426,796	96,895	1,393,741	131,633	58,735	5,483	31,581	7,535
....	1,126	9,076	300	90	....	16,321	....
....	....	1,200	....	1,068	....	200	....
....	....	....	....	36	....	1,500	....
7,851	4,151	227,873	11,828	10,141	95	188,842	2,087
....	....	....	....	....	....	....	....
3,682	....	113,365	1,700	6,295	8	8,864	....
4,858	35	19,565	430	1,928	....	4,195	....
....	....	....	....	....	....	....	....
46,770	8,976	251,011	18,582	12,579	104	96,723	3,328
30,788	1,898	299,373	25,315	13,195	23	58,498	3,423
97,522	37,738	515,213	38,937	23,753	3,706	7,795	6,276
1,972	....	93,483	4,090	2,790	3	79,926	160
22,237	24,887	307,327	19,849	12,506	539	95,103	999
551,232	135,529	950,316	114,482	68,741	9,619	14,144	4,688
100,030	83,319	717,331	119,622	36,742	1,287	14,262	3,701
3,929,113	$1,116,219	15,498,047	1,610,097	761,156	50,079	3,973,780	$144,758

RECAPITULATION.—Continued.

COUNTIES.	Flouring Mills.							Saw Mills.			
	Number of.	Runs of Stone.	Power used.		Capital invested in real and personal estate in the business.	Annual product.		Number of.	Power used.		Capital invested in real and personal estate in the business.
			Water.	Steam.		Bbls. flour made.	Value of.		Water.	Steam.	
Allegan,	9	16	8	1	$52,500	5,153	$124,401	35	18	17	$214,000
Alcona,								1	1		20,000
Alpena,								4	3	1	38,000
Barry,	8	9	8		32 000	443,350	66,638	22	17	5	57,400
Bay,	1	2		1	16,000	3,500	25,000	20		20	415,200
Berrien,	10	5	7	3	148,500	111,394	631,066	51	22	29	344,050
Branch,	2	2		2	8,686	2,250	12,500	30	14	16	82,060
Calhoun,	15		14	1	439,000	169,248	900,130	11	4	7	45,500
Cass,	8	13	6	2	58,250	26,566	156,139	27	17	10	68,800
Cheboygan,								1		1	2,300
Chippewa,								1			12,000
Clinton,	9		4	5	44,000	50,100	296,400	18	6	12	48,000
Delta,								7	2	5	324,000
Eaton,	8	19	6	3	127,800	24,416	184,875	19	12	7	56,700
Emmet,	1				2 000		1,000				
Genesee,	8	9	8	2	55,000	23,267	166,819	26	13	14	239,280
Grand Traverse,	1							2	1		4,000
Gratiot,											
Hillsdale,	15	19	10	6	83,900	14,900	183,670	43	18	24	71,600
Houghton,								3	1	3	77,000
Huron,								14	1	13	371,000
Ingham,	8	18	4	4	50,500	31,324	182,625	25	4	21	67,600
Ionia,	13		11	2	94,000	58,324	303,227	16	10	6	73,000
Iosco,								1		1	20,000
Isabella,											
Jackson,	14		12	1	196.000	64,700	409,556	9	3	6	14,600
Kalamazoo,	9		8	1	79 500	157,250	840,125	30	22	8	63,600
Kent,	17		16	1	168.500	65,541	488,495	44	37	7	170,950
Lapeer,	9	5	5	2	33,600	15,250	110,800	38	22	13	86,000
Leelenaw,								3	3		4.000
Lenawee,	15		11	5	108,100	108,452	663,305	37	10	27	120,615
Livingston,	16		15	4	92,600	18,511	196,700	17	13	4	20,100
Mackinaw,											
Macomb,	6		5	1	34,500	8,000	75,975	16	7	8	33,300
Manistee,								9	4	5	555,000
Manitou,											
Marquette,								7	5	2	36,000
Mason,								4	2	2	94,000
Mecosta,								2	2		25,000
Midland,								2		2	14,000
Monroe,	5	4	5		35,500	10,000	82,200	17	9	8	50,200
Montcalm,	1		2		8,500		15,500	8	8		54,000
Muskegon,								28	9	19	705,650
Newaygo,	2		2		9,000	800	21,120	6	3	3	43,500
Oakland,	20	8	18	2	164,100	58,814	370,856	3	2		4,500
Oceana,								4	2	2	81,000
Ontonagon,								4	1	2	12,000
Osceola,								1	1		2,000
Ottawa,	4		2	1	24,000	11,000	62,500	33	9	24	334,200
Presque Isle,											
Saginaw,	3	8		3	43,000	12 500	101,500	23	3	20	559,000
Sanilac,	2		2		7,000	2,700	15,006	9	3	6	75,500
Schoolcraft,											
Shiawassee,	5	10	5		98 500	25,784	153.828	11	6	5	33,500
St. Clair,	5		3	2	27.000	10,900	118 547	28	9	18	521,020
St. Joseph,	15		[illegible]	1	143 000	30,705	634,103	25	22	3	63,600
Tuscola,	4		3	1	13 000		28,450	8	4	4	32,000
Van Buren,	[illegible]	[illegible]	4		88 000	18.250	101.000	22	13	9	161,050
Washtenaw,	21	64	20	2	260.500	161.211	983.220	38	22	11	82,600
Wayne,	14	8	10	4	105,800	41,229	282 562	43	11	32	901,950
Total,	309	224	247	63	$2,951,336	1,786,289	$8,989,824	901	431	462	$7,607,026

RECAPITULATION.—CONTINUED.

Saw Mills. Annual product.		Aggregate of all kinds of manufactures, Mills included.				Estimated value of Real and Personal Estate.	
Feet of Lumber Sawed.	Value of.	Capital invested in real and personal estate in the business.	Hands employ'd: Males.	Hands employ'd: Females.	Value of annual products.	By Assessors.	By assistant Marshals.
27,460,000	$249,890	$366,250	415	4	$516,190	....	$3,021,847
600,000	4,050	23,150	31	...	14,651	....	219,184
2,600,000	23,300	47,600	113	....	40,437	....	....
7,931,000	61,560	106,100	93	....	167,211	$1,724,014	2,298,685
44,850,000	373,200	460,600	426	..	439,115	724,422	800,000
37,611,600	363,157	661,857	663	....	1,341,239	4,445,603	6,068,255
12,540,000	101,766	165,976	223	61	260,584	3,738,257	5,601,885
3,699,500	32,778	762,600	515	...	1,392,968	5,424,740	7,100,000
6,470,000	70,320	173,400	169	...	327,988	3,705,513	4,939,357
900,000	800	6,200	22	...	13,550	81,095	68,900
....	....	12,000	....	....	....	200,805	200,805
4,966,000	292,000	137,900	153	...	668,967	2,280,159	2,280,159
30,500,000	170,000	326,000	320	17	175,600	308,487	499,521
6,172,500	60,726	228,235	138	...	318,603	3,111,087	6,222,156
....	....	2,000	3	...	1,000	10,975	111,686
20,796,000	165,952	391,980	336	...	459,330	4,618,835	9,237,660
500,000	3,000	4,500	8	1	4,458	435,649	435,649
....	....	....	....	...	....	827,547	806,399
11,005,000	98,430	309,710	349	27	488,558	5,105,417	5,106,467
4,500,000	83,500	1,505,100	2,418	....	1,461,580	1,407,978	1,680,000
25,150,000	271,550	871,000	848	....	271,551	405,704	405,704
11,418,000	87,717	215,165	394	21	521,325	3,039,929	9,000,000
6,190,000	55,010	241,600	166	....	449,677	3,341,[illegible]	4,455,000
250,000	10,000	20,000	20	....	10,000	78,000	....
....	....	....	....	...	....	463,975	463,975
1,064,000	10,430	660,700	681	20	996,148	5,679,352	6,685,668
3,824,000	89,730	350,275	446	9	1,311,159	4,989,411	2,622,979
25,750,000	145,450	1,183,930	1,004	190	1,620,164	....	....
16,805,000	131,960	170,100	208	5	347,920	2,253,251	4,506,502
620,000	8,825	10,550	48	...	15,986	....	....
14,828,727	182,070	14,064,906	1,172	225	3,376,421	... .	10,328,323
2,428,000	20,280	176,850	144	1	293,825	3,190,816	6,181,631
....	....	3,600	16	....	6,700	202,615	403,742
5,537,000	47,840	169,100	286	1	362,641	5,074,767	7,699,220
35,000,000	218,000	569,850	502	42	278,289	605,943	605,943
....	....	7,000	....	....	42,000	73,771	73,771
3,146,523	17,377	926,100	401	...	828,074	861,670	20,000,000
18,000,000	90,000	98,700	120	31	99,850	266,978	....
140,000	13,000	25,000	6	....	13,000	376,447	....
2,000,000	14,000	14,800	37	....	14,750	657,997	848,377
6,707,136	56,743	144,706	223	47	251,413	4,059,171	4,519,787
5,800,000	29,000	68,300	75	12	50,500	907,722	1,361,584
75,140,000	464,068	735,900	653	....	536,568	986,609	1,488,138
10,700,000	75,350	57,300	97	...	105,220	964,312	964,212
835,000	2,680	886,074	401	76	740,170	9,953,812	13,942,448
6,800,000	33,000	78,200	139	22	43,650	505,916	....
1,850,000	20,400	2,177,200	1,419	....	966,100	1,251,562	4,487,000
100,000	800	2,000	3	....	800	....	....
49,500,000	213,840	470,425	492	....	555,120	2,001,259	3,113,459
....	... .	50	1	....	100	....	....
66,100,000	576,100	663,500	512	5	750,120	2,606,831	3,910,246
18,700,000	119,200	87,300	127	....	156,200	1,456,939	1,456,939
....	....	....	....	...	....	250,570	500,000
2,900,000	24,700	178,500	123	13	295,480	2,246,756	4,325,000
54,700,000	660,774	600,770	557	...	888,502	6,813,554	11,182,969
7,4[illegible]5,000	90,560	460,815	496	24	1,048,983	1,997,488	2,509,380
5,700,000	48,600	53,85[illegible]	75	1	97,050	1,172,340	....
15,700,000	146,300	297,550	212	...	336,075	2,598,780	3,248,475
8,525,700	119,397	910,650	904	164	2,000,458	8,900,000	17,800,000
56,[illegible]43,000	627,649	2,876,716	2,[illegible]	100	5,284,040	2[illegible] 567,[illegible]	27,176,010
795,606,698	6,891,769	35,308,590	21,702	1125	33,068,071	138,663,848	234,294,538

MINERAL STATISTICS.

COUNTIES.	Number of Companies.	Hands Employed.	Capital Invested.	Products.		Value of Products.
				Kinds.	Tons Raised.	
Houghton,	18	2,348	$1,911,500	Copper	2,783	$1,393,180
Marquette,	6	242	815,000	Iron.	138,800	636,400
Ontonagon, .	15	1,333	2,141,500	Copper	2,624	877,008
Total,	39	3,923	$4,868,000		144,207	$2,906,588

FISHING STATISTICS.

COUNTIES.	Capital Invested.	Annual Products.	
		Number of Barrels.	Value of.
Bay, ...	$15,000	6,000	$48,000
Berrien, . .	6,200	3,375	25,500
Chippewa,. ..	9,000	3,200	19,600
Delta, ...	5,700	2,509	15,368
Grand Traverse, .	200	86	688
Huron, . . .	9,800	4,200	30,690
Leelenaw,	4,050	1,326	10,608
Mackinac, . .	47,000	17,843	103,938
Manistee, ...	1,600	793	6,344
Manitou, ...	7,000	6,000	42,000
Marquette, . .	1,000	620	3,660
Mason,..	4,100	1,130	7,600
Oceana,.	2,200	950	6,650
Ontonagon,.	2,100	1,000	6,000
Ottawa,.	8,000	5,800	34,600
St. Clair, ...	725	850	5,090
Wayne, ...	54,700	3,375	29,300
Total, ...	$178,375	59,057	$395,636

STATISTICS

OF

MICHIGAN IN 1850,

COMPILED FROM THE

CENSUS OF THE UNITED STATES.

RECAPITULATION.

COUNTIES.	Dwelling Houses.		Number of Families.	Number of Inhabitants.				
	Whole number.	Number in Cities.		Whole number.	Colored.	Deaf and Dumb.	Blind.	Insane.
Allegan,	996	....	1,044	5,127	5	4	1	6
Barry,	1,040	....	1,055	5.072	8	2	2	3
Berrien,	2,127	....	2,156	11 417	215	4	1	8
Branch,	2,400	....	2,469	12,472	14	....	....	8
Calhoun,	3,684	....	3,762	19.169	196	5	6	5
Cass,	1,915	....	1,931	10,906	387	4	....	5
Chippewa,	187	....	187	898	15	....	....	....
Clinton,	947	....	951	5,102	2	....	1	1
Eaton,	1,325	....	1.351	7 058	3	4	1	1
Genesee,	2,253	....	2.267	12,031	14	....	6	1
Hillsdale,	2,965	....	3,026	16 159	5	3	2	1
Houghton,	116	....	116	798	....	....	....	....
Huron,	....	....	.....	*207	....	....	....	....
Ingham,	1,597	....	1,603	8,643	18	2	3	....
Ionia,	1,374	....	1,393	7.597	....	1	1	1
Jackson,	3,543	....	3,583	19 433	64	10	2	8
Kalamazoo,	2,191	....	2,210	13 179	97	5	....	6
Kent,	2,246	489	2.246	12,017	30	2	4	2
Lapeer,	1,287	....	1,296	7.026	6	2	5	1
Lenawee,	4,911	....	4,938	26 380	91	11	11	19
Livingston,	2,366	....	2,370	13,475	....	4	6	3
Macomb,	2,664	....	2,711	15.532	27	1	4	7
Mackinaw,	581	....	607	3,597	31	....	....	....
Marquette,	18	....	18	136	....	....	....	....
Mason,	12	....	12	93	....	....	....	....
Midland,	10	....	10	65	....	....	....	....
Montcalm,	164	....	165	891	....	....	....	....
Monroe,	2,536	476	2,556	14,695	54	8	12	4
Newaygo,	92	....	92	510	....	....	....	....
Oakland,	5,557	....	5,601	31,267	60	6	5	10
Oceana,	58	....	58	300	19	....	....	....
Ontonagon,	46	....	46	389	5	....	....	....
Ottawa,	1,128	....	1,134	5,587	35	1	....	2
Saginaw,	483	....	508	2 609	....	....	....	....
Sanilac,	420	....	420	2,322	....	....	1	....
Schoolcraft,	5	....	5	16	....	....	....	....
Shiawassee,	972	....	972	5,233	....	....	....	....
St. Clair,	1,817	....	1,817	10.411	23	3	....	1
St. Joseph,	2,303	....	2,316	12,717	23	2	1	2
Tuscola,	65	....	65	291	....	....	....	1
Van Buren,	985	....	1,006	5.804	2	....	1	....
Washtenaw,	5,080	....	5,080	28.569	117	6	17	7
Wayne,	7,049	3,144	7.406	42,765	699	15	15	15
Total,	71,515	4,109	72,560	397,985	2,265	105	108	129

*Balance reported with Sanilac.

RECAPITULATION.—CONTINUED.

COUNTIES.	Value of Real Estate owned.	Occupied Farms.			
		Whole number.	Acres improved.	Acres unimproved.	Cash value of.
Allegan,	$898,385	270	12,419	25,015	$405,160
Barry,	740.074	750	24,752	63.057	622,298
Berrien,	2,180,506	694	34.282	57.976	1,049,746
Branch,	2,096.483	1,463	64,141	87,886	1,609,370
Calhoun,	4,037,480	1,834	119.255	138.262	2,984,926
Cass,	1,924.804	952	59,998	80,520	1,502,701
Chippewa,	101.930	48	838	12,232	52,600
Clinton,	627,705	652	21,825	49 327	549.835
Eaton,	1,051,492	747	27,476	55,762	715,352
Genesee,	2,141,012	1,476	54,024	91,548	1.595.560
Hillsdale,	3,159 337	1,411	78,940	85,433	2,060,125
Houghton,	*52.810				
Huron,					
Ingham,	1,258,780	1,084	40.149	80,846	981,125
Ionia,	985.995	613	30.067	46.891	746,740
Jackson,	4,196,956	2.282	148,330	165,603	3,505,885
Kalamazoo,	2,971,250	1,100	73,047	80,133	1,997,320
Kent,	2,015,447	885	35,532	72,536	1,004,801
Lapeer,	1,186,153	628	34,903	39.543	782,240
Lenawee,	5,671,348	2.471	138,331	136,892	4,102,405
Livingston,	2,657 245	1,653	103.862	119,747	2,287,470
Macomb,	2,872.310	1,317	74,783	86,532	2,222,848
Mackinaw,	301.094	14	554	1,776	15,800
Marquette,	*4,350				
Mason,	19,400				
Midland,	4,195	4	207	1,281	13,575
Montcalm,	122 250	26	1,711	3,408	35,400
Monroe,	2,309,448	1,284	57,529	81,219	1,580,213
Newaygo,	54.250	12	646	699	8,200
Oakland,	7,619,091	3,559	234,428	209,574	6,541,689
Oceana,	16,460				
Ontonagon,	*81.250				
Ottawa,	580,890	204	4,914	19,128	181,497
Saginaw,	283.891	79	2,940	7,891	104,976
Sanilac,	222 550	88	3,612	4,944	78,850
Schoolcraft,	*2 020				
Shiawassee,	836.645	746	31.203	56.681	734,965
St. Clair,	1,388.638	500	37,060	50,175	636,283
St. Joseph,	2,797.097	1,354	94,266	99,930	2,526,367
Tuscola,	65,575	13	390	4,520	29,800
Van Buren,	868,219	488	21,018	36,142	510,615
Washtenaw,	7,244,735	2,546	179,714	159,547	4,979.342
Wayne,	7.318.794	1.632	83.213	106,873	3,1[illegible]8,575
Total,	$74,968,344	34,879	1,9[illegible]0,354	2,419,529	51,914,644

* Balance reported with Chippewa.

RECAPITULATION.—CONTINUED.

Value of Farming Implements and Machinery.	Live Stock, June 1st, 1850.							
	Horses.	Asses and Mules.	Milch Cows.	Working Oxen.	Other Cattle.	Sheep.	Swine.	Value of Live Stock.
$23,560	320	...	762	518	1,107	4,425	1,503	$67,929
28,439	618	....	592	451	1,816	8,486	4,312	121,549
59.486	1,609	2	1,912	847	2,368	11,302	7,199	161,800
74,54	1,726	5	3,276	1,867	4,354	21,864	6,830	254,504
129,007	3,325	3	6,366	3,778	6,357	49,663	11,369	507,217
77,682	2,065	....	2,617	1,046	2,947	17,670	8,398	212,262
4,082	88	7	71	98	53	19	111	15,620
31,278	528	....	1,552	1,125	2,083	5 085	4,788	108,671
45,15	712	1	1,858	1,288	2,563	8,857	4,055	116,416
83,814	1,654	....	3,663	2,524	4,574	25,665	6,145	267,064
117,682	2,090	....	3,885	1,953	4,982	27,862	7,199	323,808
....	......	...	.. ..	....	....	....	... ..	....
....	.. ....	...	....	....	....	....	....	....
46,089	815	....	2,419	1,896	2.464	11,523	4,062	166,942
38,649	711	2	1,58	1,266	2,365	8,447	3,336	128,030
155,888	3,457	7	6,19	4,321	6,269	51,094	11,590	501,013
142,767	2,353	....	3,934	1,868	4.330	37,674	9,113	246,126
57,388	791	...	2,163	1,641	2,649	8,1 4	4,843	174,997
49,788	933	....	1,656	1,455	2,344	16,462	3,435	165,021
201,524	4,752	4	7,53	2,792	10,321	70,385	12.154	629,244
119,375	2,217	8	4,53	3,421	4,767	32,282	8,740	382,078
101,502	2,54	2	4,4 7	1,575	5,241	35,582	7,593	311,890
866	22	....	56	20	58	....	46	3,035
....	....	...	....	.. ...	....	.... ..	....	....
....	....	...	.... ..	....	.... ..	....	....	....
525	9	...	10	16	15	37	40	1,294
2,020	49	....	72	63	66	469	158	6.575
117,927	2,835	....	4,061	2,046	5,110	19,925	10,984	286,308
725	7	....	26	26	28	8	130	2,275
385,874	6,507	1	10,597	6,924	10,608	113,804	17,633	920,273
....	....	....	....	....	....	....	.. ....	....
....	....	...	....	.. ..	....	....	....	....
8,961	90	...	538	287	837	192	1,349	21,848
5,224	145	....	289	144	387	777	479	21.536
4,391	78	....	248	192	272	774	389	17,070
.. ..	....	...	.. . ...	....	....	....	....	....
32.939	654	....	1,701	1,385	2,062	7,087	3.262	133,739
37,535	82	....	1,738	821	1,977	6,477	1.562	96,346
125,710	2,815	1	3,786	1,599	4,485	22,305	10,406	318,118
747	7	....	29	29	31	113	53	1.986
41,0 1	55	...	1,172	750	1,562	6.260	3,317	99,810
239,357	5,735	....	7,917	4,469	9,699	92,964	16,588	662,885
156,617	4,2 4	1	5,842	2,0 2	5,892	32,434	9,422	398,315
$2,748,311	57,842	44	97,557	56,203	117,043	756,382	202,588	$7,852,550

RECAPITULATION.—Continued.

COUNTIES.	Produce, during the Year						
	Wheat, bushels of.	Rye, bushels of.	Indian corn, bushels of.	Oats, bushels of.	Barley, bushels of.	Buckwheat, bushels of.	Potatoes, bushels of.
Allegan,	25,116	1,631	52,305	16,711	1,006	2,026	43,721
Barry,	79,871	929	111,609	40,442	1,572	3,021	51,837
Berrien,	88,263	144	227,650	74,175	260	3,249	60,215
Branch,	155,742	1,079	323,270	118,474	2,280	15,271	113,108
Calhoun,	390,774	3,565	334,20[illegible]	164,765	12,819	21,778	155,510
Cass,	159,997	126	422,740	122,000	1,475	4,396	64,625
Chippewa,	....	....	30	1,040	....	....	8,200
Clinton,	54,297	328	64,967	38,960	161	8,126	41,000
Eaton,	50,830	667	69,630	44,290	1,160	6,692	48,721
Genesee,	121,202	1,3[illegible]2	126,497	86,585	1,527	14,934	50,407
Hillsdale,	220,164	1,542	247,530	135,487	658	20,899	108,683
Houghton,	....	....	....	....	....	....	....
Huron,	....	....	....	....	....	....	....
Ingham,	81,687	423	95,270	58,414	277	12,981	59,790
Ionia,	76,946	2,543	75,945	44,003	1,057	7,312	57,304
Jackson,	476,617	5,266	268,725	177,237	2,980	26,478	160,115
Kalamazoo,	227,818	2,605	374,995	98,063	5,006	5,834	101,812
Kent,	69,800	4,117	93,610	59,822	2,817	12,044	74,129
Lapeer,	84,831	1,999	52,505	52,935	456	7,848	42,638
Lenawee,	318,529	3,235	393,546	177,331	2,006	38,603	138,042
Livingston,	303,594	15,474	173,197	86,894	1,496	44,157	100,312
Macomb,	182,136	2,287	160,306	157,634	2,210	21,003	59,910
Mackinaw,	....	....	....	770	....	20	4,455
Marquette,	....	....	....	....	....	....	....
Mason,	....	....	....	....	....	....	....
Midland,	300	....	1,650	200	....	....	750
Montcalm,	3,781	340	4,570	2,660	....	1,075	3,590
Monroe,	114,340	997	199,323	89,835	3,229	20,774	78,122
Newaygo,	327	....	5,200	380	....	883	2,380
Oakland,	603,786	29,854	479,458	280,538	7,065	78,004	212,508
Oceana,	....	....	....	....	....	....	....
Ontonagon,	....	....	....	....	....	....	....
Ottawa,	3,814	262	24,264	3,549	55	553	9,308
Saginaw,	4,420	106	13,935	4,235	180	999	6,635
Sanilac,	7,157	10	5,298	7,531	35	503	4,2[illegible]
Schoolcraft,	....	....	....	....	....	....	....
Shiawassee,	61,834	650	56,505	32,705	259	6,284	26,475
St. Clair,	20,285	942	42,[illegible]42	60,678	1,107	4,974	24,563
St. Joseph,	256,505	4,501	404,638	111,311	3,390	16,415	101,504
Tuscola,	470	80	1,076	315	...	20	1,040
Van Buren,	75,115	1,436	132,780	34,718	969	2,483	50,041
Washtenaw,	522,728	6,370	379,965	213,570	6,200	43,492	130,047
Wayne,	105,567	7,370	284,032	244,882	7,089	23,680	137,277
Total,	4,893,141	102,260	5,704,172	1,843,134	70,801	476,811	2,333,026

RECAPITULATION.—CONTINUED.

ENDING JUNE 1ST, 1850.							
Wool, pounds of.	Value of Orchard products.	Butter, pounds of.	Cheese, pounds of.	Hay, tons of.	Clover seed, bushels.	Maple Sugar, pounds.	Value of home made manufactures.
13,154	$2,582	64,060	6,890	3,312	97	91 970	$4,767
21,959	190	110,966	13,752	6,449	91	94,498	5,565
28,633	6,681	123,346	12.531	6,186	87	51,043	5,232
58,325	4,306	257,469	23,809	10,899	189	207.584	14,348
126,589	5,427	359,675	42 578	18,623	706	39.796	*6,941
48,343	3,355	185,215	22,700	3,853	300	107.500	7,467
....	....	....	....	366	....	2,000	....
14,638	337	135.613	5,936	5,013	82	125,024	7,761
23,969	1,211	150,174	13,367	7.202	31	210,282	7.448
72,271	2,805	295,742	30.224	16,551	360	162.266	9,019
82,620	5,952	340,121	67,318	12,478	605	170,161	17,578
....	....	....	....	....	....	....	....
....	....	....	....	....	....	....	....
28,229	843	144,080	13,243	8,620	238	166,204	9,159
23,823	866	117,769	20,386	5,596	77	118,537	*7,245
132,263	2,324	356,300	36,642	27,355	656	400	18,608
94,328	3,972	191,027	40,461	10,718	369	79,770	5,031
22,005	830	181,215	13,740	8,141	148	91,447	8,981
33,269	1,891	125,983	19,713	6,849	96	60.533	10,257
173,399	6,430	515,437	132,940	35,383	2,571	152.916	23,874
86,686	2,145	308,245	32,105	24,602	1,112	15,840	21,751
101,057	9,551	256,818	52,442	17,717	414	67,779	*35,499
....	300	1,200	....	96	....	1,100	....
....	....	....	....	....	....	....	....
....	....	....	....	....	....	....	....
128	....	600	....	50	....	....	....
942	....	5,580	....	199	....	....	253
57,098	8,341	260,469	42,494	19,000	281	26,168	9,577
....	....	1,825	....	162	....	....	20
299,590	24,472	877,856	221,152	52,134	3,128	63,097	33,595
....	....	....	....	....	....	....	....
....	....	....	....	....	....	....	....
1,166	219	30.985	2,100	1,507	1	42,365	1,256
2,406	45	14,575	1,720	1,084	....	10,475	418
2,177	....	18,415	....	1,332	....	7,255	898
....	....	....	....	....	....	....	....
21,738	1,041	110,823	16,400	7,136	110	61,157	8,927
17,681	2,163	135,715	9,940	8,068	....	1,100	1,156
68,184	3,924	270,513	26,717	12,719	758	18,395	9,565
317	....	1,170	150	77	....	3.260	142
15,994	2,940	83,704	10,085	3,567	1	63,875	7,355
235,845	15,008	589,964	117,562	38,669	8,824	63,578	25,293
95.822	11,371	433,879	63,549	42 357	365	48,912	16,268
2,007,598	$130,522	7,056,478	1,112,646	424,070	16,647	2,426,087	$341,239

* The balance of the county imperfectly reported.

RECAPITULATION.—Continued.

COUNTIES.	Flouring Mills.						Saw Mills.			
		Power used.			Annual product.			Power used.		
	Number of.	Water	Steam.	Capital invested in real and personal estate in the business.	Bbls. flour made.	Value of.	Number of.	Water.	Steam.	Capital invested in real and personal estate in the business.
Allegan,..	3	3	...	$17 000	4,600	$19,600	22	19	3	$64,600
Barry,........	2	2		6 800	4 200	16.200	17	14	3	22,875
Berrien,... ..	5	5		52,000	37,000	141,000	24	22	2	43,360
Branch,........	5	4	1	47, [illegible]	33,800	102,580	21	17	4	45,700
Calhoun,.... ..				...	...	...	...	...	...	...
Cass, ...	5	5	.	21,000	8 70[illegible]	26,400	11	10	1	13,800
Chippewa, ...		.		...	...	...	3	3	.	6,200
Clinton,....	2	2		7,000	7,000	33,000	6	6		10,000
Eaton,..........	4	4		14 000	15,230	39,520	18	16	2	25,250
Genesee,.... ..	7	7		63.300	24.427	94,305	5	5	...	15,700
Hillsdale, ...	8	6	2	79,000	27,580	120,101	24	19	5	32,100
Houghton, ...		..		...	...	...	...	...	...	...
Huron,....... ..				...	...	...	..	.	...	...
Ingham,.........	4	3	1	27,000	5,260	20,857	12	10	2	14,100
Ionia,...				...	...	...	.	...	...	...
Jackson,........	16	13	3	145,500	82.890	309,650	15	13	2	20,700
Kalamazoo,.	10	8	2	77.500	46,000	175,000	13	11	2	21,000
Kent, ...	6	6		34,000	20 544	78,844	18	18	...	40,100
Lapeer,...	7	6	1	*55,000	10 400	51,000	13	11	2	†
Lenawee, ...	17	15	2	236.500	57 233	335.065	32	14	8	88,000
Livingston, ...	11	11	...	60,500	26,775	108,500	7	4	3	11,500
Macomb, ...			..	...	...	...	..	...	.	...
Mackinaw,......		..		...	...	...	15	10	5	152,500
Marquette,.......	..	..		...	...	...		...	...	...
Mason,..		..		...	...	...	1	...	1	15,000
Midland,....		..	.	...	...	...	...	...	.	...
Montcalm,......		...	..	...	...	...	6	6	.	27,000
Monroe,...	2	2		86,500	20,075	93,318	11	8	3	27,300
Newaygo, ...			.	...	...	...	3	3	..	23,700
Oakland,.........	27	27	..	201,500	60,066	225,372	10	6	2	13,050
Oceana,.........		..		...	...	...	4	2	2	26,600
Ontonagon, ...		...		...	...	...	..	..	..	...
Ottawa,..... ..	..	..	.	...	...	...	24	11	13	144,030
Saginaw,... ...		..	.	...	...	...	8	3	5	72,100
Sanilac,....	1	1	...	2,000	800	4,000	10	7	3	58,900
Schoolcraft, ...	..		.	...	...	...	...	..	...	...
Shiawassee,......	5	5	...	31,000	11,700	36,400	7	6	1	10,500
St. Clair,.........	2	1	1	8.000	37,000	25.500	32	11	21	229,000
St. Joseph, ...	12	11	1	142.500	52,292	205,027	20	19	1	25,750
Tuscola, ...	1	1		1.500	‡	2,000	3	3	..	17,000
Van Buren,......	1	1	..	10.000	3,000	12,000	12	10	2	20,500
Washtenaw, ...	22	20	2	218,500	137,800	553,100	24	19	5	44,600
Wayne,..........	13	11	2	101,150	50,262	203,623	44	15	31	355,671
Total,.. ...	197	180	18	$1,746,050	784,634	$3,031,976	485	351	134	$1,688,186

*Invested in flour and saw mills.
†Merged with flour mills.
‡Not stated.

RECAPITULATION.—CONTINUED.

SAW MILLS.		AGGREGATE OF ALL KINDS OF MANUFACTURES, MILLS INCLUDED				ESTIMATED VALUE OF REAL AND PERSONAL ESTATE.	
Annual product.			Hands employ'd				
Feet of Lumber Sawed.	Value of.	Capital invested in real and personal estate in the business.	Males.	Females.	Value of annual products.	By Assessors.	By assistant Marshals.
12,895,000	$76,700	$113,900	129	2	$155,780	$674,323	$1,348,646
5,625,000	29,300	83,975	63	....	65,300	369,590	492,786
7,790,000	50,000	144,760	187½	...	325,565	832,454	2,497,362
6,220,000	39,265	141,550	140	...	239,095	750,781	1,989,296
......	......	......	......	...	......	1,582,485	3,878,602
2,332,000	12,990	41,100	43	....	49,725	826,486	826,486
850,000	8,500	674,960	822	...	395,460	150,312	150,312
1,530,000	9,010	21,175	25½	2	58,900	529,510	529,510
3,660,000	21,820	58,45	83	..	123,678	570,979	1,600,000
5,200,000	38,725	104,525	132	1	181,148	744,577	Not reported
6,335,000	40,495	122,220	142		188,399	650,000	875,000
......	......	....	....	..	......	......	......
......	......	......	......	..	......	Ret'd with	Tuscola.
3,610,000	22,660	51,450	52	..	62,388	638,006	2,031,351
......	......	......	......	.	......	......	......
2,480,000	16,960	250,475	361	20	524,422	1,449,298	4,037,602
5,200,000	35,465	186,300	189	39	355,714	777,906	1,036,482
11,425,000	65,475	149,350	245	...	269,144	800,669	1,007,537
5,400,000	35,100	78,650	106	..	126,695	Not stated.	Not stated.
7,740,000	33,950	473,850	539	37	784,856	2,277,181	2,884,723
8,227,000	21,430	90,850	86½	...	180,240	755,917	1,133,725
......	......	......	......	...	......	830,465	2,491,395
20,250,000	109,550	176,381	422	...	206,481	169,279	169,279
......	......	......	......	...	......	......	......
3,000,000	16,500	16,900	45	...	22,200	......	......
......	......	......	......	...	......	......	......
6,000,000	26,000	27,000	80	...	29,100	Not stated.	Not stated.
4,820,000	32,830	146,100	155	1	201,440	1,031,701	1,031,701
6,500,000	31,550	27,850	109	..	48,662	......	......
3,030,000	22,780	250,555	236	30	713,058	2,280,644	5,837,052
6,100,000	32,000	23,500	83	....	37,700	......	......
......	......	......	......	...	......	......	......
49,320,000	307,480	153,540	323	..	337,548	435,856	671,178
6,975,000	54,85	75,665	113		65,150	318,037	897,546
6,725,000	53,775	66,000	99	..	72,795	130,638	861,276
......	......	......	......	..	......	......	......
1,500,00	9,990	71,075	75	...	110,474	353,954	951,948
34,450,00	316,800	324,125	543	6	473,400	851,009	2,537,151
5,590,000	37,605	259,045	278	8	441,482	1,001,510	2,379,825
1,055,000	8,600	20,500	23	...	15,600	33,502	100,506
4,600 00	27,000	43,500	85	...	67,300	493,820	750,039
6,145,000	43,223	475,070	529½	39	1,004,263	3,259,261	4,490,380
43,523,500	533,325	1,068,205	1,783½	117	2,173,323	1,657,363	3,803,221
301,157,500	$2,221,798	5,965,551	8,383½	302	$10,111,488	$27,280,518	$52,781,977

MINERAL STATISTICS.

Counties.	Number of Companies.	Hands Employed.	Capital Invested.	Products. Kinds.	Products. Tons Raised.	Value of Products.
Branch, ..	1	25	$15,000	Iron.	2,700	$15,000
Kent, ...	1	7	7,900	Plaster	1,500	6,000
Kalamazoo, ..	1	10	14,000	Iron.	1,890	16,000
Counties of U. Peninsula	24	706	614,360	Copper.	1,507	386,960
Total, .	27	748	$651,260		7,597	$423,960

STATISTICS

OF

MICHIGAN IN 1840,

COMPILED FROM THE

CENSUS OF THE UNITED STATES.

COMPILED FROM UNITED STATES CENSUS.

COUNTIES.	Whole No. of Inhabitants.	Live Stock, June 1st, 1840. Horses and Mules.	Neat Cattle.	Sheep.	Swine.
Allegan,	1,783	132	1,511	107	2,266
Barry,	1,078	117	991	86	1,807
Berrien,	5,011	941	4,984	2,407	10,067
Branch,	5,715	714	5,211	744	13,224
Calhoun,	10,599	1,567	9,557	8,057	18,808
Cass,	5,710	1,496	7,179	5,524	11,411
Chippewa,	534	21	83	14	48
Clinton,	1,614	112	1,621	294	2,560
Eaton,	2,370	90	2,102	108	3,188
Genesee,	4,268	418	3,468	1,007	6,540
Hillsdale,	7,240	755	6,926	1,804	10,630
Ingham,	2,498	112	2,516	172	4,358
Ionia,	1,923	200	1,866	270	3,202
Jackson,	13,130	1,533	12,565	3,920	21,674
Kalamazoo,	7,380	1,559	7,061	8,694	13,665
Kent,	2,587	238	1,271	222	2,460
Lapeer,	4,265	329	3,813	1,197	6,207
Lenawee,	17,889	1,970	14,917	6,034	22,973
Livingston,	7,430	855	7,931	1,903	10,952
Macomb,	9,716	1,482	7,193	8,959	8,969
Mackinaw,	923	47	96	6	65
Monroe,	9,922	1,688	8,364	3,010	9,281
Oakland,	23,646	3,561	20,651	19,656	39,218
Ottawa,	208	4	12	....	18
Oceana,	496	22	269	....	492
Saginaw,	892	244	1,066	....	1,462
Shiawassee,	2,103	190	2,143	875	3,808
St. Clair,	4,606	770	3,101	1,075	3,929
St. Joseph,	7,068	1,542	7,865	3,980	18,864
Van Buren,	1,910	240	2,125	538	3,422
Washtenaw,	20,571	0,719	22,208	19,278	30,141
Wayne,	24,173	3,576	14,574	10,181	17,092
Total,	212,267	30,144	185,190	99,618	205,890

COMPILED FROM UNITED STATES CENSUS.

COUNTIES.	Produce, during the Year ending					
	Wheat, bushels of.	Rye, bushels of.	Indian corn, bushels of.	Oats, bushels of.	Barley, bushels of.	Potatoes, bushels of.
Allegan,	13,815	30	14,735	15,424	646	23,792
Barry,	12,884	....	9,435	13,775	563	13,255
Berrien,	56,685	240	97,603	53,692	2,792	35,535
Branch,	67,317	31	89,085	70,222	4,073	74,243
Calhoun,	176,630	85	140,971	179,177	20,553	132,319
Cass,	95,101	780	177,925	98,833	1,868	58,363
Chippewa,	....	....	....	322	....	3,065
Clinton,	18,632	80	15,296	11,310	100	17,038
Eaton,	15,896	....	14,492	11,209	940	22,918
Genesee,	37,397	218	17,675	26,766	982	41,442
Hillsdale,	80.256	50	82,757	71,741	4,837	75,230
Ingham,	23,127	....	18,923	10,947	48	24,951
Ionia,	32,382	240	14,784	16,695	1,100	23,500
Jackson,	180.649	771	167,870	190,087	11,898	147,068
Kalamazoo,	161 168	500	125,023	157,866	5,979	71,355
Kent,	18,750	170	13,320	17,320	440	16,700
Lapeer,	35,472	90	19.801	26,009	3,922	36,351
Lenawee,	167,891	3,468	199,538	151,111	5.989	112,434
Livingston,	84,943	....	82,081	77,945	3.623	93,647
Macomb,	81,064	7,387	71,028	69,792	1,344	80,881
Mackinaw,	....	....	20	614	....	2,016
Monroe,	42,856	2,103	74,407	68,794	2,199	83,016
Oakland,	264,965	6,157	254,902	238,005	4,514	329,807
Ottawa,	....	....	....	....	....	100
Oceana,	1,226	15	3,950	2,235	47	7,741
Saginaw,	4,125	20	9,837	2,841	....	16,929
Shiawassee,	19,584	....	13,772	10,937	206	23,007
St. Clair,	10,836	726	11,443	12,641	956	40,657
St. Joseph,	131,451	2,438	148,944	112,125	11,323	66,386
Van Buren,	15,640	120	28,587	16,176	835	20,832
Washtenaw,	216,597	2,941	220,096	284.181	31,050	210,224
Wayne,	89,769	5,576	138,739	94,989	4,975	204,318
Total,	2,157,108	34,236	2,277,039	2,114,051	127,802	2,109,205

COMPILED FROM UNITED STATES CENSUS.

June 1st, 1840.			Value of home made manufactures.	Grist and Flouring Mills.		Number of Saw Mills.	Capital invested in Mills.
Wool, pounds of.	Value of the product of the Dairy.	Hay, tons of.		Number of.	Bbls. Flour made.		
239	...	657	...	8	4,700	15	$202,275
265	$497	677	...	...	...	3	1,800
1,959	16,018	2,579	$2,651	10	11,000	27	154,575
1,692	660	451	750	8	3,000	15	93,100
3,676	19,475	6,796	2,780	15	16,300	29	215,200
10,481	11,696	832	8,760	6	8,000	22	55,000
39	...	89	...	...	...	1	...
215	...	984	...	...	...	...	...
134	4,839	817	160	3	...	8	16,500
1,302	8,040	1,941	2,958	3	1,050	10	35,500
3,745	5,626	4,064	2,216	3	...	16	46,500
338	2,099	563	525	1	...	6	11,900
315	208	466	...	2	...	9	31,700
4,255	19,529	12,298	3,931	7	16,500	25	141,850
4,362	9,743	3,929	621	6	...	22	11,400
566	3,250	970	...	3	2,000	18	133,000
1,250	1,476	2,634	945	5	...	14	42,200
7,429	16,950	6,294	5,827	12	6,500	44	246,650
3,945	10,659	9,956	1,247	8	3,600	14	35,700
13,057	620	6,884	6,920	5	7,2[illegible]0	12	74,500
...	400	97	570	...	...	...	...
3,786	12,654	6,411	4,953	7	2,000	11	44,400
33,859	56,903	18,435	29,031	38	64,650	41	231,900
...	...	10	...	...	...	...	...
...	...	193	...	...	...	12	103,500
...	255	1,109	...	1	...	6	41,900
583	2,147	502	1,000	1	800	8	42,900
1,909	471	1,716	779	5	80	15	85,000
4,298	9,022	2,426	2,336	7	6,600	11	28,000
900	6,052	1,842	1,079	2	...	8	34,800
29,427	64,536	20,573	26,541	18	28,800	41	220,000
19,349	17,191	14,110	8,375	11	21,100	28	78,450
153,375	$301,052	130,805	$113,955	190	202,880	491	$2,460,200

POPULATION OF THE UNITED STATES.

STATES AND TERRITORIES.	CENSUS OF 1820.	CENSUS OF 1830.	CENSUS OF 1840.	CENSUS OF 1850.	CENSUS OF 1860.*
Maine,	298,335	399,455	501,793	583,169	619,958
New Hampshire,	244,161	269,328	284,574	317,976	326,072
Vermont,	235,764	280,652	291,948	314,920	315,827
Massachusetts,	523,287	610,408	737,699	994,499	1,123,494
Rhode Island,	83,059	97,199	108,830	147,541	174,621
Connecticut,	275,202	297,675	309,978	370,704	460,670
New York,	1,392,812	1,918,608	2,428,921	3,097,394	3,851,563
New Jersey,	277,575	320,823	373,306	489,555	676,084
Pennsylvania,	1,049,458	1,348,233	1,724,033	2,311,786	2,916,018
Delaware,	72,749	76,748	78,085	91,532	112,353
Maryland,	407,350	447,040	420,019	583,034	731,565
Virginia,	1,065,379	1,211,405	1,239,797	1,421,661	1,593,199
North Carolina,	638,829	737,987	753,419	868,903	1,008,342
South Carolina,	502,741	581,185	594,398	668,507	715,371
Georgia,	340,987	516,823	691,392	905,999	1,082,797
Alabama,	127,901	309,527	590,756	771,671	955,917
Mississippi,	75,448	136,621	375,651	606,555	887,158
Louisiana,	153,407	215,739	352,411	517,739	666,431
Tennessee,	422,813	681,904	829,210	1,002,625	1,146,140
Kentucky,	565,317	687,917	779,828	982,405	1,145,567
Ohio,	581,434	937,903	1,519,467	1,980,408	2,377,917
Indiana,	147,178	343,031	685,866	988,416	1,350,802
Illinois,	55,211	157,445	476,183	851,470	1,691,238
Missouri,	66,586	140,445	383,702	682,043	1,201,209
District of Columbia,	33,039	39,834	43,712	51,687	75,321
Michigan,	8,896	31,639	212,267	397,654	754,291
Arkansas,	14,273	30,388	97,574	209,639	440,775
Florida,	......	34,730	54,477	87,401	145,694
Wisconsin,	......	......	30,045	305,191	768,485
Iowa,	......	......	43,112	192,214	682,002
Texas,	......	......	......	212,592	600,955
California,	......	......	......	92,578	384,770
Oregon,	......	......	......	13,293	52,566
New Mexico,	......	......	......	61,547	92,024
Utah,	......	......	......	11,380	50,000
Minnesota,	......	......	......	6,077	172,793
Kansas,	......	......	......	......	143,645
Nebraska,	......	......	......	......	28,893
Dakotah,	......	......	......	......	4,880
Washington,	......	......	......	......	11,624
Total,	9,638,131	12,866,020	17,069,453	23,191,074	31,646,490

* As reported by Sup't. Kennedy of the U. S. Census Bureau.

ERRATA.

Page 45, total in Cities, "1,555," should be "1,553."
Page 51, total by Assessors, "$5,524,740," should be "$5,424,740."
Page 59, " " "$2,705,513," " "$3,705,513."
Page 78, total No. of occupied farms, "178," should be "1,781."
Page 90 and 91, Meegeezee erroneously included in the total of Grand Traverse.
Page 107, Capital invested in manufactures in Huron, "$305,000," should be "$371,000;" "$66,000," invested in Dwight, being omitted.
Page 107, value of products of manufactures in Huron, "$196,150," should be "$271,551;" "$75,401," products of Dwight being omitted.
Page 118, acres unimproved in Ionia, "97,478," should be "99,478."
Page 131, total feet of lumber, "1,654,000," should be "1,064,000."
Page 133, total dwelling houses, "4,787," should be "4,687."
Page 139, feet of lumber in Brady, "1,325," should be "1,325,000;" total of the Co., "7,590,325," should be "8,824,000."
Page 187, value of real and personal estate in Marquette, as given by Marshals, "$2,000,000," should be "$20,000,000."
Page 209, wool in Big Prairie, "227," should be "277."
Page 210, total of steam saw mills in Newaygo should be "3."
Page 216, total of Indian corn, "890,866," should be "870,866."
Page 227, total value of products of saw mills in Oceana, "$38,000," should be "$33,000."

INDEX.

www.ingramcontent.com/pod-product-compliance
Lightning Source LLC
LaVergne TN
LVHW011200110826
845150LV00006B/1275

9781425572976